SCHOLASTIC

MASTERING SCIENCE

Course Book 7

Published by Scholastic India Pvt. Ltd.

A subsidiary of Scholastic Inc., New York, 10012 (USA)

Publishers since 1920, with international operations in Canada, Australia, New Zealand, the United Kingdom, India, and Hong Kong.

For information regarding permission, write to:
Scholastic India Pvt. Ltd.
A-27, Ground Floor, Bharti Sigma Centre
Infocity-1, Sector 34, Gurgaon (Haryana) 122001, India
Email: education@scholastic.co.in

Layout design and typeset: Mansi Bansal

Series editor: Sonia Kapoor

First edition: 2010
Reprinted: 2011 (twice), 2012, 2013, 2014, 2015, 2016, 2017, 2019 (twice), 2020, 2023, 2025

ISBN-13: 978-81-8477-492-4

Contents

Introduction

Mastering Science is a comprehensive series targetted at the middle school. Devised within the framework recommended by the CBSE, this series aims to spark the students' interest in science, encourage them to actively participate in the learning process, and gain a thorough understanding of scientific terms and concepts. The aim of this series is to encourage students to be curious about scientific phenomenon and explore them logically.

The main features of the series:

- It has been designed keeping in mind the thematic and activity-oriented approach recommended by the CBSE.
- Difficult-to-understand concepts and everyday scientific phenomenon are explained in a clear, concise and lucid manner.
- Colourful illustrations, numerous photographs and examples help students gain a clear understanding of the topics under discussion.
- The series complies with the **Comprehensive and Continuous Evaluation** (CCE) approach recommended by the CBSE. To make it more convenient for teachers, an evaluation sheet that provides for a thorough understanding of the student's capabilities and grasp of the lessons is provided with all books in the series.
- Amazing facts relevant to the topic under discussion are provided in every lesson in a section titled **Factastic**.
- The **Think it Over** section comprises inferential questions that encourage students to think independently. This is in tune with the Higher Order Thinking Skills (HOTS) emphasised by the CBSE.
- The **Explore** and **Learn More** sections encourage the student to gather, classify and understand

information. This reinforces the concepts within the chapter and forms a tool for independent learning for the students.

- **Circle Time** provides students a platform to share their ideas and understanding of topics with their peers.
- Every lesson is followed by a **Revision** section to help revise and reinforce concepts.
- Hands-on and easy-to-do experiments encourage analysis and reasoning, allowing the students to confidently carry out the procedure and reach a logical conclusion.
- Difficult words are explained in a glossary on the page where they appear.
- Brainteasers, puzzles and riddles, which form a part of every chapter, add a fun element to the text.

Biman Basu is the author of several popular science series and is the editor of a popular Indian science monthly. A former scientist with the prestigious Council of Scientific and Industrial Research (CSIR), Biman Basu has over thirty years of experience in writing for children. He has scripted several TV science documentaries and published more than 1,000 articles on popular science topics in various publications. He is the winner of the 'NCSTC National Award for Science Popularisation in 1994', awarded annually by the Department of Science and Technology, Government of India. He was conferred the 'AWIC Honour 2007' by the Association of Writers and Illustrators for Children for his contribution to children's literature.

1 Nutrition in Plants

All living organisms need food. Food provides the energy required for the growth and maintenance of all living organisms. Different organisms need different kinds of substances for nutrition. Human beings need proteins, carbohydrates, fats, fibres, vitamins and minerals. These are obtained from both plant and animal sources. Humans consume different plant parts such as fruits, stem, seeds, roots, leaves and tubers. Humans also consume plant-eating animals and so depend on plants for food indirectly as well.

Green plants are the only living organisms that make their own food in the presence of sunlight, from raw materials provided by nature. Known as **autotrophs**, the mode of nutrition in green plants is called autotrophic (*auto* = self; *trophos* = nourishment). Organisms that use chemical energy are called **chemoautotrophs**. These include certain bacteria that live in the roots of leguminous plants. These bacteria use nitrogen from air and convert it into nitrates, which plants can take up as food.

Plants are autotrophs

Non-green plants, such as fungi, some bacteria and certain flowering plants, do not have chlorophyll and hence cannot make their own food. They depend on others for their food and are thus called **heterotrophs** having a heterotrophic (*heteros* = other; *trophos* = nourishment) mode of nutrition.

autotrophic: organisms that can make food from simple inorganic sources by photosynthesis
leguminous: plants that bear seeds in pods
heterotrophic: organisms deriving their nutritional requirements from complex organic substances

Cells

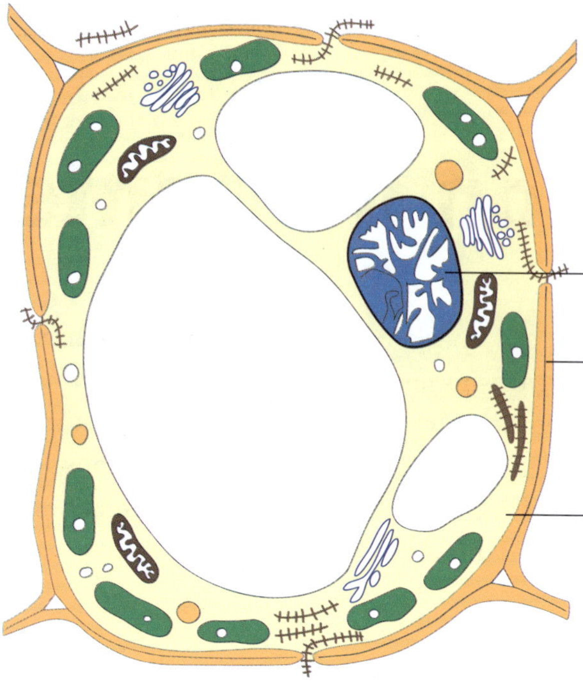

Plant cell

Before understanding plant nutrition or how plants make their own food, it would be better to know something about the structure of living cells. The **cell** is the most basic unit of life. There are millions of different types of cells. Some organisms, such as amoeba and bacteria, are made up of a single cell. However, usually groups of cells form organisms such as human beings. A living cell is extremely tiny and cannot be seen with a naked eye. It can only be seen under a microscope.

A typical cell is enclosed by a thin outer boundary called the **cell membrane** that protects it from the outside environment. The cell membrane regulates the movement of water, nutrients and wastes into as well as out of the cell. The working parts of the cell are inside the cell membrane. Most cells have a distinct, centrally located spherical structure called the **nucleus**. The nucleus is surrounded by a jelly-like substance called the cytoplasm.

Factastic

The word cell comes from the Latin *cellula*, meaning 'a small room'.

Food production in green plants

Leaves are the food factories of plants. The process by which plants make their food from carbon dioxide and water is called **photosynthesis** (photo = light; synthesis = to combine) and begins when light falls on leaves (both sunlight and artificial light can power this process). Chloroplasts, which are cell organelles in the plant's leaves, contain a green pigment called **chlorophyll**, which helps the leaves capture

cytoplasm: the material within a living cell, excluding the nucleus
chloroplast: specialised part of cells of green plants containing chlorophyll that carry out photosynthesis

the energy of the sun. This energy is used to synthesise food using carbon dioxide and water. Carbon dioxide from the air enters the leaf through tiny holes called stomata. Water and minerals are absorbed by the roots and transported to the leaves through channels in the stem called **xylem**. In the leaf, carbon dioxide combines with water in the presence of chlorophyll through a chemical reaction to produce a simple carbohydrate. Oxygen is produced in the process and is released into the air.

carbon dioxide + water → carbohydrate + oxygen

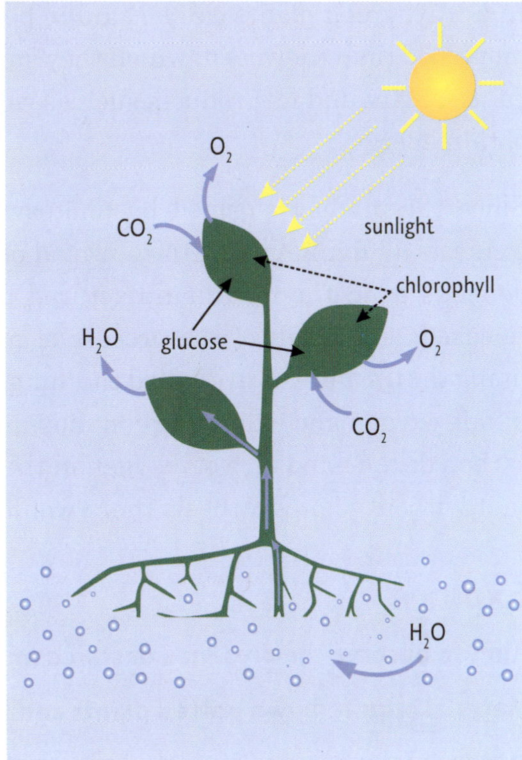

Photosynthesis

Factastic

Apart from leaves, photosynthesis also takes place in other green parts of the plant such as green stems and green branches. Most desert plants do not have leaves but have spines to reduce the loss of water by transpiration. Photosynthesis in these plants is carried out in the stems.

The carbohydrates produced as food are then transported through tubes in the leaf to the stems, fruits and roots of the plants. These tubes are called **phloem**.

Some of the carbohydrate is used immediately by the plant for energy; some is converted and stored as starch.

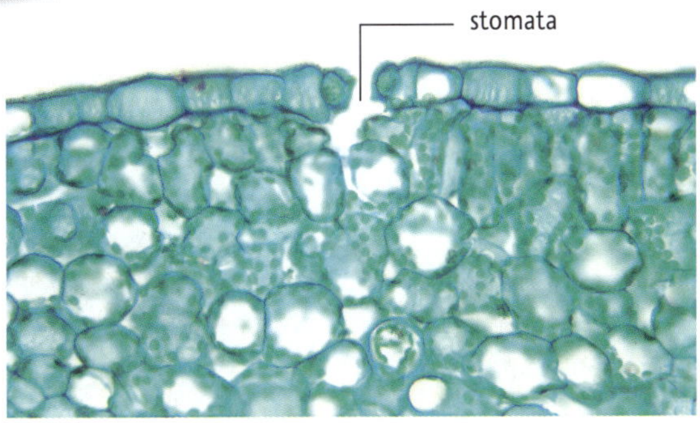

Structure of a leaf showing stomata

stomata: the minute pores in the leaf or stem of a plant through which gases and water vapour can pass

In a way, green plants can be said to be storing the sun's energy as food. Plants produce more food than they need, which they store in stems, roots, seeds or fruits. We can directly eat the plant and its products such as rice, wheat grains, apples, mangoes or potatoes and obtain energy.

Since the products formed by photosynthesis form the base of the food chain, which connects all living things, the survival of almost all living organisms directly or indirectly depends upon the food manufactured by green plants. In addition, the oxygen that is released as a result of the process of photosynthesis is essential for the survival of all living things. Forests are called the 'lungs of the earth' because animals including humans, inhale oxygen and exhale carbon dioxide in the process of respiration, and plants take in carbon dioxide and give off oxygen in the process of photosynthesis. We can thus conclude that without photosynthesis there would be no life on earth.

Explore

Aim: To observe the presence of starch in leaves.

Material required: two potted plants and iodine solution

Method: Take two similar potted plants. Keep one plant in complete darkness for three days and the other plant exposed to light After three days, take a few leaves from each plant and test for the presence of starch using iodine solution. Do leaves from both the plants show the presence of starch?

Now keep the plant, which was earlier kept in the dark, in light for three days and then test the leaves for starch. Do you find starch in the leaves? Can you explain your observations?

Leaves during autumn

Sometimes plants have leaves that are not green. Plants, such as crotons, have colourful leaves. These plants have chlorophyll in their leaves, but also large amounts of red, brown and other pigments that mask the green colour. In autumn, due to shorter days and reduced availability of water, chlorophyll production in many trees stops and hence their leaves turn yellow or red before falling off.

Algae

Among the common organisms that produce their own food are algae, which are often seen as slimy, green patches in ponds or in other stagnant water bodies. Algae also contain chlorophyll and can produce their own food by the process of photosynthesis, producing oxygen as a by-product.

Besides carbohydrates, plants also produce other substance such as proteins and fats. Pulses, lentils and chickpeas are all plant seeds that are rich sources of proteins, and mustard, sesame, sunflower and coconut are rich sources of oils and fats.

Plants cannot make protein from pure carbohydrate, because proteins contain nitrogen and sometimes sulphur. They get the nitrogen required for producing proteins from nitrates in the soil. Fertilizers provide plants with nitrates. As mentioned earlier, some bacteria living near the roots of plants, are able to convert atmospheric nitrogen into soluble nitrates. Plants absorb these soluble nitrates along with water. Plants get the sulphur required for the production of proteins from sulphates present in the soil.

Parasitic plants

Although most plants can make their own food, some of them lack chlorophyll and cannot produce their own food. Such plants grow on other green plants and use food produced by them. In other words, they have a heterotrophic mode of nutrition. A common example is the dodder or *Cuscuta* (known in India as *amar bel*) which is a commonly seen yellow thread-like plant that wraps itself around the stems and branches of trees. The dodder plant does not have leaves or any chlorophyll. Since it cannot make its own food, it has to depend on readymade

algae: chlorophyll-containing mainly aquatic plants lacking true stems, and roots and leaves

Dodder or *Cuscuta* plant

food from the plants it climbs on. The plant on which it climbs is called a **host**. Since it derives valuable nutrients from the host, it is called a parasite. Sometimes a parasitic plant can even kill its host by depriving it of nutrients.

Insectivorous plants

Nitrogen and calcium are essential nutrients that plants need for growth. There are places, such as bogs and marshy areas, where the soil is poor in nutrients. Plants growing in such areas often have novel means of getting their nutrients. They trap and digest insects. Such insect-eating plants are called **insectivorous** plants, or **carnivorous** plants. These plants may be green or of some other colour. They are able to carry out photosynthesis but lack a few key nutrients, which they obtain from insects.

Pitcher plant

There are various kinds of insectivorous plants that use different methods for trapping insects. A common example is the 'pitcher plant' in which the leaf is modified into the shape of a pitcher. The tip of the leaf forms a lid that can open and close the mouth of the pitcher. The pitcher is filled with a liquid and has hair along the walls, which are directed downwards. When an insect lands in the pitcher, the lid closes and the trapped insect gets entangled in the hair. Over a period of time, the insect is digested by the digestive juices secreted in the pitcher.

Circle Time

Visit your city's botanical garden or the botany department of the nearest university and observe pitcher plants. Observe how they trap and digest insects.

Saprotrophs

Saprotrophs are organisms that feed on dead and decaying matter. They include most fungi, which are seen growing on

parasite: an organism that lives in or on another organism (its host) and benefits by deriving nutrients from the host

bread as mould or cultivated as mushrooms for food. Mushrooms can also be seen growing on rotting wood during the rainy season. Saprotrophs cannot make their own food and so are heterotrophs. Saprophytes are useful scavengers and can break down organic matter into nutrients that are easily assimilable by green plants.

Unlike green plants, fungi have a different mode of nutrition. They secrete digestive juices on the dead and decaying matter and convert it into a solution and then absorb nutrients from it. This mode of nutrition in which organisms take in nutrients in the form of a solution from dead and decaying matter is called saprotrophic (*sapros* = rotten; *trophos* = nourishment) nutrition.

Fungal spores are generally present in the air. When they land on wet and warm things, they germinate and grow, often spoiling things on which they grow. A moist bread slice has adequate nutrition and moisture necessary for mould spores to germinate and grow. That is why if bread is kept open in a humid and warm place for a few days, it gets covered with mould. Fungi also grow on pickles, leather articles, clothes and other objects that are left in hot and humid weather for a long time.

Explore

Take a slice of bread and moisten it with a few drops of water. Leave it in a humid and warm place for four days. When you look at the slice of bread after four days, you may see patches of various colours—white, green, brown, etc. Examine the patches under a microscope or a magnifying glass. What do you see? Can you guess where the mould came from?

Mould on bread

Edible mushrooms

Many fungi, such as yeast and mushrooms are useful, but some fungi cause diseases in plants, animals and humans. The common antibiotic, penicillin, is obtained from a greenish-blue mould of the *Penicillium* species.

Wild mushrooms

saprotrophic: an organism that feeds on or derives nourishment from decaying organic matter

Symbiosis in plants

Although in most places organisms are seen to compete for food and space, however, there are organisms that live together and share shelter and nutrients for mutual benefit. Such associations are called **symbiotic**. In its most common usage, symbiosis is used to describe the intimate association between two species that mutually benefit from this association. These associations are obligatory ones in which neither organism can survive independently in nature. For example, certain fungi live in the roots of trees in a symbiotic system called mycorrhiza. The tree provides nutrients to the fungus, in return, receives help from the fungus in absorbing water and nutrients from the soil. This association is very important both for the tree and for the fungus.

Lichens on tree trunks

Lichens are composite organisms that characteristically form a crust-like or branching growth on rocks or tree trunks. In lichens, the chlorophyll-containing partner, which is an algae, and the fungi live together. The fungi provides shelter, water and minerals to the algae, in return, the algae provides food, which it prepares by photosynthesis.

Replenishing soil nutrients

When plants are grown in a plot of land, they take up nutrients from the soil, which in turn becomes deficient in those nutrients. That is why farmers and gardeners have to supply manure or fertilisers regularly to the soil to replenish the nutrients. Fertilisers and manures contain plant nutrients such as nitrogen, potassium, phosphorous, etc., which need to be added from time to time to enrich the soil. It is good to have the soil tested in a lab before adding fertiliser to it to find out what nutrients are needed.

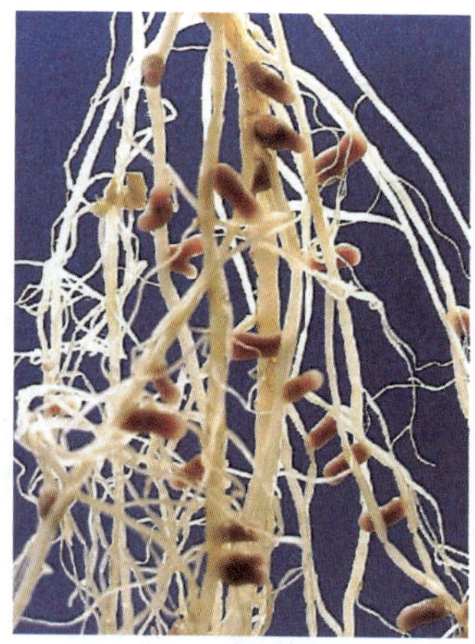

Rhizobium on the roots of leguminous plants

symbiotic: a mutually beneficial relationship between different organisms
mycorrhiza: a fungus that grows in association with the roots of a plant in a symbiotic relationship
lichen: composite organism formed of algae and fungi that characteristically form a crust-like or branching growth on rocks or tree trunks

Usually crops require a lot of nitrogen to make proteins and hence after the harvest, the soil becomes deficient in nitrogen. Although nitrogen gas is available in plenty in the air, plants cannot use it directly in the way they can use carbon dioxide. Plants can only absorb soluble forms of nitrogen from the soil through their roots.

The bacterium *Rhizobium* can take up atmospheric nitrogen and convert it into soluble forms of nitrates. But, *Rhizobium* cannot make its own food. So it lives in the roots of gram, peas, *moong*, beans and other plants called legumes and provides them with nitrogen. In return, the plants provide food and shelter to the bacteria thus setting up a symbiotic relationship. This association is of great significance to farmers because they can add nitrogen to the soil by simply growing leguminous crops instead of adding nitrogen fertiliser to the soil.

Activity

When rainwater falls on plants, it makes them wet. If observed closely, most leaves become wet. However, some of them do not let water accumulate on them and instead let it roll off. The lotus leaf is one such example that has an extremely waxy coating and hence water does not stay on it. As soon as drops of water fall on the lotus leaf, they form small balls and roll off.

Observe this interesting fact with the leaves of several plants. Tick the correct column based on your observations.

	Name of the plant	Water rolls off the leaf (waxy leaf)	Water does not roll off the leaf (not-so waxy leaf)
1.	lotus plant		
2.	rubber plant		
3.	banyan tree		
4.	hibiscus		
5.	grass		

Revision Time

- ✶ All living organisms need food to get energy for their growth and maintenance.
- ✶ Green plants are the only living organisms that make their own food from raw materials provided by nature.
- ✶ Green plants are autotrophs.

* The process by which plants make their food using carbon dioxide and water in the presence of chlorophyll and sunlight is called photosynthesis.
* Complex chemicals, called carbohydrates, are produced during photosynthesis and oxygen is released into the air.
* Oxygen released during photosynthesis is utilised by other living organisms for their survival.
* Green plants store the sun's energy as food, which is consumed by all animals including humans.
* The dodder or *Cuscuta* plant (known in India as *amar* bel) is a parasite and cannot make its own food. It has to steal readymade food from the host plants it climbs on.
* Some plants, such as the pitcher plant, which grow in soil that is poor in nutrients, often have novel structures that help them trap and digest insects.
* Mushrooms are fungi that get their nutrition from dead or decaying matter and are known as saprotrophs.

Quiz Time

1. Answer the questions.

a. How do autotrophs get nutrition?

b. What is special about leguminous plants?

c. Which cell organelle helps in photosynthesis?

d. Why would there be no life on earth without green plants?

e. Where do carnivorous plants get their nutrition from?

2. Fill in the blanks.

a. The ________________ is the most basic unit of life.

b. Carbon dioxide from air enters the leaf through tiny holes called ________________.

c. Dodder or *Cuscuta* is a ________________ plant.

d. ________________ are organisms that feed on dead and decaying matter.

e. Lichens are ________________ organisms that characteristically form a crust-like or branching growth on rocks or tree trunks.

3. **Indicate whether the statements are true or false.**

a. Green plants can make their own food with the help of sunlight and so are called heterotrophs. True False

b. In plant leaves, the cytoplasm contains chlorophyll, which helps the leaves to capture the energy of the sun. True False

c. The slimy, green patches often seen in ponds or in other stagnant water bodies are lichens. True False

d. The dodder plant has a heterotrophic mode of nutrition. True False

e. The pitcher plant uses poison to kill insects. True False

4. **Explain the terms.**

a. heterotroph b. chloroplast c. symbiosis

d. saprotroph e. mycorrhiza

5. **Project work**

a. Match the terms given in Column I with those in Column II.

Column I	Column II
pea	saprotroph
amar bel	parasite
lichens	symbiont
mushroom	legume
mycorrhiza	composite

b. Collect different types of plants along with the roots. For example, a pea plant, a piece of *amar bel* anchored to a tree branch or stem, a money plant (*Philodendron*) growing in a bottle of water, an orchid plant growing on a tree and some creeper that climbs on walls. Examine the roots of each plant. Are they similar? Do the roots of the pea plant have something special? What are they? Where do the roots of *amar bel* grow? Record your observations in a table with sketches of each type of root.

Think it over

1. **Why do the leaves of some trees turn yellow or red before falling?**
2. **Since aquarium plants remain completely submerged in water, from where do they get carbon dioxide for photosynthesis?**

2 Nutrition in Animals

Green plants can make their own food, but animals have to depend on plants for food. Animals eat plants either directly, or indirectly by eating animals that eat plants. There are certain animals that eat only plants and these are called herbivores while those that eat only other animals are called carnivores. Some animals eat both plants and animals and they are called omnivores.

All organisms, including humans, require food for the growth, repair and functioning of their bodies. Food supplies all the

Herbivores: Giraffe, horse, zebra and monkey

nutrients required for healthy growth. Nutrition in animals depends not only on the nutrients present in food but also on the mode of intake of the food and its utilisation in the body. All food contains complex substances such as carbohydrates, proteins and fats. The body cannot utilise these substances in their complex form. The food consumed is broken down into simpler substances by a process called digestion. The digested food can be easily absorbed by the body.

herbivore: an animal that feeds chiefly on grass and other plants
carnivore: an animal that feeds on the flesh of other animals
omnivore: an animal that feeds on both animal and plant matter
digestion: the process by which food is converted into simple substances that can be absorbed by the body

Carnivores: Shark, owl and tiger

Omnivores: Bear, ants and frog

Modes of eating

The manner in which and the kind of food that different animals consume varies widely. Butterflies, bees and sunbirds live on nectar, which they suck from flowers, while infants of humans and many other animals feed on mother's milk. Cows and buffaloes chew cud, while snakes, such as the python and anaconda, swallow the animals they prey on. Some whales and flamingos feed upon tiny food particles floating in water, by filter feeding. This is a form of procurement where food particles or small organisms are strained from water.

Factastic

A star fish has the ability to push its stomach, which is located on the underside of its body, out of its mouth in order to digest prey that is too big to swallow. It can crush oyster and clam shells and eat the soft animal inside.

cud: partially digested food that is brought up from the first stomach to the mouth again for further chewing by ruminants such as cattle and sheep

Digestion in humans

Breaking down food into simpler forms is called **digestion**. Digestion is both mechanical and chemical. In mechanical digestion, food is physically broken down into smaller particles by chewing. Chemical digestion makes use of enzymes, which are proteins that help in the simplification of food matter.

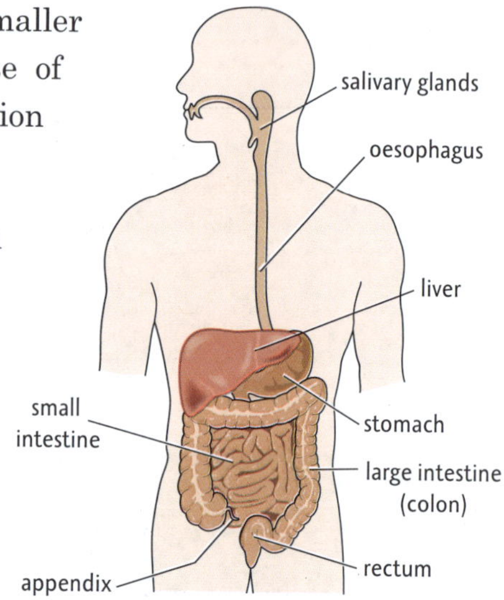

Human digestive system

The food that we eat passes from our mouth through the digestive system, which helps the body break down and absorb food. Salivary glands in the mouth secrete saliva and start the digestion process. The organs that make up the digestive tract, which is also known as the **alimentary canal**, are the mouth, oesophagus, stomach, small intestine, large intestine, rectum and anus. The digestive tract is a series of hollow organs joined in a long, twisting tube from the mouth to the anus. Inside these hollow organs is a mucus-secreting lining called the mucosa. The mucosa contains tiny glands that produce juices to help digest food. The digestive juices contain enzymes that convert complex substances of food into simpler ones that the body can absorb. The digestive tract also has a layer of smooth muscle that helps in breaking down the food and moving it to the end of the tract.

Explore

Aim: To observe the conversion of complex food substances into simple food.

Material required: test tubes, boiled rice and iodine solution

Method: Take a few teaspoonfuls of boiled rice and two test tubes. In one test tube, put one teaspoonful of the boiled rice. Wash your mouth and put some boiled rice in it. Chew it for a few minutes and take it out. Put one teaspoonful of this chewed boiled rice along with the saliva from your mouth into the other test tube. Add 3–4 ml of water in both the test tubes and shake them well. Now add 2–3 drops of iodine solution to each test tube and observe. Does the colour change in both the test tubes? What has happened to the boiled rice that you had chewed for a few minutes? What did saliva do to the starch in boiled rice?

The **liver** and **pancreas** are two digestive organs which produce digestive juices that reach the intestine through small tubes called **ducts**. The **gall bladder** stores the digestive juices until they are needed in the intestine. Some parts of the nervous and circulatory systems also play important roles in the digestive system.

enzyme: any of the several proteins that are produced by cells and act as catalysts in biochemical reactions
mucosa: mucus-secreting membrane lining all body cavities or passages

The mouth

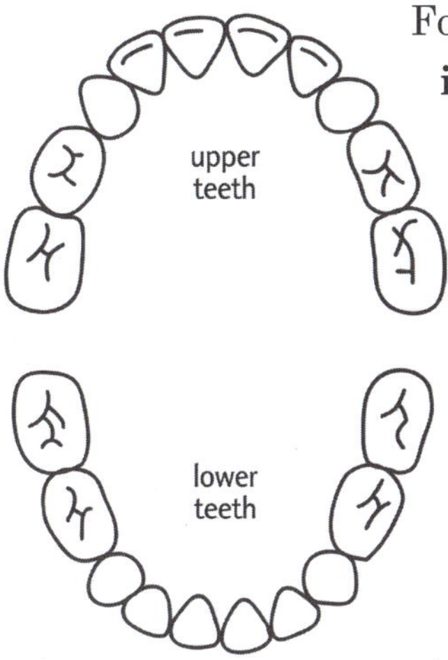

Children's milk teeth

Food is taken into the body through the mouth by a process called **ingestion**. Large pieces of food need to be chewed to break them down into smaller pieces before swallowing. Humans use their teeth to bite and chew food. The number of teeth that an individual possesses is age dependent. Humans grow two sets of teeth during their lifetime. The first set of teeth grows during infancy and fall off at the age between six and twelve years. These are termed **milk teeth**. The second set that replaces them are the **permanent teeth**, which may last throughout life or fall off during old age. Children upto the age of six have around twenty milk teeth, which fall off and give way to the thirty-two permanent teeth that adults possess. Gradually, permanent teeth replace all the milk teeth. Each tooth is rooted in a separate socket in the gums.

All the thirty-two teeth in our mouth are not similar; they vary in appearance and perform different functions. The teeth are classified into four groups: incisors, canines, premolars and molars. In each jaw, there are four incisors, two canines, four premolars and six molars. The incisors are located in the front of the mouth and are used for cutting or gnawing. Canines are pointed, conical teeth located between the incisors and premolars and are used for tearing food. The premolars and molars, situated at the back of the mouth, are mainly used for chewing and grinding.

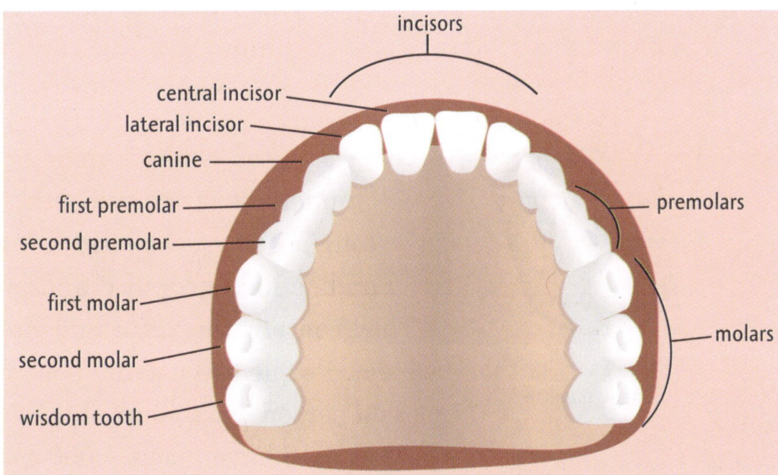

Adult teeth

incisor: a tooth for cutting or gnawing; located in the front of the mouth in both jaws
canine: pointed, conical teeth (two in each jaw) located between the incisors and the premolars
molar: the grinding teeth in the rear part of the mouth

Care of teeth

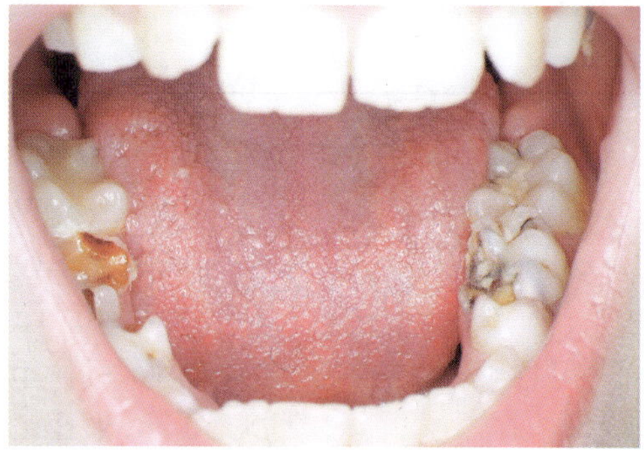

Tooth decay

The tough, shiny and white outer surface of the tooth, called the **enamel**, is very hard, but it can get damaged by acids formed because of eating food. If teeth are not cleaned properly after eating sweets, many harmful bacteria begin to grow and live in them. These bacteria break down the sugars in the food that we consume and release acids, which gradually dissolve the enamel and damage the teeth. This is called **tooth decay**. If not treated in time, it causes severe toothache and in extreme cases the tooth may need to be removed. Chocolates, sweets, cold drinks and other products containing sugar are the major causes of tooth decay. It is necessary to clean the teeth well after eating so that no food particle remains trapped in or sticking to the teeth. Brushing the teeth well at least twice a day is usually recommended to prevent tooth decay.

The tongue

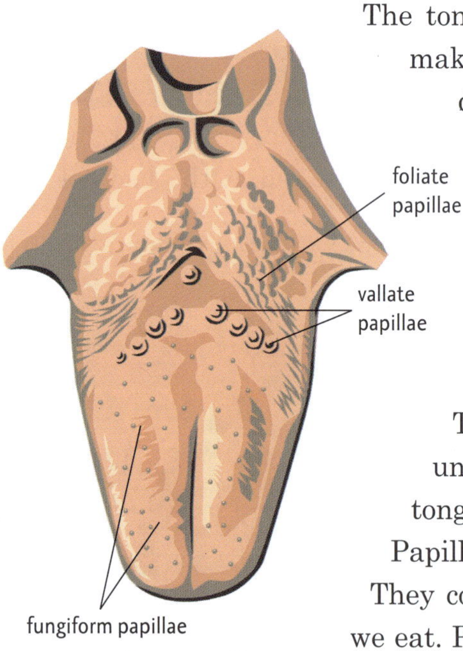

Tongue papillae

The tongue is made up of many groups of muscles, which makes it very strong. These muscles run in different directions to carry out all the functions of the tongue. The front part of the tongue is very flexible and can move around, working with the teeth to create different types of words when we speak. This part also helps us eat by moving food around the mouth while chewing. The tongue pushes the food inside the mouth so that the rear teeth can grind it.

The top of the tongue is rough and bumpy while the underside is very smooth. This is because the top of the tongue is covered with a layer of bumps called papillae. Papillae help grip food and move it around while chewing. They contain the taste buds, which help us taste whatever we eat. People are usually born with about 10,000 taste buds, but as a person ages, some of these taste buds die. Hence, an old person may have about 5,000 taste buds! Some typical tastes that the taste buds can detect are sweet, sour, bitter and salty.

papillae: small nipple-shaped protuberances on a tongue concerned with taste and touch

Circle Time

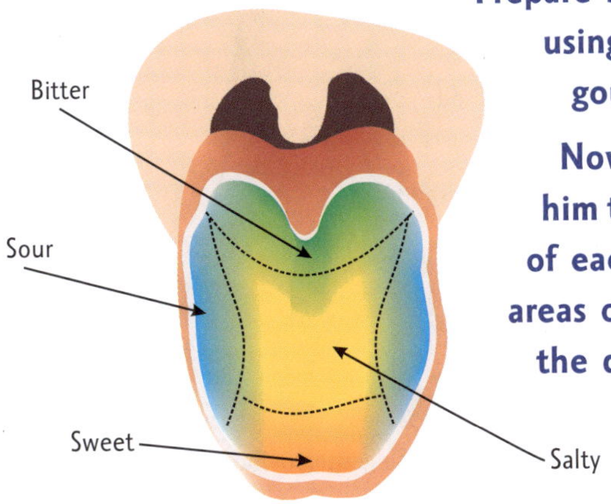

Tongue–taste regions

Prepare samples of sweet, sour, bitter and salty solutions using sugar, lemon juice, crushed neem leaves or bitter gourd and common salt, respectively.

Now, blindfold one of your classmates and ask her/him to stick out his/her tongue and hold still. Put a drop of each of the above samples one by one on different areas of the tongue–front, sides and back, as shown in the drawing–using a clean toothpick for each sample. Ask the classmate to identify in which areas of his/her tongue he/she could detect the sweet, sour, bitter and salty substances. Repeat this activity with other classmates. Do you find any difference in the perception of taste between your classmates?

The muscles at the back of our tongue help us make certain sounds, like the letters 'k' and hard 'g' (like in the word 'go'). The rear part of the tongue is important for eating as well. Once the food is ground and mixed with saliva, the rear muscles start to work. They move and push a small bit of food at a time along with the saliva into the oesophagus, which is the food pipe leading from the throat to the stomach.

Since the food pipe runs adjacent to the wind pipe, which carries air from the nostrils to the lungs, food particles occasionally get into the wind pipe thus causing coughing or choking. This may happen particularly while eating in a hurry or while laughing or talking while eating. Normally, when food is being swallowed, a flap-like valve closes the passage of the windpipe and guides the food into the food pipe. However, talking or laughing while eating does not allow the valve to close properly and food particles could enter the windpipe and cause choking.

The oesophagus or food pipe

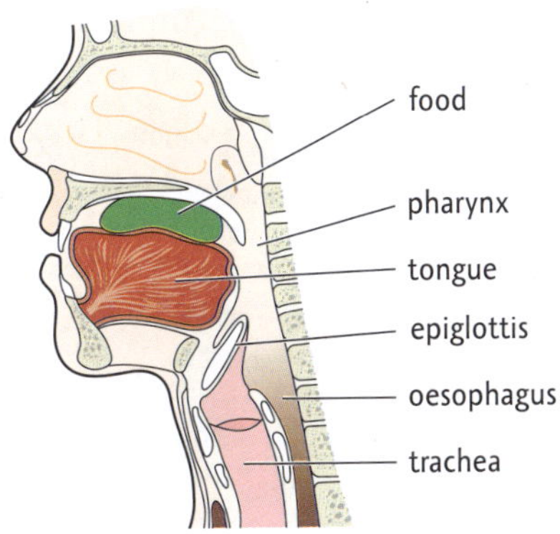

The food that is swallowed is pushed down by the movement of the wall of the oesophagus. Similar movement also takes place throughout the alimentary canal and pushes the food downward. The food then reaches the junction of the oesophagus and stomach where a ring-like muscle closes the passage between the two organs. When food approaches, the muscle relaxes and allows the food to pass through to the stomach. At times the food is not accepted by the stomach and is vomited out.

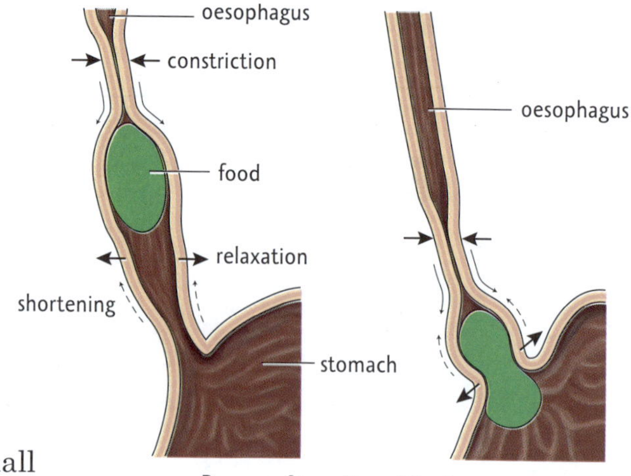

Process of ingestion of food

The stomach

The human stomach is a muscular, elastic, pear-shaped bag, lying hortizontal in the abdominal cavity beneath the diaphragm. It is located between the oesophagus and the small intestine. The size and shape varies according to the position of the body and the amount of food inside it. The capacity of the stomach of an adult is about 2 litres. Food enters the stomach from the oesophagus. The contents of the stomach empty into the duodenum. The duodenum is the first section of the small intestine.

The stomach functions as the primary organ of the digestive tract. The inner lining of the stomach secretes digestive enzymes and hydrochloric acid to help in food digestion. The digestive juices break down the proteins into simpler substances. A mucous layer protects the lining of the stomach from the acid.

The stomach carries out three mechanical tasks. The muscle of the upper part of the stomach relaxes to accept large quantities of the swallowed food and liquid material. This is then mixed with the digestive juices in the lower part of the stomach by the action of its muscles. Finally, the stomach empties its contents slowly into the small intestine.

The small intestine

The partially digested food mixed with the digestive juices from the stomach enters the small intestine. It then mixes with the juices of the two other digestive organs, namely, the pancreas and the liver. The pancreas produces a juice that contains enzymes to break down the carbohydrate, fat and protein in food. Other enzymes that are active in the process come from glands in the wall of the intestine.

diaphragm: a muscular partition separating the abdominal and chest cavities; functions in respiration
duodenum: the first section of the small intestine
bile: a digestive juice secreted by the liver and stored in the gall bladder; aids in the digestion of fats

The liver produces yet another digestive juice known as bile. Bile is stored between meals in the gall bladder. At mealtime, it is squeezed out of the gall bladder through the bile ducts and into the small intestine. Bile mixes with the fat in food and helps dissolve it. After the fat is dissolved, it is digested by enzymes from the pancreas and the lining of the intestine.

Factastic
In a grown-up person, the small intestine is about 7.5 metres long and the large intestine is about 1.5 metres long.

Most of the digested molecules of food, as well as water and minerals, are absorbed through the small intestine. The lining of the small intestine contains many folds that are covered with tiny hair-like projections called villi. The villi, in turn, are covered with microscopic projections called microvilli. These structures create a very large surface area through which nutrients can be absorbed. The digested food can now pass into the blood vessels that are present in the wall of the intestine. This process is called **absorption**.

The absorbed substances are transported to different organs of the body where they are used to build complex substances, such as the proteins required by the body. This process is called **assimilation**. In the body cells, glucose combines with oxygen to produce carbon dioxide, which is transported through blood to the lungs and is exhaled out. The reaction also releases energy, which is essential for us.

The food that remains undigested and unabsorbed then enters the large intestine.

The large intestine

The large intestine is a part of the digestive system where waste products from the food that was eaten are collected and processed into faeces. It is wider and shorter than the small intestine and performs several functions—it reabsorbs water and maintains the fluid balance of the body; it absorbs certain vitamins; processes undigested fibre; and stores waste before it is eliminated as faeces. The faecal matter is removed through the anus from time-to-time. This is called egestion.

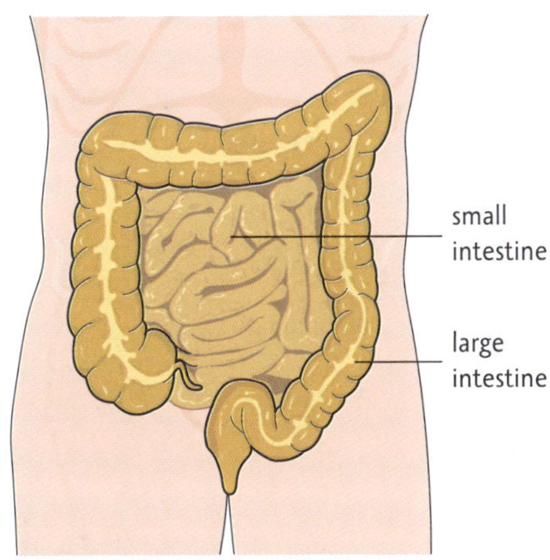

Small and large intestines

villi: minute, hair-like projection on mucous membrane
egestion: the act of expelling faecal matter from the body
diarrhoea: frequent and watery bowel movements

Diarrhoea

Diarrhoea is a condition where one passes watery stool frequently. It may be caused by an infection, food poisoning or indigestion. Diarrhoea is very common in India, particularly among children. If it is not controlled in time, it can be fatal as there may be excessive loss of water and salts from the body. The immediate remedial measure to make up for the lost water and salts in the body is to give the patient plenty of **oral rehydration solution** (ORS), which is boiled and cooled water with a pinch of salt and sugar dissolved in it.

Digestion in grass-eating animals or ruminants

Grass-eating animals, such as goats, sheep, cows and buffaloes, have a very special way of digesting their food. They cannot digest the food they eat in one go because they lack the enzymes to break down cellulose, which is a type of carbohydrate present in the cell walls of plants. Ruminants have a very special digestive system that allows them to live exclusively on plants, whose nutrients remain locked in cellulose.

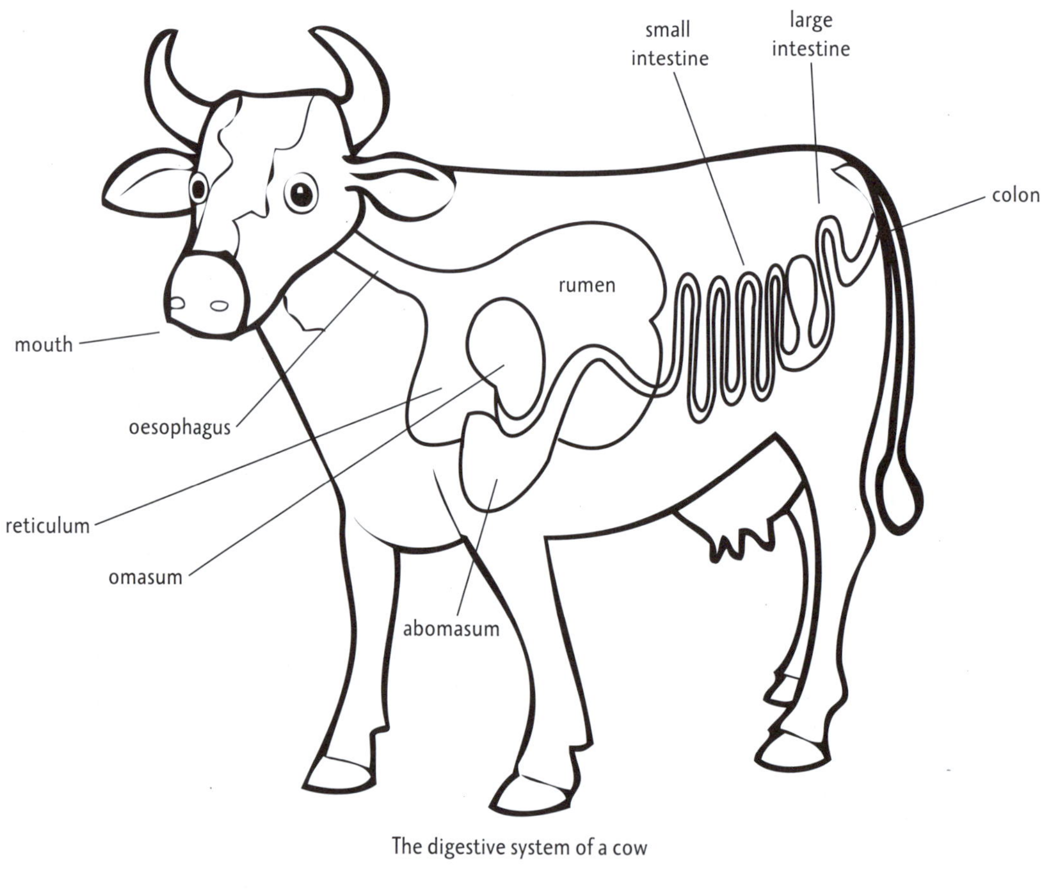

The digestive system of a cow

Unlike other mammals that have one stomach, a cow or buffalo has a complicated stomach with four chambers. The four chambers include: rumen, reticulum, omasum and abomasum. When a cow or a buffalo eats something, the food is partly chewed and swallowed and passed into the rumen, or the first chamber. The digestion process begins in the rumen. Bacteria in the cow's rumen help to break down the cellulose. The partly digested food is called the cud. Later the cud returns to the mouth in small lumps and the animal chews it again. This process is called rumination and the animals that ruminate are called ruminants. Chewing the food again allows the ruminant to get as much nutrition as possible from its food.

Feeding and digestion in amoeba

Amoeba is a microscopic single-celled organism found in pond water. An amoeba has a cell membrane, a rounded, dense nucleus and many small bubble-like vacuoles (tiny cavities filled with fluid) in its cytoplasm. Constantly changing its shape and position, the amoeba pushes out one, or more finger-like projections, called pseudopodia or false feet, for movement and capturing food. The amoeba is an omnivore, feeding on both plants and animals. Its diet includes bacteria, microscopic plants, such as the diatoms, minute algae, microscopic animals, such as other protozoa, nematodes and even dead organic matter.

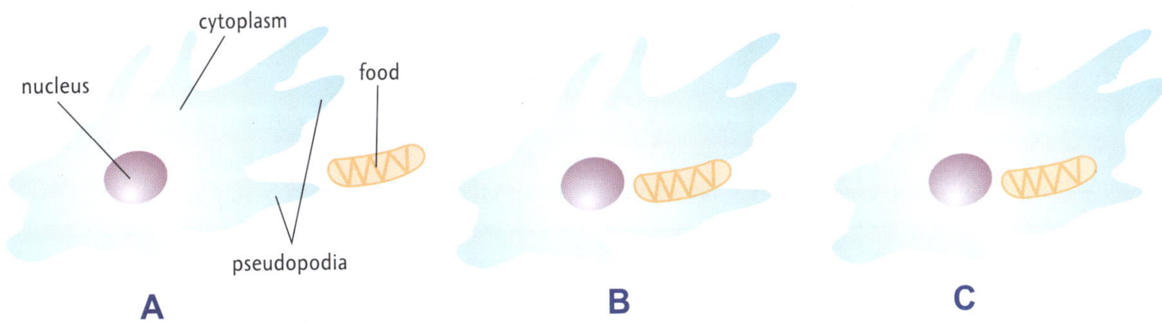

Amoeba—ingestion through circumvallation

rumen: the first chamber of the stomach of a ruminant where food is collected and returned to the mouth as cud for chewing
ruminant: any of various cud-chewing mammals having a stomach divided into four compartments.
pseudopodia: a temporary projection used by some micro-organisms as an organ of feeding or locomotion

Since it is a unicellular organism, an amoeba does not have any specialised structure or organ for ingestion. The amoeba takes in its food through the general body surface with the help of pseudopodia. When the amoeba senses food, it pushes out pseudopodia around the food particle and surrounds it. The food is ingested at the point where it comes in contact with the cell surface, with the help of pseudopodia. The food is then acted upon by digestive juices in **food vacuoles** and gradually the digested food is absorbed. The absorbed substances are then used for growth, maintenance and multiplication. The undigested residue of the food is expelled outside by the vacuole.

Activity

Our tongue can sense sweet, salty, bitter and sour tastes. Write the correct taste in front of the food items mentioned below. Also mention the part of the tongue that senses the flavours of each food item—sides, back, tip, etc.

	Food item	Taste
1.	ice cream	
2.	cooked vegetable	
3.	a slice of lime	
4.	*karela* (bitter gourd)	
5.	pastry	
6.	ginger	
7.	honey	
8.	potato chips	
9.	chocolate	
10.	raw mango	

Answers: 1. sweet (tip), 2. salty (middle), 3. sour (sides), 4. bitter (back), 5. sweet (tip), 6. bitter (back), 7. sweet (tip), 8. salty (middle), 9. sweet (tip), 10. sour (sides)

Revision Time

* Animals have to depend on plants for food and nutrition either directly by eating plants or indirectly by eating animals that eat plants.
* Nutrition in animals depends not only on the nutrients present in food but also on the mode of intake of the food and its utilisation in the body.
* The modes of feeding vary in different organisms.
* Breaking down food into simpler parts is called digestion. Digestion is both mechanical and chemical.

* Chemical digestion makes use of certain chemicals called enzymes, which help in the simplification of food matter.
* The food that we eat passes from our mouth through the digestive system.
* Organs that make up the digestive tract are the mouth, oesophagus, stomach, small intestine, large intestine, rectum and anus.
* Digestion is a complex process involving: (i) ingestion, (ii) digestion, (iii) absorption, (iv) assimilation and (v) egestion.
* The digestive juices, which contain enzymes, convert complex food substances into simpler ones that the body can absorb.
* Humans grow two sets of teeth during their lifetime. The first set, termed as milk teeth, fall off between the ages of six and twelve. The second set of teeth are the permanent teeth, which may last throughout life or fall off during old age.
* Taste buds on the tongue can detect sweet, sour, bitter and salty tastes.
* The stomach functions as the primary organ of the digestive tract.
* Most of the digested molecules of food, as well as water and minerals, are absorbed through the small intestine.
* The large intestine is the part of the digestive system where waste products from the food that was eaten are collected and processed into faeces.
* Ruminants, such as cows and buffaloes, use a two-step process for digestion. They quickly swallow their leafy food and store it in the rumen. Later, the food is brought back into the mouth and the animal chews it again.
* Amoeba uses its false feet or pseudopodia to ingest food.

Quiz Time

1. Answer the questions.

a. Why does food need to be digested to be useful to the body?

b. Where does digestion take place in the human body?

c. What causes tooth decay?

d. Why is the stomach not dissolved by the acid it contains?

e. Where is bile produced and stored?

2. Fill in the blanks.

a. Digested food can be easily ________________ by the body.

b. Digestion makes use of certain chemicals called ________________.

c. The ________________ stores the liver's digestive juices until they are needed in the intestine.

d. The premolars and molars, situated in the rear part of the mouth, are mainly used for ________________.

e. The inner lining of the stomach secretes digestive enzymes and ________________ to help in food digestion.

3. Indicate whether the statements are true or false.

a.	Enzymes are proteins that help in the simplification of food matter.	True	False
b.	The incisors are located in the rear part of the mouth in both jaws and are used for chewing and grinding.	True	False
c.	Swallowed food is pushed down by the movement of the wall of the stomach.	True	False
d.	Most of the digested molecules of food, as well as water and minerals, are absorbed through the large intestine.	True	False
e.	A cow has a complicated stomach with four chambers.	True	False

4. Explain the terms.

a. enzyme

b. alimentary canal

c. digestive juices

d. assimilation

e. ruminant

5. Project work

a. Make a list of animals, birds and insects. Use reference books or the internet to find out what they eat and which of the following modes they use for feeding: fluid feeding, bulk feeding, filter feeding, deposit feeding and phagocytosis. Record your findings in the table on the next page.

Animal	What it eats	Mode of feeding
mosquito		
earthworm		
flamingo		
sunbird		
crow		
cow		
spider		
whale		
amoeba		
butterfly		
python		
starfish		

b. Talk to your classmates, friends and neighbours and find out from them at what age they lost their first tooth. Enter the data in the table given below. From the table, find the average age at which children lose their milk teeth.

S. No.	Name	Age at which first tooth fell

Think it over

1. **Why are diarrhoea patients in hospitals usually given a glucose drip?**
2. **Why is oral rehydration solution advised for patients with diarrhoea?**

3 Fibres and Fabrics

All fabrics are made by weaving or knitting yarn, or threads of different kinds. Yarn is actually made when several thin strands of natural or synthetic fibres are spun together. Spinning twists the fibres making them stay together and gives strength to the yarn. There are many sources from which fibres are obtained. Vegetable fibres include cotton, flax, hemp and jute. Among the fibres obtained from animals, wool and silk are most prominent. Wool is obtained from the fleece of sheep or goat while silk is obtained from the cocoon of the silkworm. Different methods are used to obtain fibres from animals and to process them into yarn and fabric.

Wool

Wool is obtained mainly from sheep and certain other animals such as goats, yak, camels and rabbits. It is primarily made of a fibrous protein called keratin, which is the main constituent of hair and feathers. Wool has many unique properties that makes it well suited for textile production and can be woven or knitted.

fleece: the woolly covering of a sheep or goat
cocoon: a silky case spun by the larvae of many insects for protection as pupae
silkworm: the commercially bred caterpillar of the domesticated silk moth, which spins a silk cocoon from which silk fibre is obtained
keratin: a fibrous protein forming the main structural constituent of hair, feathers, hoofs, claws, horns, etc.

Wool is obtained from sheep

Like humans who have different types of hair on the body and the head, animals too have different types of hair on their body. The hairy skin of the sheep has two types of fibres that make up its fleece—coarse hair and fine soft underhair or 'downs' close to the skin. It is the fine underhair that provides the fibres for making wool. Some breeds of sheep have softer and better quality underhair than others and these are specially bred for making wool. This method of breeding animals for their special quality is called **selective breeding**. Although most of the wool available in the market comes from the fleece of sheep, it is not the only source of wool. For example, one of the finest wools used for weaving expensive pashmina shawls comes from the pashmina goat, which is a special breed of goat found in Jammu and Kashmir. The pashmina goat sheds its winter coat every spring, which is collected and is hand spun to produce pashmina wool. The fleece of sheep called Merino provide the merino wool. Merino wool comes from Australia, South Africa and South America. The fibres are so fine that a one mile long string would weigh only 0.3 gm.

Pashmina goat

Yak

In Ladakh and Tibet, the hair of the yak is used to make wool. Yaks usually shed their soft underhair annually, which is gathered and spun into yak wool. Angora wool is obtained from angora goats, found in hilly regions such as Jammu and Kashmir. The fleece of the angora goat is soft and silky and the whitest known in the trade. It is also known as **mohair**.

underhair: a covering of soft downy hairs lying underneath the outer hairs of an animal's coat

Llama

Camel

Factastic

The wool produced by the vicuña, a South American member of the camel family and a relative of the llama and the alpaca, is the finest, warmest and the most expensive wool in the world. A metre of vicuña wool fabric may fetch prices that range from US$ 1,800 to US$ 3,000.

The fur on the body of camels and three other camel-like animals, llama, alpaca and vicuña found in South America, is also used as wool.

Alpaca

Sheep rearing

Sheep are reared in many parts of India for wool. In the hills in Arunachal Pradesh, Himachal Pradesh, Jammu and Kashmir, Sikkim and Uttaranchal, the plains of Gujarat, Haryana, Punjab and Rajasthan and in the south in Andhra Pradesh and Karnataka, sheep rearing is a regular vocation.

Sheep breeds of India

Breed	States where found
Gurez	Mountainous areas of Jammu and Kashmir
Bhakarwal	Lower hills of Himalayas
Rampur bushir	Himachal Pradesh, Uttaranchal
Lohi	Rajasthan, Punjab
Nali	Rajasthan, Punjab
Marwari	Rajasthan, Gujarat
Sonali	Rajasthan
Nalore	Andhra Pradesh
Deccani	Andhra Pradesh
Mandya	Karnataka

Processing fibres into wool

The processing of wool involves four major steps—shearing followed by sorting and grading, making yarn and, lastly, weaving into fabric.

- Raw wool is obtained by shearing sheep. Shearing means removing the fleece by cutting, which is usually done once a year. Machines similar to those used by barbers are used to shave the fleece off sheep skin. Usually, the fleece is removed during the hot weather so that it grows back in winter to provide protection to the animal. Shearing does not hurt the sheep just as cutting hair does not hurt us because hair is merely dead strands of protein without any nerve endings.

Shearing

- The fleece that is obtained straight off a sheep after shearing is known as grease wool because it contains a high level of grease called **lanolin**, as well as dirt and dead skin that needs to be **scoured** or cleaned. The process of scouring may be as simple as a bath in warm water, or as complicated as an industrial process using detergent and alkali, and specialised equipment. It is during this step that the lanolin (grease of wool), is separated off and later used to make cosmetics and soaps.

Picking

Spinning

shearing: cutting the wool off sheep or other animals
scouring: removing dirt or unwanted matter

- After scouring, the wool is passed through a series of rollers and dryers and when dried, it is carded. The carding process involves passing the wool through rollers that have thin wire teeth.

Weaving

- After carding, the processes used in making yarn vary slightly, depending on the length of the fibres. Wool manufacturers knit or weave yarn into a variety of fabrics. The longer fibres are made into wool for knitting sweaters and the shorter fibres are spun and woven into woollen cloth. Wool may also be dyed at various stages of the manufacturing process and undergo finishing processes to give them the desired look and feel.

Wool is used to make sweaters, dresses, coats, suits and jackets. It is also made into blankets and carpets.

Factastic

Wool catches fire at a higher temperature than cotton and some synthetic fibres. And even when it catches fire, the flame does not spread quickly. After burning, wool does not melt or drip; it forms a char, which is insulating and self-extinguishing.

Knitting

Silk

Silk is also an animal fibre. It is a natural protein fibre produced by **silkworms**, some forms of which can be woven into textiles. The best-known type of silk is obtained from cocoons made by the larvae of the mulberry silkworm, *Bombyx mori*, reared in captivity. The rearing or culture of silkworms for obtaining silk is called **sericulture**. India produces plenty of silk on a commercial scale.

The silkworm is actually the **caterpillar** of a moth. The female silk moth lays eggs, from which hatch larvae called caterpillars. The caterpillar is a voracious eater and consumes lots of leaves of the tree on which it lives. It grows rapidly in size and after some time stops eating. The caterpillar then prepares to form **pupa**, which is the next stage in its life cycle. It begins spinning a protective **cocoon** by moving its head from side to side in a figure '8' pattern. During cocoon formation, the caterpillar secretes fibre made of a **protein** that hardens on exposure to air and becomes silk fibre. Soon, the caterpillar completely covers itself with silk fibres.

Steps in making silk

Even as the cocoon is spun, the further development of the moth continues inside the cocoon. If the silkworms are allowed to mature and break through the cocoon, a mature moth emerges after about two weeks. But this can destroy the cocoon and the silk it is made of. So before the moth emerges, the cocoon is plunged into boiling water to kill the growing moth inside and dissolve the glue holding the cocoon together. The end of the silk is then located and pulled out from the cocoon onto a spindle to be made into thread. About the size and colour of a cotton ball, the cocoon is constructed from one continuous strand of silk about 1.5 km long.

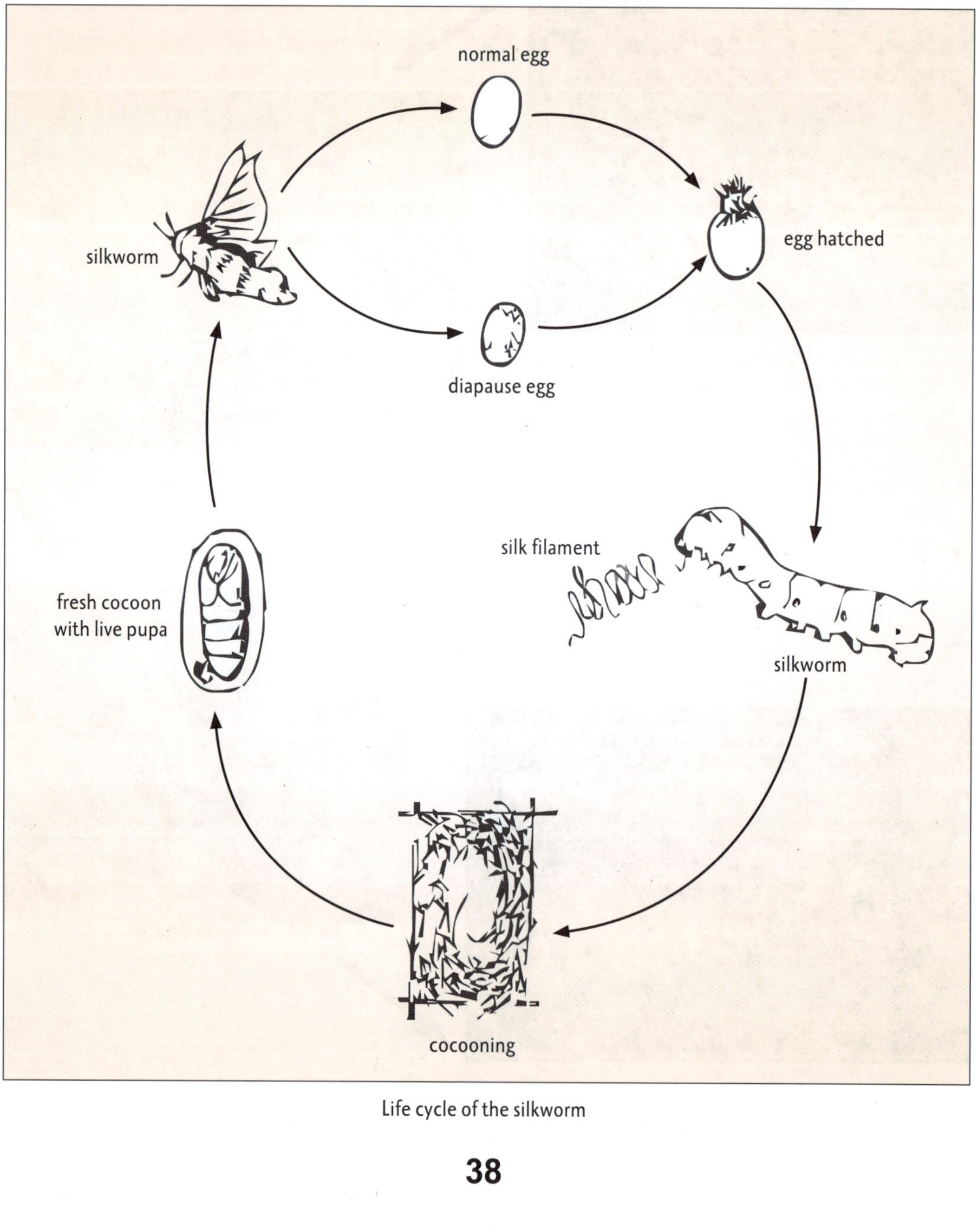

Life cycle of the silkworm

Tassar silkworm

Eri silkworm

There are several different varieties of silk moths that look very different from one another and the silk yarn they produce differ in texture and colour. The different varieties —*tassar* silk, *mooga* silk, *eri* silk—are obtained from cocoons spun by different types of moths. However, the most common silk moth is the mulberry silk moth, which feeds on mulberry leaves. Mulberry silk is soft, lustrous and elastic and can be dyed in beautiful colours.

Mooga silkworm

Factastic

Ancient stories indicate that silk was first discovered in China by Empress Si Ling Chi. The story goes that the empress was relaxing under a mulberry tree, enjoying a cup of tea. A silkworm cocoon fell from the tree and landed in her tea cup. As she removed it, the fine thread started to unravel. The secret of Princess Si Ling Chi's discovery was guarded by the Chinese for hundreds of years. It was considered the cloth of the gods and emperors and produced great wealth within the country. The Chinese secret to silk production lasted so long because of the threat of severe punishment. Anyone found guilty of selling or transporting silkworms, cocoons or mulberry trees was put to death.

Rearing silkworms

Silk is produced at silk farms by rearing silkworms for the production of raw silk. A female silk moth lays hundreds of eggs at a time. The eggs are laid on specially prepared paper. After the eggs hatch, the caterpillars or silkworms are fed fresh mulberry leaves. After about 35 days, the caterpillars stop eating. By this time, the caterpillars would have moulted or shed their skin four times and would be 10,000 times heavier than when they hatched and ready to begin spinning a cocoon. A straw frame is placed over the tray of caterpillars and each caterpillar begins spinning a cocoon. Within three days, the caterpillar spins enough silk to be completely encased in a cocoon.

The silk farmers then collect the cocoons to obtain silk. The cocoons are put in boiling water and the silk filament is drawn by pulling. The process of taking out threads from the cocoon is called reeling the silk. Reeling is done in special machines, which unwind the threads or the filaments of silk from the cocoon and wind them on a spool. The silk filaments are then spun into silk threads, which are woven into silk cloth either by hand looms or by machines.

Brainteaser

Why is a new quilt warmer than an old one?

Answers: A new quilt is fluffy and not compressed. As a result, more air is enclosed inside. Air is a bad conductor of heat and does not allow the heat to pass across making it more warm. When the quilt is not so new, it becomes compressed with repeated use and washing, thus enclosing lesser air than it did initially, making it less warm.

Revision Time

- Wool and silk are animal fibres.
- Wool comes from the hair of sheep, yak and other animals.
- The hairs of camel, llama, alpaca and vicuña are also processed to yield wool.
- In many Indian states, sheep are reared for wool.
- Silk is produced by the silkworm, the caterpillar of the silk moth.
- Silk fibres are made of a protein.
- The silk cocoon is constructed from one continuous strand of silk about 1.5 km long.
- There are several different varieties of silk moths that produce silk yarns of different texture and colour.
- The rearing or culture of silkworms for obtaining silk is called sericulture.
- The process of taking out threads from the cocoon is called reeling the silk.
- The silk filaments are spun into silk threads, which are then woven into silk cloth either by hand looms or by machines.

reeling: winding onto a reel

Quiz Time

1. Answer the questions.

a. What is wool made of?

b. Which part of the sheep's fleece provides fibres to make wool?

c. What is the raw wool obtained straight off a sheep after shearing known as and why?

d. From what stage in the life cycle of a silk moth, is silk obtained?

e. What are the longer and shorter wool fibres used for?

2. Fill in the blanks.

a. Some breeds of sheep have softer ________________ than others.

b. One of the finest wool used for weaving the expensive pashmina shawl comes from the pashmina ________________.

c. Before the fleece can be used for commercial purposes, it needs to be ________________.

d. The best-known type of silk is obtained from cocoons made by the larvae of the ________________ silkworm.

e. The process of extracting threads from the cocoon is called ________________ the silk.

3. Indicate whether the statements are true or false.

a.	The fleece of the angora goat is also known as pashmina.	True	False
b.	Shearing is the second step in wool production.	True	False
c.	Wool catches fire at a higher temperature than cotton and some synthetic fibres.	True	False
d.	The rearing or culture of silkworms for obtaining silk is called sericulture.	True	False
e.	Silk cocoons are put in cold water and the silk filament is drawn by pulling.	True	False

4. Explain the terms.

a. underhair

b. mohair

c. scouring

d. pupa

e. fleece

5. Project work

a. Collect pieces of silk cloth of various types from a tailor's shop. Mark each with a number and look at each sample closely through a microscope in your school lab. Observe all the samples at the same magnification. Make pencil sketches of what you see through the microscope and mark each sketch with the number put on the sample.

Take the sample home and identify the sample by discussing it with an adult. After identification, paste the samples in your scrap book along with the sketches you have made. Do you find any link between the structure of the fibre as seen under the microscope and the texture of the silk?

Try and collect pictures of different moth varieties, the caterpillars of which produce different types of silk. See if any of them produce the kind of silk you have collected as samples. You may paste the pictures of the moths along with the samples and your sketches in your scrapbook.

b. This project should be done under adult supervision. Take a few strands of pure silk, nylon, cotton and pure wool thread. Light a candle and carefully bring the tip of the different threads to the flame. Remove them quickly and find out what the smoke from each smells like. Does it smell like burning hair, burning paper or something else? Record your observations in a table as given on the next page.

Burnt strands of thread

Material of thread	Smoke smells like
silk	
nylon	
cotton	
wool	

From your observations, what conclusion do you draw about the chemical nature of the different fibres?

Think it over

1. **Why should woollen and silk garments always be washed with mild detergents?**
2. **Why is a woollen blanket used to smother a fire?**

4 Heat

In our daily life, we come across things that are cold and those that are hot. Water, kept in the fridge, and ice cream are cold while a steaming cup of tea or coffee is obviously hot. An object may be mildly hot or warm, or it may be mildly cold; the degree of heat varies. Sometimes it is possible to tell whether an object is hot or cold by simply touching it with our hand or any other body part, but this is not an accurate measurement. Certain factors, such as the temperature of the hand or fingers touching the object, play a role in determining whether the object is percieved as hot or cold. For example, if you put your left finger in ice-cold water and your right finger in warm water for some time and then put both your fingers in water at room temperature, your right finger will feel that the water is hot while your left finger will feel that the water is cold.

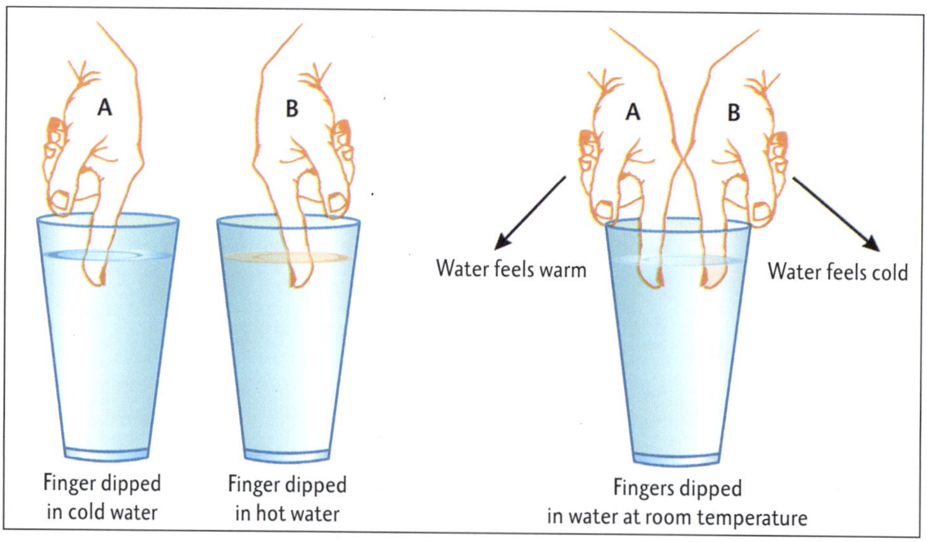

Dipping fingers in water at three different temperatures

Caution!

It is dangerous to touch a hot object without knowing how hot it is; it may cause severe burns!

temperature: the degree of hotness or coldness of a body or environment

> **Factastic**
> In 1742, Swedish astronomer Anders Celsius originally created a 'reversed' version of the modern Celsius temperature scale in which the boiling point of water was fixed as 0°C and the freezing point of water as 100°C. In 1744, the year Celsius died, the famous Swedish botanist Carolus Linnaeus reversed Celsius's scale, fixing the melting point of ice as 0°C and the boiling point of water as 100°C.

A more reliable method of identifying whether an object is hot or cold is to measure its **temperature** with an instrument. Temperature is a measure of the hotness or coldness of an object. The higher the temperature, the hotter an object is and the lower the temperature, the colder it is. Temperature can have a negative value as well.

To measure any condition or object, the basic requirement is some unit of scale. For example, to measure the length of a place or an object, one can use a metre, centimetre, yard or inch scale. Similarly, there are different scales for measuring temperature. The most commonly used is the **Celsius scale** in which the normal freezing point of water is 0 degree and the boiling point is 100 degrees, which is written as 0°C and 100°C, respectively. The Celsius scale is a centigrade scale, which means that the temperature range between the freezing and boiling points of water is divided into 100 equal parts.

There is another scale, mostly used in the United States and a few other countries, which is called the **Fahrenheit scale**. In this scale, the freezing point of water is taken as 32 degrees Fahrenheit, written as 32°F, and the boiling point of water as 212°F. Here, the scale is divided into 180 equal parts between the freezing and boiling points of water.

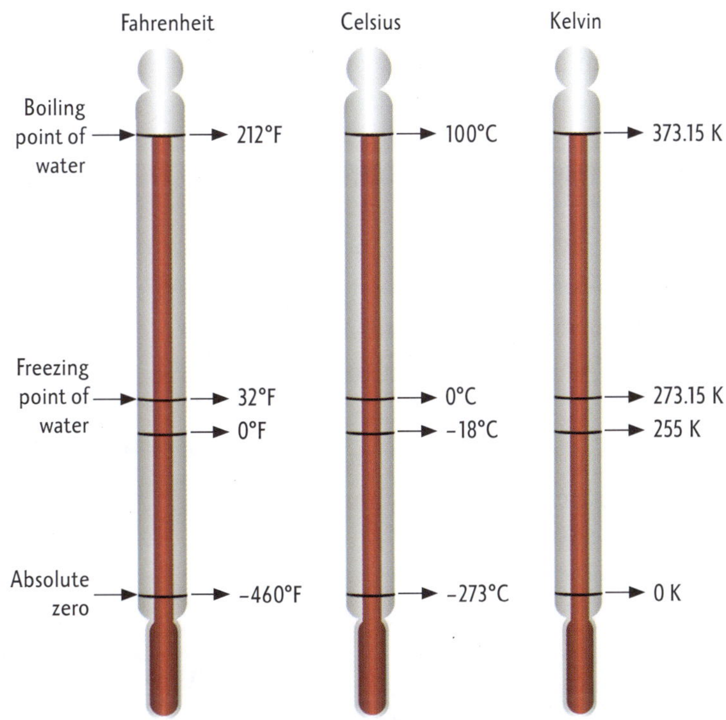

Temperature scales

Scientists mostly use a **Kelvin scale** in which temperature is measured in 'Kelvin'. In this scale, the freezing point of water is 213.15 K and the boiling point of water is 313.15 K. The degree sign is not used with the Kelvin temperature. The temperature of zero Kelvin (0 K) is called the 'absolute zero'. In the Celsius scale, absolute zero is –273.15°C. In the Kelvin scale the temperature range between the freezing and boiling points of water is divided into 100 equal parts.

Factastic

Although matter can be heated to millions of degrees Celsius, according to laws of thermodynamics, nothing can be cooled to absolute zero; that is, 0K or –273.15°C.

Thermometer

A thermometer (Greek *thermo* = warm and *meter* = to measure) is a device to measure temperature by using materials that change in some way when they are heated or cooled. It consists of a mercury or alcohol-filled bulb attached to a small tube with a narrow bore. When in contact with heat, the liquid in the bulb expands and when in contact with cold, it contracts and correspondingly the length of the liquid column in the tube increases or decreases. Modern thermometers are calibrated in standard temperature units such as Fahrenheit or Celsius.

The clinical thermometer

A clinical thermometer is used for measuring human body temperature. Like any other thermometer, it also consists of a mercury-filled bulb attached to a small tube with a narrow bore. A clinical thermometer has a constriction or kink in the thin bore close to the bulb. As the temperature rises, the force of expansion pushes the mercury up the thin tube through the constriction, but when the thermometer is removed from the

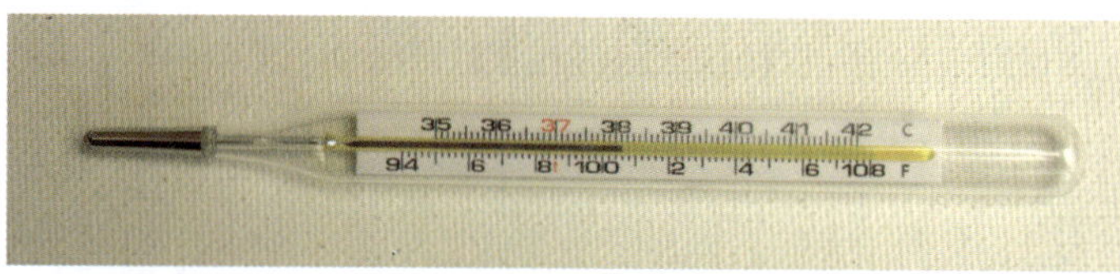

Clinical thermometer

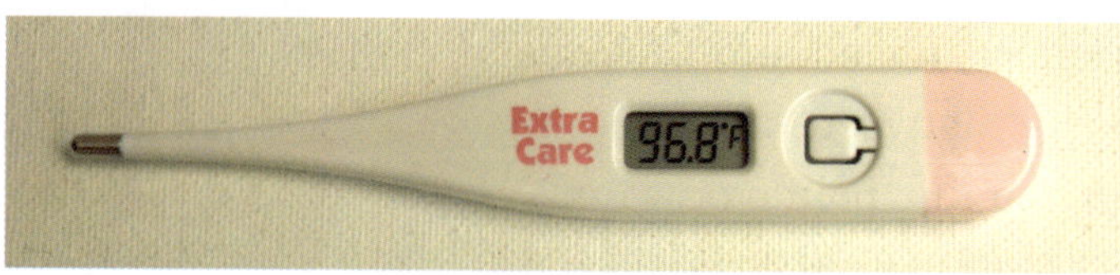

Digital thermometer

thermometer: an instrument for measuring temperature
clinical thermometer: a thermometer used to measure body temperature

body and the temperature possibly falls, the column of mercury breaks at the constriction and cannot return to the bulb, thus remaining stationary in the tube. This is necessary to show the correct reading, because otherwise the thermometer will always show a temperature lower than the body's actual temperature. Before the thermometer is reused, it has to be shaken with some force to bring the mercury column back into the bulb.

Factastic

In the conventional clinical thermometers, there is a possibility of breaking and thus spilling the mercury. Mercury is a toxic substance and is very difficult to dispose off. Nowaday digital clinical thermometers are available which do not use mercury and give the reading in clear digital form.

Reading on the thermometer

A clinical thermometer can read temperatures from 35°C to 42°C because it is designed to measure the temperature of the human body, which is usually in that range. The normal body temperature is 37°C. In the Fahrenheit scale, which was used in India earlier, the normal body temperature is 98.5°F. A body temperature higher than 37°C or 98.5°F may indicate fever, but may vary marginally from person to person.

To check for the exact reading, the thermometer needs to be held at eye level and parallel to the floor.

Usually the temperature scale is marked with long and short lines. The longer lines mark full degrees and half degrees. For example, the long lines indicate temperatures of 95, 95.5, 96, 96.5... and so on. The shorter lines mark 0.1 degrees and hence to read the correct temperature, one has to look very carefully at where the mercury column ends. If the mercury column is not seen clearly, the thermometer can be slightly rolled between the fingers until the column is visible.

Correct way of reading a clinical thermometer

Precautions while reading a clinical thermometer

- **The thermometer should be washed before and after use, preferably with an antiseptic solution to avoid spreading infection.**
- **Ensure that the mercury column is below the 35°C mark before use.**
- **The thermometer may be placed either in the mouth, under the tongue or under the armpit. In both cases, ensure proper contact of the skin with the bulb.**
- **The thermometer may be taken out after one minute and temperature recorded.**
- **The thermometer should be read by holding it at eye level and parallel to the floor.**
- **The thermometer should be handled delicately, taking care not to hit it against any hard object.**
- **The thermometer should never be held by the bulb while noting a reading.**

A clinical thermometer should not be used for measuring the temperature of any object other than the human body. If its bulb is exposed to a temperature higher than 42°C, it may break and spill the mercury. Hence, it should not be brought near a flame or exposed to direct sunlight.

The laboratory thermometer

The **laboratory thermometer** is used for different purposes including for measuring the boiling or melting points of substances. It is usually much bigger in length than a clinical thermometer and can measure temperatures in the range of –10°C to 110°C. The markings on the scale are similar to those on a clinical thermometer.

A laboratory thermometer is usually used in a vertical position. For example, to know the temperature of a liquid in a beaker, the bulb of the thermometer is dipped in the liquid and held vertically. In such a case, it is necessary to see that the thermometer bulb does not touch the bottom or the sides of the beaker or else the correct temperature may not be ascertained.

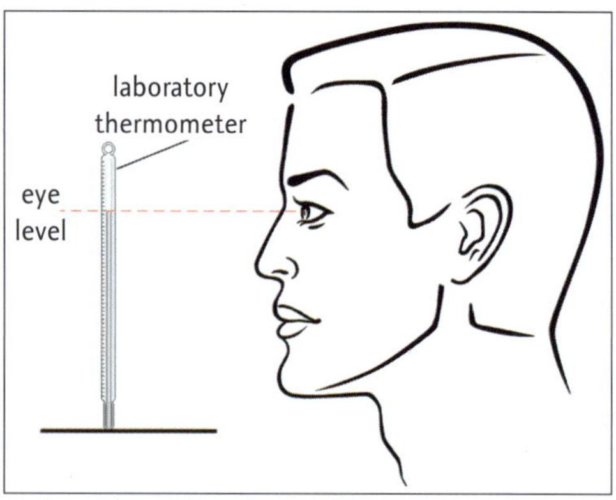

Correct way of reading a laboratory thermometer

Unlike the clinical thermometer where the temperature is read after taking the thermometer away from the body, the temperature in a laboratory thermometer has to be read while the bulb is dipped in the liquid of which the temperature is being measured. Since there is no kink in the mercury column, the laboratory thermometer will only show the temperature of the surroundings as soon as it is taken out of the liquid.

Explore

Take some hot water in a beaker. Take a laboratory thermometer and dip it in the beaker carefully. Wait for a few minutes and note the temperature. Now, take the thermometer out of the beaker and watch carefully what happens to the mercury column. Does it remain where it was when the thermometer was dipped in hot water? Why does the mercury column show a fall?

Now take water with ice in another beaker. Dip the thermometer in it and wait for some time. Note the temperature. Take out the thermometer and watch the mercury column. Does it remain steady? Why does the mercury column rise?

From what you have observed, do you think it is possible to measure body temperature with a laboratory thermometer accurately?

Factastic

The highest and the lowest temperatures of the previous day, as reported in weather reports, are measured by an alcohol-mercury thermometer called the maximum-minimum thermometer in which two tiny spring-loaded steel markers pushed by a mercury column record the two temperatures. The markers have to be brought back to the starting points using a magnet every day before recording the day's maximum and minimum temperatures.

Brainteaser

Can a mercury thermometer be used to measure temperature in the Arctic and Antarctic regions?

Answer: No. Mercury thermometers cannot be used in regions that have extremely low temperatures. Instead, alcohol thermometers are used in such areas since the freezing point of mercury is −39° C and that of alcohol is −112° C.

How heat flows

It is common experience that when a metal pan is placed on a stove it becomes hot, but after it is removed from the flame it cools down. The metal pan heats up because heat from the stove flame is transferred or flows into the metal pan. As long as the pan remains on the flame, it remains hot. But when it is removed from the flame, heat no longer flows into the pan; instead, now heat flows from the hot pan to the surroundings and hence the pan cools down. At the same time, the surrounding air and the table on which the hot pan is kept become warm till, after some time, they all cool down to room temperature.

Heat always flows from a hotter object to a colder object till both reach the same temperature, or attain equilibrium. There are three ways in which heat flows: by conduction, convection and radiation. When a metal pan is placed on a stove, the heat from the flame flows directly into the metal and heats it through conduction. Similarly, if a metal spoon is dipped in a cup of hot coffee, the other end of the spoon also gets hot after some time. In solid objects, heat is usually transferred by conduction.

Conduction

Convection

Radiation

Materials that allow heat to flow through them easily are **conductors** of heat. All metals are conductors, but the rate of heat flow varies in different metals. Heat flows much faster through copper and silver than through stainless steel or iron. That is why copper vessels or copper-lined vessels are often preferred for cooking because, being good conductors of heat, they help save fuel. On the other hand, materials, such as glass, plastic, rubber and wood, do not allow heat to flow through them. That is why the wooden handle of a sauce pan does

equilibrium: a stable situation where nothing changes
conduction: the process by which heat is directly transmitted through a material without the movement of the material
convection: the transfer of heat through a fluid (liquid or gas) caused by the motion of molecules
radiation: transfer of heat energy without a medium

not get hot when the pan is put on a stove. Such materials, which are poor conductors or non conductors of heat, are called **insulators**.

Water is a bad conductor of heat. But if water in a beaker is put on a burner, the entire water heats up and not only the water that is at the bottom and nearer to the flame. Initially, the water at the bottom of the beaker is heated by conduction and being lighter, the hot water rises up. Simultaneously, cold water from the sides moves down towards the source of heat at the bottom. This water also gets hot and rises and again water from the sides moves down. This process continues till all the water gets heated. This mode of heat transfer within a fluid caused by the tendency of warmer and less dense material to rise is called convection.

Explore

Fill two-thirds of a test tube with water. Place it on a tripod over a wire gauze. Let the water in the test tube stand for a while. Carefully drop a crystal of potassium permanganate at the bottom of the tube using a straw. Light a candle or a burner with low flame and place it under the test tube just below the potassium permanganate crystal. Watch what happens. How does the water in the test tube become coloured? What is the process known as?

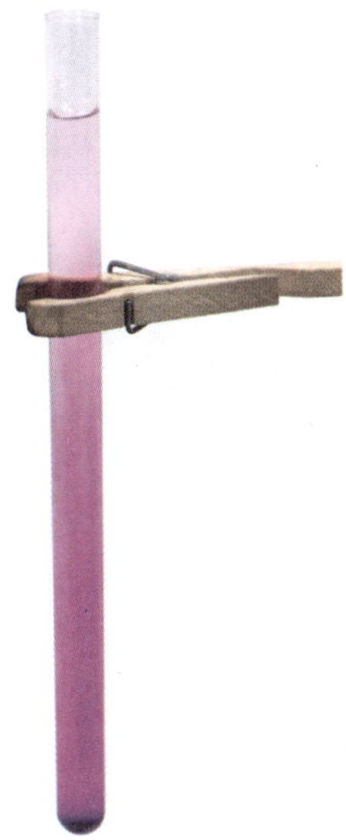

Air is also a bad conductor of heat; it is also heated by the same process as water. Smoke from a fire rises due to convection. If a candle is lit, more heat is felt if a hand is placed well above the flame than by keeping the hand near the flame on the side. This is because hot air from the flame rises up.

The third mode of transfer of heat is radiation. When there is a camp fire, the heat from it can be felt from a distance. This is due to the transfer of heat by radiation. Hot objects when kept in the open get cold due to the transfer of heat to the surroundings by radiation. All hot bodies radiate heat. When this heat falls on some object, a part of it is reflected, a part is absorbed and a part may be transmitted. The temperature of an object increases when it absorbs radiated heat. The earth also gets heated when it absorbs the heat radiated by the sun.

The transfer of heat by conduction and convection requires a medium—solids, liquids and gases. However, the transfer of heat by the radiation method does not need any medium. That is why the earth is able to receive the heat radiated by the sun across 150 million km of space, which is a vacuum.

Sea and land breezes

Sea and land breezes are wind and weather phenomena associated with coastal areas. When sunlight falls on earth during the day, both land surface and the oceans get heated. Land area heats up faster than the oceans because water, with its high heat capacity, takes a longer time to heat up. As the land area heats up, it also heats the air above it, causing the hot air to rise due to convection. At the same time, cooler air from the sea moves in towards the land to take its place. The air moving from the sea towards the land is called the sea breeze.

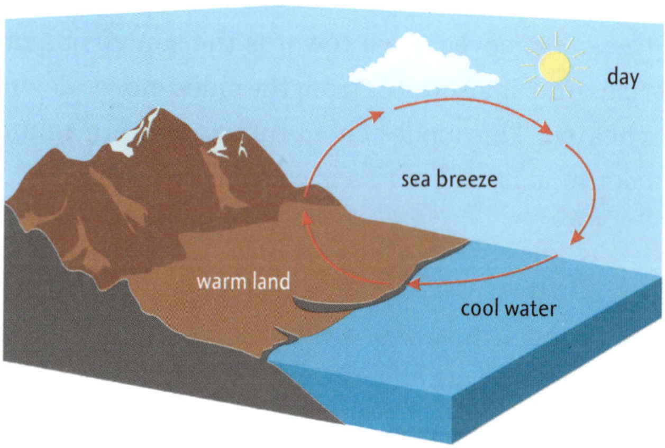

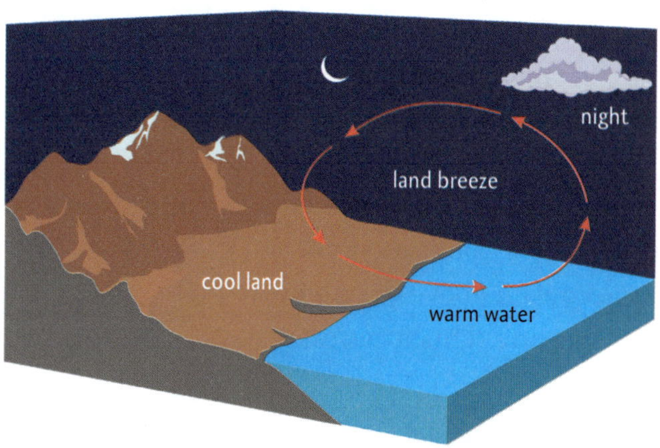

Flow of heat in sea and land breezes

At night the opposite happens. After sunset, the land cools faster than the sea by radiating heat. In contrast, the sea takes longer to cool because water loses heat slowly. Now, air over the sea being hotter rises and is replaced by cool air moving in from the land. This is known as land breeze. Both sea breeze and land breeze are caused by the transfer of heat to the air by a combination of conduction and convection.

Colour and heat

The amount of heat absorbed by an object that is exposed to the sun depends on the colour of the object and the material it is made of. As a general rule, a dark colour, such as black, absorbs more heat than a lighter colour such as white. This is because a dark-coloured object absorbs radiation of all the colours including heat radiation from the sun, whereas white colour reflects almost all the colours and absorbs very little. That is why choosing the right colour of clothes for winter and summer is important.

heat capacity: the amount of heat needed to raise the temperature of a body by 1°C
sea breeze: wind blowing from sea to land during the day
land breeze: wind blowing from land to sea during night

Explore

Take two identical beakers. Paint the outer surface of one, matt-finish black and of the other dull white. After the paints are dry, pour equal amounts of water in each and leave them in the mid-day sun for about an hour.

Measure the temperature of water in both the beakers with a laboratory thermometer. Is there any difference in the temperatures of the water in the two beakers? Which one do you find hotter to touch? Can you explain why?

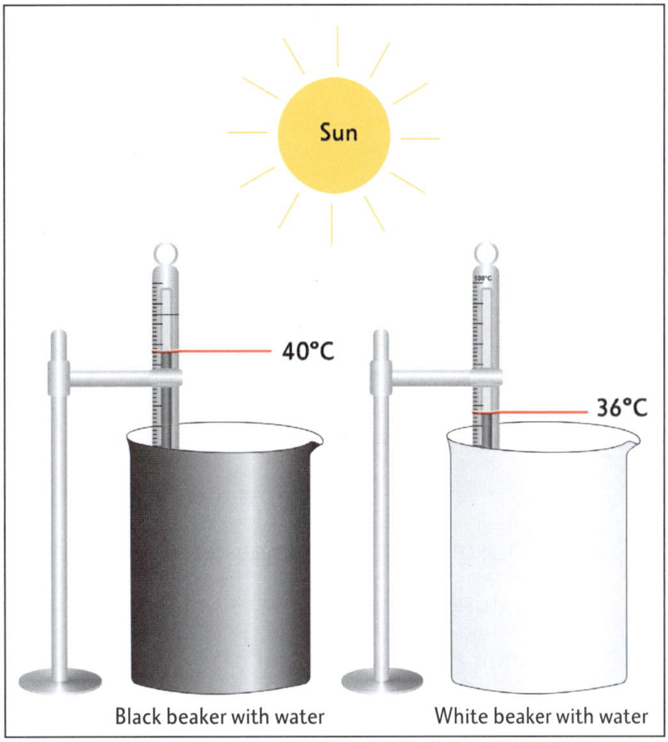

Black absorbs more heat than white

Empty the two beakers and let them cool to room temperature. Now, fill them with equal amounts of hot water at the same temperature—about 70°C. Leave the beakers in the shade. Note the temperature of water in the two beakers after about 15 minutes. Do they show the same temperature? Water in which of the beakers cools faster? Can you explain why?

Summer clothes

Going out in the sun dressed in a dark-coloured dress in summer would be unwise because a dark-coloured dress would absorb more heat from the sun making it very uncomfortable. But a dark-coloured dress would be quite comfortable in winter when the outside temperature is low and a little warmth is welcome. Therefore, dark-coloured clothes should be preferred in winter whereas light coloured clothes would be more comfortable in summer.

Apart from colour, the dress material also matters in the choice of dress for summer and winter. Woollen dress material is preferred in winter, whereas cotton is the favoured dress material for summer.

Wool has two important properties that makes it ideal for winter wear. Wool is a good insulator, so it does not allow the body heat to go out and keeps the body warm in winter. Second, the air trapped within wool fibres offers additional insulation to keep the body heat in, helping to keep the body warm.

Brainteaser

What is the space above a mercury column in a thermometer filled with?

Answer: It is originally a vacuum which may later contain some amount of mercury vapour in it.

Revision Time

- In our daily life we come across things that are cold and things that are hot.
- Our sense of touch is not always a reliable guide to the degree of hotness of an object.
- Temperature is a measure of the hotness or coldness of an object.
- A thermometer is a device for measuring temperature.
- A clinical thermometer is used for measuring only human body temperature; for other purposes, the laboratory thermometer is used.
- The normal average temperature of the human body is 37°C.
- Heat always flows from a hotter object to a colder object till both come to the same temperature or attain equilibrium.
- Heat can flow in three ways: by conduction, convection and radiation.
- In solids, heat is usually transferred by conduction.
- In liquids and gases, heat is transferred by convection.
- No medium is required for the transfer of heat by radiation.
- Materials that allow heat to flow through them easily are called conductors of heat.
- All metals are conductors of heat but heat flows at different rates through different metals.
- Materials that conduct heat poorly or do not conduct heat are called insulators.
- Sea and land breezes are wind and weather phenomena associated with coastal areas.
- Dark-coloured objects absorb heat better than light-coloured objects.
- Woollen clothes keep us warm during winter because wool is a poor conductor of heat and the air trapped between the fibres provides insulation.

Quiz Time

1. Answer the questions.

a. Why is a laboratory thermometer not used to measure body temperature?

b. Why is it necessary to shake a clinical thermometer before measuring body temperature?

c. What are the different modes of transfer of heat?

d. What are materials through which heat can flow easily called?

e. What are sea and land breezes?

2. Fill in the blanks.

a. The hotness of an object is determined by its ______________.

b. A ______________ thermometer cannot be used to determine the temperature of boiling water.

c. When water is heated from the bottom, heat is transferred by ______________.

d. Materials that allow heat to flow through them easily are called ______________ of heat.

e. During the day, the land surface heats up faster than the sea giving rise to the ______________ breeze.

3. Match the following.

a. sun's heat	i. absorption
b. rising smoke	ii. insulation
c. thermometer	iii. radiation
d. warmth of wool	iv. conduction
e. black cooking pot	v. convection

4. Indicate whether the statements are true or false.

a. In the Kelvin scale, the boiling point of water is 213.15°K.	True	False
b. The metal handle of a saucepan gets hot when the pan is put on a stove because of conduction.	True	False
c. Transfer of heat by radiation is not possible without a medium.	True	False

d. When placed in the sun, a light-coloured object becomes hotter than a dark-coloured object. True False

e. In coastal areas, land breeze occurs during the day. True False

5. Project work

a. Find out from reference books or by talking to a physician why a clinical thermometer has to be kept under the tongue or under the armpit for taking body temperature. Why can't the thermometer be used on other parts of the body?

Ask the physician to measure the body temperature of 10 or 15 students of your class. See if all of you have the same body temperature. If not, ask the physician the reason.

b. Carefully place a beaker of boiling water on a table. Collect an assortment of objects made of different materials such as a stainless steel spoon, a plastic spoon, a 15-cm wooden scale, a 15-cm steel scale, a glass rod, steel scissors, divider from a geometry box, a large iron nail and a pencil.

Put these objects in hot water in the beaker so that only one end of each object is immersed in water and the other end is above water. Wait for a few minutes, then touch the dry end of each object to feel how hot it is. Record your observations in the table given below.

Object	Material it is made of	Becomes hot
stainless steel spoon	metal	yes
plastic spoon		
wooden scale		
steel scale		
glass rod		
steel scissors		
geometry divider		
iron nail		
pencil		

Which materials are good conductors of heat?

Think it over

1. **How does a *tandoor* cook or bake?**
2. **How does coffee remain hot in a thermos?**

5 Acids, Bases and Salts

For thousands of years people have known that vinegar, lemon juice and certain other food items taste sour. However, it was not until a few hundred years ago that it was discovered why these things taste sour. The reason is that they are all **acids**. The term acid, in fact, comes from the Latin term *acere*, which means sour.

Many substances of daily use have either acids or bases in them. For example, orange juice and lemon juice contain citric acid. These juices, and others, also contain ascorbic acid, a substance more commonly known as vitamin C. Salads are often flavoured with vinegar, which contains dilute acetic acid. Curd contains lactic acid and grapes contains tartaric acid.

Fruits containing acids

You will see other acids, such as hydrochloric acid, sulphuric acid and nitric acid, in a chemistry laboratory. These acids are called mineral acids because they can be prepared from minerals. Mineral acids are generally stronger than household acids, and need to be handled with great care because they can burn skin and clothing.

Soaps

Baking powder

Factastic

Our body contains several types of acids. Each cell in our body contains deoxyribonucleic acid or DNA, the carrier of genetic information. Proteins, that build part of our cells are made of amino acids. The fats in our body contain fatty acids.

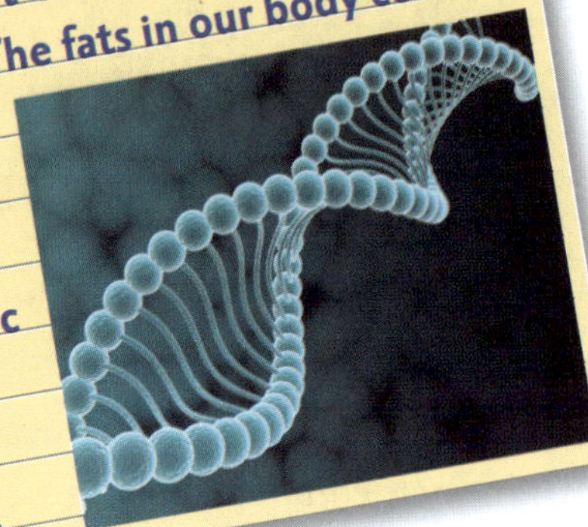

Our stomach secrets hydrochloric acid to aid in digestion.

A **base** is a chemical that has a bitter taste. When a base is added to an acid, neutralisation occurs and a **salt** is formed. A solution of ammonium hydroxide, often used in homes for cleaning, milk of magnesia, used to treat acidity and baking soda are all bases. Limewater—a water solution of slaked lime or *chuna*—is also a base. Lye or sodium hydroxide, used in the manufacture of soap, is another familiar example of a base.

deoxyribonucleic acid: a self-replicating material present in nearly all living cells, associated with the transmission of genetic information
amino acid: a nitrogen-containing organic acid that is the basic unit of proteins
fatty acids: organic acids occurring as compounds in fats and oils
neutralisation: making an acidic or basic substance chemically neutral
litmus paper: paper stained with litmus, used to test acidic and basic substances

Factastic

The first definition of acids and bases was given by the seventeenth-century Irish chemist Robert Boyle. He defined acids as sour tasting and corrosive to metals. They change litmus paper red and become less acidic when mixed with bases, while bases (which he called alkalies) feel slippery, change litmus paper blue and become less basic when mixed with acids.

A bitter taste and slipperiness are characteristics of all bases. It is the presence of a base that gives unflavoured milk of magnesia or baking soda their bitter taste. If a drop or two of household ammonia or moist baking soda is rubbed between our fingers, we get the slippery feeling of a base. Wet soap is also slippery because of the presence of a base.

Substances, such as vinegar, lemon juice, curd and tamarind, which contain acids, are called **acidic** substances. On the other hand, substances, such as household ammonia and baking soda, are said to be **basic**.

Explore

Take samples of lemon juice, orange juice, curd, baking soda, tamarind, green mango, grapes, vinegar and salt and taste each of them. Can you make out which of these are acids, which are bases and which are salts on the basis of their taste? Look up a reference book or the internet and find out which of them are acidic and which are basic. Do any of them contain an acid but do not taste sour? Can you tell why?

Testing for acids and bases

Acids and bases can be differentiated on the basis of their sour and bitter tastes, respectively. However, instead of tasting, which can be dangerous with unknown substances, there is a better and safer way of testing for the presence of acidic and basic substances. Using special coloured substances called indicators, we can detect the presence of acids or bases. The indicators change their colour when added to a solution containing an acidic or a basic substance. A large variety of indicators are available and most are natural colouring materials. Litmus, turmeric, petals of the hibiscus or China rose flower and red cabbage are some of the indicators found in nature.

Litmus

Litmus is the most commonly used indicator for testing acidic and basic substances in a laboratory. It is a water-soluble mixture of ten to fifteen different natural dyes extracted from lichens. When dissolved in distilled water, it produces a purple-coloured solution.

lichens: a simple slow-growing plant, which typically forms a low crust-like growth on rocks and trees

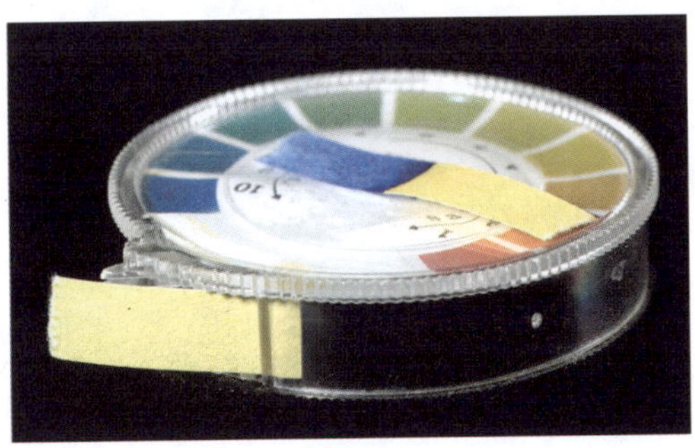

Litmus paper

Explore

Make separate solutions of salt, lemon juice, baking powder, washing soda, sugar, vinegar, detergent, lime water, curd and an aerated soft drink in different test tubes. In another test tube, take plain distilled water. Take strips of red and blue litmus paper. Using a dropper, place one drop of each solution on separate strips of red and blue litmus paper and note any change in colour. Also check for change in colour of the litmus paper with plain distilled water.

From change in colour of the litmus papers, can you identify the acidic and basic solutions?

Litmus indicator is available in the form of a solution or as litmus paper. Litmus paper strips are made by soaking in litmus solution and drying. The strips are available as red and blue litmus paper. Red litmus paper is prepared by treating the paper with a mild acid to make it turn red. Blue litmus paper is prepared in a similar way by treating the paper with a mild alkali. If red litmus paper is dipped in a basic solution, it turns blue, and if blue litmus paper is dipped in an acidic solution, it turns red.

The solutions that do not change the colour of any litmus papers are known as neutral solutions and are neither acidic nor basic. When litmus solution is added to an acidic solution it turns red, but when added to a basic solution, its colour becomes blue.

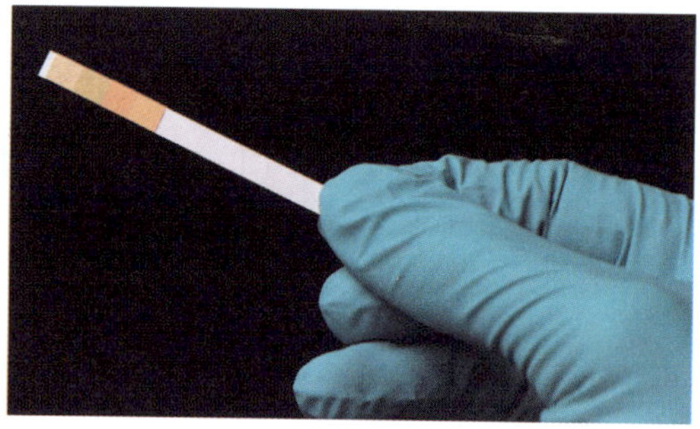

Testing with litmus paper

Turmeric

Turmeric is widely used in Indian cooking and is available in every household. The yellow colour of turmeric can be used as an indicator for the presence of basic substances. Turmeric does not change colour in an acidic or neutral medium, but in the presence of a basic substance, its colour changes to dark pink or red.

Turmeric

Turmeric stain

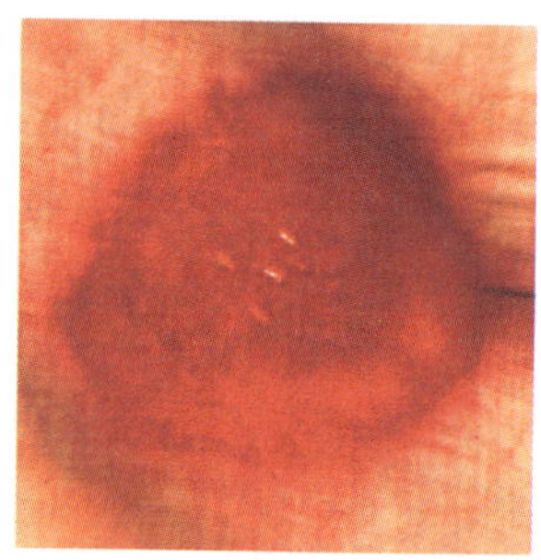

Turmeric stain after dipping in a base/alkali

Explore

Take a tablespoon of turmeric powder in a test tube. Add 20 ml of water to it. Mix well and dip a few strips of blotting paper in the mixture. Take out the strips and dry them thoroughly.

Prepare solutions of different substances such as salt, lemon juice, baking powder, washing soda, sugar, vinegar, detergent, lime water, curd and an aerated soft drink. Using a dropper, put one drop of each solution on the dry turmeric paper strips.

From the change in colour can you tell which of the solutions are basic? Are these the same solutions that had turned red litmus blue?

China rose or Hibiscus flower

The colourful flowers of China rose, or Hibiscus, contain natural dyes that can be used as indicators to test for acidic and basic solutions.

Hibiscus flower

Explore

Aim: To check the acidity of various solutions using a China rose indicator.

Material required: China rose flowers, conical flask and solutions of salt, lemon juice, baking power, washing soda, sugar, vinegar, detergent, lime water, curd and an aerated soft drink

Method: Collect a few fresh red China rose, or Hibiscus, flowers. Take a few petals and boil them in about 10 ml of distilled water for five minutes in a small conical flask. Filter the solution and use as an indicator.

Prepare solutions of different substances, such as salt, lemon juice, baking powder, washing soda, sugar, vinegar, detergent, lime water, curd and aerated soft drink, as done earlier. Take about 5 ml of each solution in test tubes and add five drops of the China rose extract indicator to each of them. The China rose indicator turns dark pink in acidic solutions and green in basic solutions. Record your observations. Do they match with the observations as with the litmus and turmeric tests?

Red cabbage

Red cabbage

Red cabbage juice contains a natural acidity indicator that changes colour according to the acidity of the solution. It shows red to violet colour in acidic solution and blue to green colour in basic solution.

Explore

Aim: To check the acidity of various solutions using red cabbage.

Material required: red cabbage, solutions of: salt, lemon juice, baking powder, washing soda, sugar, vinegar, detergent, lime water, curd and an aerated soft drink

Method: Take a red cabbage and grate it into small pieces. Place the grated cabbage in water in a container. Boil the mixture for 20 minutes, until the liquid turns a dark purplish colour. Pour the dark purple-coloured liquid into a glass or jar through a strainer.

Prepare solutions of different substances such as salt, lemon juice, baking powder, washing soda, sugar, vinegar, detergent, lime water, curd and an aerated soft drink. Take about 5 ml of each solution in test tubes and add five drops of the red cabbage extract indicator to each. The red cabbage indicator turns red to violet in acidic solutions, depending on the level of acidity, and blue to green in basic solutions. Record your observations. Do they match with the observations with the litmus, turmeric and China rose indicator tests?

Red cabbage extract

The four natural colour indicators described here can also be used to test a few strong acidic and basic substances such as hydrochloric acid, sulphuric acid, nitric acid and sodium hydroxide. But these materials need to be handled very carefully, as they are highly corrosive and can cause skin burns.

Acid–base neutralisation

Acidic and basic substances have contrasting properties. If the two are mixed in the right amounts, they react and **neutralise** each other, producing a **salt**, which may be neutral or mildly acidic or basic. The word 'neutralisation' is used because the acidic and basic properties of the two substances are destroyed or neutralised. The reaction also produces water molecules in addition to the salt.

For example, if hydrochloric acid is mixed with just the right amount of sodium hydroxide solution, the acid will be neutralised and the mixture will contain a solution of common salt or sodium chloride in water. That is, after neutralisation, the resulting solution is neither acidic nor basic.

Hydrochloric acid + Sodium hydroxide → Sodium chloride + Water
(HCl) (NaOH) (NaCl) (H_2O)

The reaction also produces some heat.

Explore

Aim: To observe the acidic and basic nature of solutions.

Material required: **dilute hydrochloric acid, sodium hydroxide solution, conical flasks, test tubes and phenolphthalein indicator**

Method: **Take dilute hydrochloric acid in a beaker and add few drops of the phenolphthalein indicator to it.**

Now, with a tube, add sodium hydroxide solution drop-by-drop to the beaker containing dilute hydrochloric acid and phenolphthalein. Shake the beaker gently and look for any change in colour. Continue adding the sodium hydroxide solution till a pink colour appears. Phenolphthalein turns pink in basic solution.

phenolphthalein: a colourless crystalline solid that turns pink in basic solution and is used as an indicator

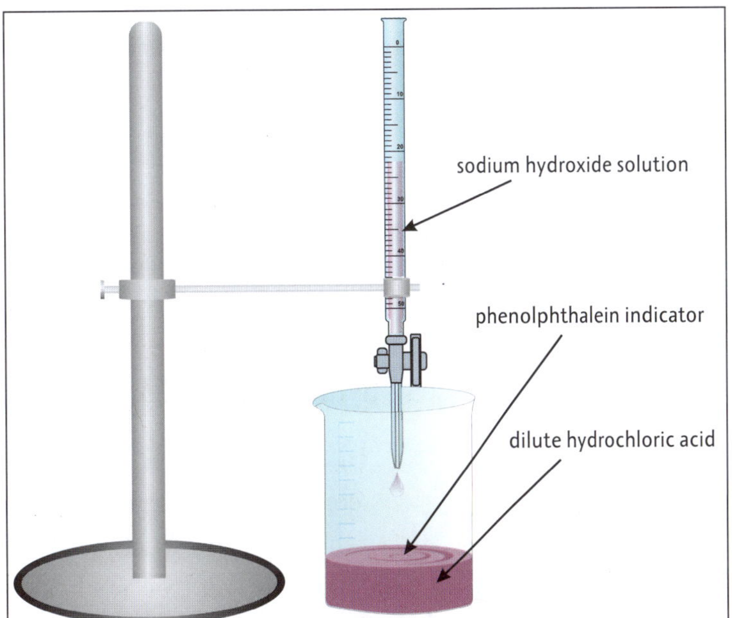

Add a drop of dilute hydrochloric acid to the beaker and see if the pink colour disappears. Does the solution turn pink again if one more drop of sodium hydroxide solution is added to it? What do these observations show?

Neutralisation reactions in everyday life

Acidity

Stomach acid, also referred to as **gastric acid**, is a digestive liquid consisting of hydrochloric acid that is produced in the stomach. The contents of stomach acid work to digest food and kill harmful bacteria ingested into the system. But, too much of acid in the stomach causes acidity and heartburn, and can often lead to **ulcers**, which may be painful.

The excess acid in the stomach can be neutralised by antacids, such as milk of magnesia, which contains magnesium hydroxide.

Acid in red ant bite

The bite of red ants causes a burning sensation because the body of ants contains formic acid. When the red ant bites, it injects the acidic liquid into the skin. The simplest way to neutralise the acid is by rubbing moist baking soda or boric powder on the wound. Calamine solution, which contains zinc carbonate, an alkali, is also effective.

Red ants

Acidic and basic soils

The excessive use of chemical fertilisers makes the soil acidic. Most food crops grow well in a neutral or slightly acidic soil and not in very acidic soil. When the soil becomes too acidic, it can be treated with bases, such as quick lime (*chuna*) or slaked lime (calcium hydroxide), to neutralise the acid.

In places where rainfall is scanty, the soil is often basic, containing large amounts of calcium, sodium and magnesium. Such basic soil may be neutralised by adding organic matter such as sawdust, compost, wood chips or

heartburn: a form of indigestion felt as a burning sensation in the chest, caused by acid regurgitation into the oesophagus
formic acid: a colourless irritant acid present in the fluid emitted by some ants

sulphur to it. Organic matter on decomposition releases acids that neutralise the basic nature of the soil.

Acid rain

Statues are damaged as a result of acid rain

Acids are present not only in certain fruits and on laboratory shelves, but they are also produced in nature, due to human activity. When any type of fuel is burnt, lots of different chemicals are produced as gases, that mix with air. Power stations, factories and cars burn fuel and produce polluting gases. Some of these gases (especially nitrogen oxides and sulphur dioxide), react with the tiny droplets of water in the clouds to form sulphuric and nitric acids. The rain from these clouds then falls as a very weak acid solution and is known as acid rain. Acid rain is primarily a result of air pollution and it can cause damage to buildings, historical monuments, plants, animals, statues, vehicles, pipes and cables. The worst affected are things made from marble, limestone or sandstone, as these types of rocks are particularly sensitive to acids.

Activity

Aim: To make an egg behave like rubber.

Material required: a glass of vinegar, one hard-boiled egg with its shell intact

Method:

Take the hard-boiled egg and place it in a glass of vinegar for a few days and do not move it. After 3–4 days, you will see some scum formation. Remove the egg from the vinegar and wash it, rinsing off the scum. Now if you press the egg, it will feel like rubber.

Explanation: The vinegar (which is acidic in nature), dissolves the calcium carbonate shell, leaving behind the inner membrane or skin of the egg. The egg thus feels rubbery!

acid rain: rainfall made so acidic by atmospheric pollution that it causes environmental harm, chiefly to forests, lakes and buildings

pollution: the presence of a substance in the environment which has harmful or poisonous effects

Brainteaser

Name a citrus fruit that contains more sugar than strawberries.

Answer: Lemon

Revision Time

- ✶ Acids are sour in taste and corrode metals.
- ✶ Bases are bitter in taste and feel slippery to touch.
- ✶ Indicators are substances that show different colours in acidic and basic conditions.
- ✶ Acids turn blue litmus red and bases turn red litmus blue.
- ✶ If acidic and basic substances are mixed in the right amounts, they react together and neutralise each other, producing a salt.
- ✶ Polluting gases emitted by industries cause acid rain by combining with cloud droplets.

Quiz Time

1. Answer the questions.

a. What are the common characteristics of acids and bases?

b. What is the source of litmus and what is it used for?

c. What acid is present in vinegar?

d. What is the salt produced when hydrochloric acid reacts with sodium hydroxide?

e. What is acid rain?

2. Fill in the blanks.

a. Orange juice contains ascorbic acid, a substance more commonly known as ____________________.

b. When a base is added to an acid, ____________________ occurs and a salt is formed.

c. A ____________________ taste and a slippery feel are characteristics of all bases.

d. Litmus, turmeric and China rose can be used as natural ________________.

e. The bite of red ants causes a burning sensation because it contains ________________ acid.

3. Indicate whether the statements are true or false.

	Statement		
a.	Salads are often flavoured with vinegar, which contains dilute hydrochloric acid.	True	False
b.	An indicator is a substance that shows different colours in acidic and basic solutions.	True	False
c.	Phenolphthalein turns pink when added to an acidic substance.	True	False
d.	Excessive use of chemical fertilisers makes the soil acidic.	True	False
e.	Litmus is obtained from the flowers of the Hibiscus plant.	True	False

4. Match the following.

a.	lemon	i.	lactic acid
b.	stomach	ii.	ascorbic acid
c.	grapes	iii.	hydrochloric acid
d.	vinegar	iv.	tartaric acid
e.	curd	v.	acetic acid

5. Project work

a. Prepare lime water in a bottle by dissolving some quicklime (*chuna*) in water. Stir the solution well and keep it for some time. Pour a little of the solution from the top into a beaker. Add a few drops of phenolphthalein indicator to it. It should show a deep pink colour. Take a straw and keep blowing into the lime water. What happens after some time? Why does the pink colour disappear?

b. Take a few samples of acids and other liquid chemicals available in your school lab and also a few common liquids available in the school and test for their acidic or basic nature using the four natural indicators discussed in this chapter. Enter your observations in the table given on the next page.

S. No.	Substance	Colour with litmus	Colour with turmeric	Colour with China rose	Colour with red cabbage	Acidic or basic
1.	hydrochloric acid					
2.	vinegar					
3.	milk					
4.	lemon juice					
5.	soda water					
6.	sulphuric acid					
7.	nitric acid					
8.	washing soda solution					
9.	baking soda solution					
10.	buttermilk					
11.	salt solution					
12.	ammonium chloride solution					
13.	sodium hydroxide					

Do all the indicators show consistent results with acidic, basic and neutral substances?

Think it over

1. **Why is carbonated water often prescribed to treat acidity?**
2. **Why is it advised that concentrated acid be poured into water for diluting it rather than pouring water into the acid?**

6 Physical and Chemical Changes

Changes constantly occur around us. Iron objects rust, ice melts into water, wet clay dries up, milk becomes sour, candles burn, chalk sticks get worn out, fruits rot and so on. Broadly all these changes can be divided into two categories—**physical changes** and **chemical changes**. In a physical change, the material that undergoes the change remains chemically unchanged. But in a chemical change, the original material itself changes into a new substance.

Physical change

A physical change is a change in the form of matter but not in its substance or its chemical nature. A physical change involves a change only in the physical properties such as shape, size, colour and the state of a substance. For example, if a piece of paper is cut up into small pieces, it still remains paper; only the shape and size of the paper changes. There is no change in the texture or colour of the paper. Similarly, if sugar is dissolved in water, this too is a physical change because if the water is allowed to evaporate, the sugar crystals would remain.

Circle Time

Make five groups in your class. Each group may do one of the following activities:

a. Take some ice in a small stainless steel bowl; melt it by keeping it in the sun. Now, place this bowl of water in a freezing mixture prepared by mixing crushed ice with salt. Wait for some time till the water freezes.

b. Crumple a few sheets of paper into tight balls. Then open them up into flat sheets again.

c. **Crush a chalk stick into powder. Add a little water to the chalk powder and mix it into dough. Carefully roll the dough into the shape of a chalk stick and allow it to dry.**

d. **Take a large iron nail and carefully hold it with a pair of tongs. Carefully take its tip over the flame of a burner. Let it glow red. Remove the nail from the flame and allow it to cool.**

e. **Take some water in a beaker and put it to boil on a tripod. Hold an inverted metal pan a little above the water boiling in the beaker. Look at the inside of the pan after a few minutes.**

What type of changes are observed in each of the activities mentioned? Record the changes observed in each case. Why do you think they are physical changes? Did the substances subjected to the change revert to their original form in all cases?

Crumpled ball of paper

Crumpled paper obtained as a flat sheet

Another example of a physical change is seen when ice melts into water. Ice and water have the same chemical composition—H_2O. Here also, only the form or state of a substance is changed; the chemical nature of the substance undergoing the change remains unchanged.

An important property of a physical change is that it is mostly reversible; that is, the substance undergoing physical change can be brought back to its original state. For example, a cup of water freezes when cooled and becomes liquid when heated.

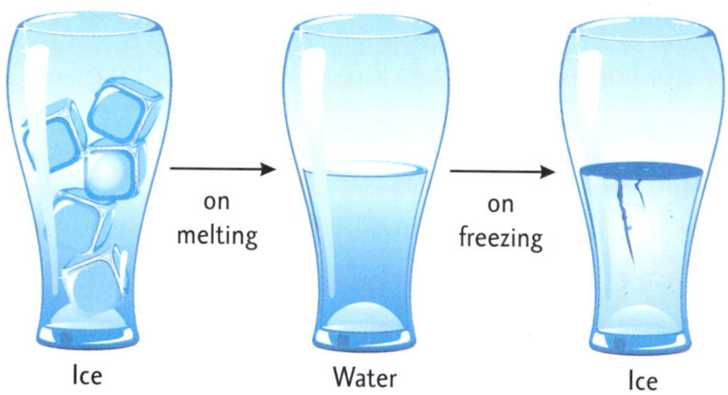

Conversion of ice to water is a physical change

Chemical change

A chemical change occurs when one kind of matter is changed into a different type of matter. A chemical change involves a chemical reaction in which new substances are formed and energy is either given off or absorbed. A chemical change usually involves a change in one or more chemical property of a substance like change in colour, release of gas, the formation of a precipitate

precipitate: material deposited in the solid form in a solution

and the absorption or release of heat. For example, if a sheet of paper is burned rather than crumpled or cut into pieces, it changes into a gas called carbon dioxide and heat is evolved. Similarly, if sugar is added to a cake recipe and baked, it undergoes a chemical reaction and changes into a new substance. When iron rusts, a new substance called iron oxide is formed by a chemical reaction between iron and oxygen, and in the process iron is lost.

Unlike a physical change, a chemical change is not reversible; that is, the substance undergoing a chemical change cannot be brought back to its original state by any simple process. For example, the sugar added to a cake recipe can not be brought back to its original form after the cake is baked. The rust that is formed on iron objects as a result of a chemical reaction, is a substance different from iron and cannot be turned back into iron by any simple means.

Rusting of iron

The rusting of iron is a chemical change. It is common to see rust on old iron gates, iron nails, iron pipes, steel furniture, old bridges, old car and truck bodies, iron shovels and spades. The reddish-brown coating of rust produced on the surface of iron objects is an oxide of iron formed by the action of oxygen in the air in the presence of moisture.

Iron (Fe) + Oxygen (O_2) + Water (H_2O) → Rust (Iron oxide, Fe_2O_3)

The presence of both oxygen and

Factastic

The iron pillar in the Qutub Minar Complex in New Delhi is a classic example of production of high quality iron. The pillar is said to be more than 1,600 years old and stands about 6.7 m high. The weight of the pillar is about 6,500 kg. Despite remaining exposed to the atmosphere for so long, the pillar has not rusted, which is a demonstration of the high degree of accomplishment in the art of iron making by ancient Indian iron and steel makers.

Rusting of iron

Application of paint to prevent rusting

moisture are essential for rusting to occur. If iron objects are left open in dry air, they will not rust. On the other hand, if the amount of moisture is very high, as in coastal areas, rusting occurs much faster.

The only way to prevent rusting is, therefore, to prevent iron objects from coming in contact with oxygen and water. This can be done in two ways. One, by applying a coat of paint or grease, rusting of iron can be prevented. Second, iron can be protected from rusting by applying a thin layer of zinc on its surface. Steel and iron structures, such as bridges, grills of buildings and ship hulls, need regular application of paint for protection against rusting.

The process of depositing a layer of zinc on iron is called galvanisation. The iron pipes used in homes to carry water are galvanised to prevent rusting. Corrugated iron sheets used as roofing are also galvanised to prevent rusting.

Stainless steel contains chromium that prevents it from rusting. Chromium reacts with oxygen to form a thin film that acts as a protection layer on steel.

Factastic

What prevents stainless steel objects from getting rusted is the presence of the metal, chromium. Stainless steel contains at least 12 per cent chromium that protects it from stains. The chromium in the steel combines with oxygen in the atmosphere to form a thin, invisible layer of chrome-containing oxide, called a passive film, which acts as an effective barrier against rusting.

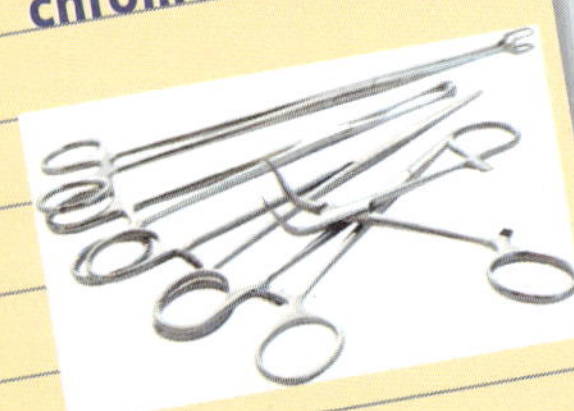

Iron in copper sulphate

When iron nails are put in an acidified solution of copper sulphate, a chemical change takes place. Iron reacts chemically with copper sulphate by dissolving in the solution, forming iron sulphate, which gives a light green colour to the solution. Copper is released in the

galvanisation: coat iron or steel with a protective layer of zinc solution and is deposited as a brown coating on the iron nails.

$$\underset{(CuSO_4,\ \text{blue})}{\textbf{Copper sulphate solution}} + \underset{(Fe)}{\textbf{Iron}} \rightarrow \underset{(FeSO_4,\ \text{green})}{\textbf{Iron sulphate solution}} + \underset{(Cu,\ \text{brown})}{\textbf{Copper}}$$

Explore

Take some copper sulphate crystals from your school laboratory. (Be careful while handling it because it is poisonous. Wash your hands after use.) Powder the blue crystals, take a teaspoonful of the crushed crystals in a beaker and add water to dissolve it. Add a few drops of sulphuric acid with a dropper to the solution. Mix well and pour half of the solution into another beaker.

In one of the beakers, drop a few clean iron nails and leave the other as it is. Look at the solutions in the two beakers after about an hour or so. Do you observe any change?

Note the colour of the solution into which the iron nails had been put. Is the colour the same as the colour of the solution in the other beaker? Is there any change in the colour of the nails? What is the brown deposit on the nails?

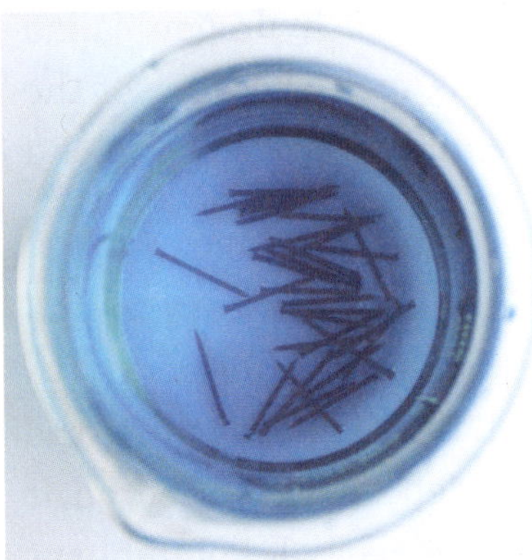

Copper sulphate solution with iron nails

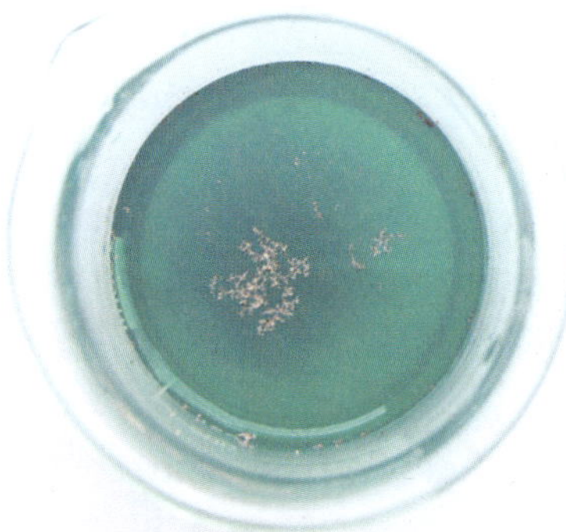

Copper sulphate solution and sulphuric acid with iron nails

Brown deposit on iron nails

Baking soda in vinegar

Another simple chemical change occurs when baking soda is added to vinegar. During this chemical reaction, carbon dioxide is released. If the reaction is carried out in a small conical flask with a stopper, the gas can be passed with the help of a bent glass tube into a test tube containing lime water. The gas turns lime water milky.

Vinegar + Baking soda → Carbon dioxide + Sodium acetate
(CH_3COOH) ($NaHCO_3$) (CO_2) (CH_3COONa)

When carbon dioxide is passed through lime water, another chemical change takes place.

Carbon dioxide + Lime water → Calcium carbonate + Water
(CO_2) ($Ca(OH)_2$) ($CaCO_3$) (H_2O)

Being insoluble in water, the calcium carbonate formed in the reaction turns lime water milky.

Thus, when baking powder is added to vinegar, a chemical change occurs in which new substances (carbon dioxide and sodium acetate) are produced.

Burning of a candle

The burning of candle is a good example of a chemical change. A candle is made up of a substance called **paraffin wax**, which is a compound of carbon and hydrogen called **hydrocarbon**. When a candle is lighted, the wax around the wick melts because of the heat and vapours are formed. It is these vapours that catch fire and form the flame of a candle.

Soot deposition on metal

When a candle burns, it is easy to find out the new substances formed. If a clean metal plate is held touching the flame, a black deposit is formed on it which is **soot** (fine particles of unburnt carbon). If a cold metal plate is held a little above the flame, tiny droplets of water, formed by the condensation of water vapour can be seen on it. Also, since a candle contains carbon, carbon dioxide is also formed. In effect, the burning of candle produces three new substances—soot, water vapour and carbon dioxide. Energy is also evolved during the reaction.

Wax	+	Oxygen	→	Carbon	+	Water	+	Carbon dioxide
(Hydrocarbon)		(O_2)		(C)		(H_2O)		(CO_2)

It is the glowing particles of carbon in the flame that make the candle flame luminous.

Browning of cut fruits

Action of air on cut apple

One of the very common everyday examples of a chemical change is seen when cut fruits are kept exposed to air for some time. The most common example is the browning of cut apples.

Apples and many other fruits contain certain chemicals called phenols. Phenols when exposed to air react with oxygen after the fruit is cut and produce dark-coloured substances, which give a brownish colour to the cut surface. This is also a chemical change because the brown surface cannot become white again. But the browning of cut apple can be prevented by coating the cut surface with lemon juice or sugar syrup, which prevents its reaction with oxygen.

Extracting iron from iron oxide

Chemical changes are all around us and they are important in our lives. Combustion reactions help release energy to cook our meals and move our vehicles. Oxidation–reduction reactions keep the batteries in our cell phones and laptops functioning. Chemists are able to identify unknown substances by observing how they react with a known substance. We are able to identify if fruits or food items are spoiled, if they emit a foul smell. This foul smell is a result of foul-smelling substances being produced during the rotting process.

phenols: a class of weakly acidic organic compounds containing a benzene ring

Useful materials, such as metals, plastics, adhesives, dyes, paints and medicines, which we see around us are products of chemical changes. For example, if a metal is to be extracted from an ore, such as iron from iron ore, it has to go through a series of chemical changes. Most medicines are the end products of a chain of chemical reactions.

Signs of a chemical change

- Original substance and form may be lost (as in the burning of a sheet of paper, or a candle)
- A new substance may be formed (as in lime water turning milky due to exposure to carbon dioxide)
- Heat or light may be given off or absorbed (as in burning of wood or coal, or cooking)
- Sound may be produced (as in the explosion of fire crackers)
- A change in smell may take place or a new smell may be given off (as in rotting or fermentation)
- A colour change may take place (as in the baking of a cake, or the toasting of bread)

Fire crackers

The burning of coal, wood, gas or other substances is also a chemical change and is always accompanied by the production of heat. Apart from heat, the burning of fire crackers also produce light, sound and harmful gases that pollute the air.

Common salt is usually obtained by the evaporation of sea water. However, the crystals that are obtained are not pure and are small in size. But, it is possible to obtain large crystals of pure substances from their solutions by a process called crystallisation. The formation of crystals is an example of a physical change. Crystallisation is used in industry to obtain substances in their pure state.

crystallisation: form or cause to form crystals

Crystallisation requires slow cooling of a saturated solution of the salt of which crystals are to be grown. For growing large crystals, the saturated solution often needs to be seeded with a tiny crystal, called a seed crystal, made of the same material.

Explore

Aim: To grow crystals from saturated solutions.

Material required: alum, beaker and water

Method: Mix two tablespoons of powdered alum in half a beaker of water. Heat and stir until the alum dissolves. Keep adding alum powder till no more of it dissolves in the solution. Filter the solution if necessary. Pour two tablespoonfuls of the clear solution onto a petri dish and set is aside for 24 hours. By that time, the bottom of the petri dish will be covered with tiny crystals of alum, which can be used as seed crystals.

Take the remaining solution of alum, add two tablespoonfuls of water to it and heat it again. Add a little more alum powder till no more of it dissolves. Now drop two or three carefully selected seed crystals into the solution, cover it and keep it aside where it will not be disturbed for quite some time. For growing large crystals, the saturated solution needs to be cooled very slowly. Growing good quality single crystals takes time. It may take up to four weeks to grow a large alum crystal.

The same method can be used to grow crystals of any other salt that dissolves in water.

Growing crystals

Brainteaser

What is full of holes but can still hold water in it?

Answer: A sponge

seed crystal: a small piece of single crystal from which, typically, a large crystal of the same material is to be grown

Revision Time

- ✶ A physical change is a change in the form of matter that does not change its chemical nature.
- ✶ A chemical change occurs when one kind of matter is changed into a different kind of matter.
- ✶ The rusting of iron is a chemical change that can be prevented by painting or galvanising the iron surface.
- ✶ Cooking always leads to a chemical change.
- ✶ One of the very common example of a chemical change is seen in the browning of exposed cut fruits.
- ✶ Substances such as metals, plastics, adhesives, dyes, paints and medicines are products of chemical changes.
- ✶ The formation of crystals is an example of a physical change. Crystallisation is used in industry to obtain substances in their pure state.

Quiz Time

1. Answer the questions.

a. Why is the setting of curd considered a chemical change?

b. What kind of change occurs when baking powder is added to lime juice and why?

c. What are the methods used to prevent iron from rusting?

d. Why does stainless steel not get rusted when exposed to air and moisture?

e. Mention any two signs of a chemical change.

2. Fill in the blanks.

a. Changes in which new substances are formed are called ____________ changes.

b. When iron nails are put in copper sulphate solution, the colour of the solution changes to light green due to the formation of ____________ .

c. When carbon dioxide is passed through lime water, a precipitate of ____________ is formed.

d. Stainless steel contains ____________________, which protects it from rusting.

e. Unlike a physical change, a chemical change is not ____________________.

3. Indicate whether the statements are true or false.

a. In a chemical change, the material that undergoes a change remains chemically unchanged.	True	False
b. When iron rusts, a new substance called iron oxalate is formed by a chemical reaction between iron and oxygen.	True	False
c. When iron nails are put in a solution of copper sulphate, copper is released in the solution.	True	False
d. When baking powder is added to vinegar, sulphur dioxide gas is evolved.	True	False
e. The browning of a piece of apple is a chemical change.	True	False

4. Give five examples of chemical changes and justify in each case why they should be considered as chemical changes.

5. Project work

a. Make a list of fermentation reactions that you can think of and classify them as 'good' or 'bad' depending on whether they are useful to us or not. Describe the new products formed in each case and explain why they are good or bad.

b. Find out from reference books or the internet what chemical changes go on in a dry cell used in a torch and a car battery. Both produce electricity through a chemical change. But why can a car battery be used again and again after charging while a dry cell cannot?

Think it over

1. Why does a tin-plated iron sheet with scratches get rusted more easily than a scratched galvanised iron sheet?

2. When quicklime is put in water, a lot of heat is evolved. Is it a physical or a chemical change?

7 Weather, Climate and Animal Adaptations

The weather changes daily and from place to place. It forms an integral part of our lives and affects our day-to-day functioning. It affects many things that we do, such as the clothes we wear, the food we eat, where we live and how we travel. The weather is of great interest to people everywhere, from meteorologists (scientists who study weather) to farmers and horticulturists whose crops depend on ambient weather conditions. The weather is of concern to

WEATHER

Max. 34.1°C (-1)/Min. 29.4°C (+2)
Moonrise: Tuesday - 2.35 pm
Moonset: Wednesday - 01.11 am
Sunset: Tuesday - 7.19 pm

Sunrise: Wednesday - 5.36 am
Generally cloudy sky; rain/thundershowers likely. Max. & min. temperatures on Tuesday likely to be 35°C & 28°C. Max. humidity was 79% and min. 66%.

Weather report

Rain

meteorologists: scientists who study the processes and phenomena of the atmosphere, especially as a means of forecasting the weather

Floods

the civil aviation industry as well. Bad weather often leads to delay or cancellation of flights resulting in inconvenience to passengers as well as financial loss for the aviation industry.

Drought

Weather phenomenon such as floods, droughts, cyclones, etc., can have a profound effect on human life and on the economy.

What is weather?

The *Oxford English Dictionary* defines weather as "the condition of atmosphere at a certain place and time, with reference to the presence or absence of sunshine, rain, wind, etc." Weather is primarily concerned with the air or the atmosphere at any place at any time—whether it is warm or cold, wet or dry and cloudy or windy. Weather has several components, which are nothing but individual physical features of the atmosphere.

Factastic

The various parameters, such as temperature, humidity, air pressure, etc., that meteorologists use to forecast weather are called the elements of weather.

On any single day, the weather can be different at different places. For example, in deserts, it rains very rarely. In a tropical jungle, it is always hot. Even at one particular place, the weather does not remain the same throughout the day; it keeps changing through the day. It may be cool and pleasant in the morning, sultry in the afternoon followed by rains in the evening and then pleasant weather again—all in the span of a single day.

atmosphere: an envelope of gases surrounding the earth
humidity: a quantity representing the amount of water vapour or moisture in the atmosphere
elements: the various parameters such as temperature, humidity, air pressure, etc., that meteorologists use to forecast weather

Most newspapers carry daily weather reports that have information about the temperature, humidity and rainfall during the past 24 hours at any place and also give a forecast of the weather for that day. The weather reports are prepared by meteorologists, who collect data on temperature, wind, etc., from weather stations in different cities and also receive data and pictures from satellites and use supercomputers to make weather forecasts.

Satellite image of clouds over the earth

If the daily weather reports over a week for any place are compared, it is clear that all seven days of the week do not have the same maximum and minimum temperatures, humidity or rainfall. There may be considerable variation, depending on the season. The weather at any place is the day-to-day condition of the atmosphere with respect to the temperature, humidity, rainfall, wind speed, etc.

Explore

Record information about your city's temperature, humidity and rainfall over a span of a week. You can source this information from the weather report printed in your local newspaper.

Tabulate the data for the whole week. What do you observe? Did the maximum and minimum temperatures and the humidity levels remain the same on all days of the week? Did it rain every day?

Make a similar table during the monsoon season. Did the humidity level remain the same? Did it rain every day? Can you explain why?

The sun and the weather

The sun is reponsible for the earth's weather patterns. It is the sun's heat that creates winds, clouds, cyclones and other weather phenomena.

supercomputer: a particularly powerful and fast mainframe computer
weather forecast: an estimate of the approaching weather
maximum temperature: the highest temperature recorded at a place on a single day
minimum temperature: the lowest temperature recorded at a place on a single day

The sun is actually a star—a medium-sized star—and is the source of all energy on earth. The core of the sun consists mainly of hydrogen, which is the lightest element. In the core of the sun, hydrogen atoms undergo thermonuclear fusion to produce helium atoms. During this process, an enormous amount of energy is released, which the sun radiates. The earth receives this energy in the form of heat and light. Almost every activity on the planet depends on a regular supply of the sun's heat and light. Without sunlight, no plants can grow and without plants no animals or humans can survive. The absence of sunlight for a considerable period of time can wipe out several species. This is supposed to have happened 65 million years ago when a giant asteroid hit the earth. It is believed that this collision produced a thick blanket of dust and ash cutting off sunlight and leading to the extinction of dinosaurs and many other species.

Since the earth is shaped like a sphere and it rotates on an axis that is tilted at an angle to the plane of the earth's orbit, not all parts of the globe receive the same amount of sunlight all the time. This causes the uneven heating of the earth's surface, oceans as well as the atmosphere, which plays an important role in determining the weather at any place.

The latitude or the distance from the equator also plays an important role in deciding the weather of a place. In general, a place nearer to the equator, will have an average temperature that is higher than a place further away from the equator. A place close to the poles will, on an average, experience very low temperatures, which may fall quite low in winters. The weather on mountains often changes unpredictably. This is due to sudden changes in wind direction and cloud formation at higher altitudes.

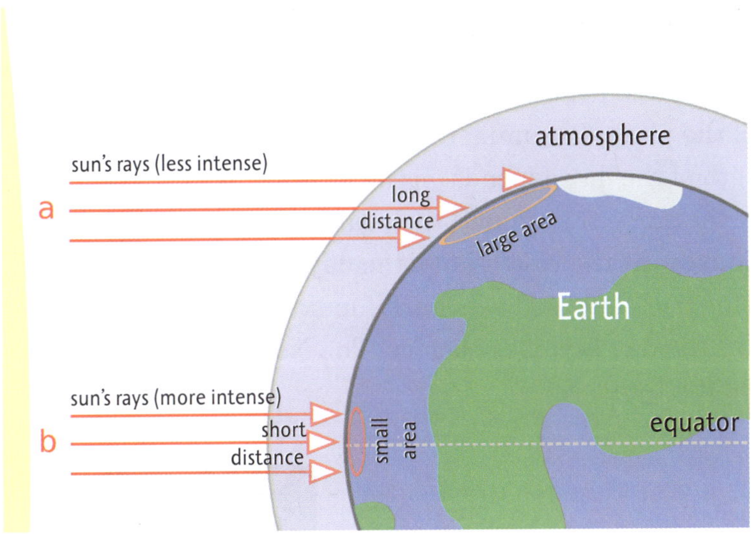

Weather forecasts

Weather is a highly complex system that is difficult to predict. A daily weather forecast involves the work of thousands of observers and meteorologists all over the world, and the work of thousands of computers. Modern computers have made weather forecasting more accurate than ever. Weather satellites orbiting the earth take photographs of clouds and send them to receiving stations on earth. Forecasters use the observations from the earth's surface as well as from space, along with formulae and rules based on the experience of what has happened in the past, and then make their forecast. But it is not always that the forecast made by the local meteorological office turns out to be correct.

Meteorologists use special thermometers called **maximum** and **minimum thermometers** to record the daily maximum and minimum temperatures. These thermometers use alcohol and a moving column of mercury in combination with two tiny, spring-loaded, steel markers in the thermometer capillary. When alcohol in the bulb expands at high temperatures, it pushes the mercury column up, which in turn pushes one marker towards high temperature end in the thermometer scale. As the temperature falls, the alcohol in the bulb cools and pulls the mercury column in the opposite direction. The mercury column now pushes the second steel marker towards the lower temperature, but the first marker remains stuck in the thermometer capillary at the highest temperature reached. Similarly, the second marker remains stuck at the minimum temperature reached. Both the markers are reset from outside with a magnet before recording the temperatures for the next day. Generally, the maximum temperature of the day occurs in the afternoon while the minimum temperature occurs early in the morning.

The time of sunrise and sunset at a place depends not only on the month of the year or season, but also on the latitude of the place. In summer, the sun rises early and sets late, making the day long. But the length of the day depends on the latitude. Near the equator, the length of day remains almost the same throughout the year. But as one moves north of the equator, the day becomes longer. At the North Pole, the day is almost 24-hour long in mid-summer. In winter, the sun rises late and sets early, making the days short. As one moves north from the equator, the day becomes shorter. The North Pole experiences an almost 24-hour long night in mid-winter.

Measuring rain

Rainfall is measured in millimetres. It is actually the height up to which the accumulated water would rise if all the rain fell on a perfectly flat surface, and indirectly gives a measure of the volume of water falling as rain. Thus, if it rained 200 mm over an area of 10 km^2, then the total volume of rain water would be $[(10\times1000\times100\times10)^2 \times 200]$ mm^3. Converted into litres it is 2×10^{10} litres, or 2,00,00,000 m^3. A rain gauge is a device for measuring rainfall. It is designed to collect the rain falling over a certain area, the volume of

Rain gauge

rain gauge: a device for measuring the amount of rainfall which can be measured with a measuring cylinder and the amount of rainfall can be computed in millimetres.

> **Factastic**
> Rain gauges are believed to have been used in India more than 2,000 years ago. In Kautilya's *Arthashastra*, there is a mention of the use of rain gauges to set precise standards of grain production. Each of the state's storehouses was equipped with a standardised rain gauge to classify land for taxation purposes.

Most standard rain gauges have a wide funnel leading into a measuring cylinder of such diameter that one millimetre of rain measures one centimetre when it collects inside. The funnel prevents the falling rain drops from splashing and spreading outside the funnel periphery. Standard meteorological gauges have a funnelled aperture of 150-170 cm and are set 30 cm above ground level. Normally, the cross-sectional area of the funnel is ten times that of the measuring cylinder. Rainfall as low as 0.02 mm can be measured with this instrument. Rainfall less than 0.02 mm is considered 'trace'.

Climate

Climate can be defined as the typical condition of the atmosphere near the earth's surface at a certain location on the earth. But it should not be confused with weather, which changes from day to day, or seasons that change in a regular cycle during the year. Even during a particular season, the weather may vary widely at the same place. In Delhi during summer, for example, the day temperature may rise to 45°C and on the next day, after a dust storm, may drop by a few degrees. But overall, summers in Delhi are always very hot. It is the climate that makes one area of the world a desert, another a grassland, another a rainforest, and yet another an icy expanse.

Climate is broadly the long-term weather of an area, taken over a period of at least thirty years. It includes the region's general pattern of weather conditions, seasons and weather extremes such as hurricanes, droughts or rainy periods. When the temperature of a place is shown as above or below normal (+ or –), the 'normal' is the average of the past 30 years or more. So also is the case with rainfall. During the monsoons, the same place may get very little rain in one season and too much of it in another and it may vary from year to year. Thus, climate is sometimes referred to as 'average' weather for a given area; it is the sum of all statistical weather information that helps describe a place or region.

> **climate:** the weather conditions prevailing in an area in general or over a long period

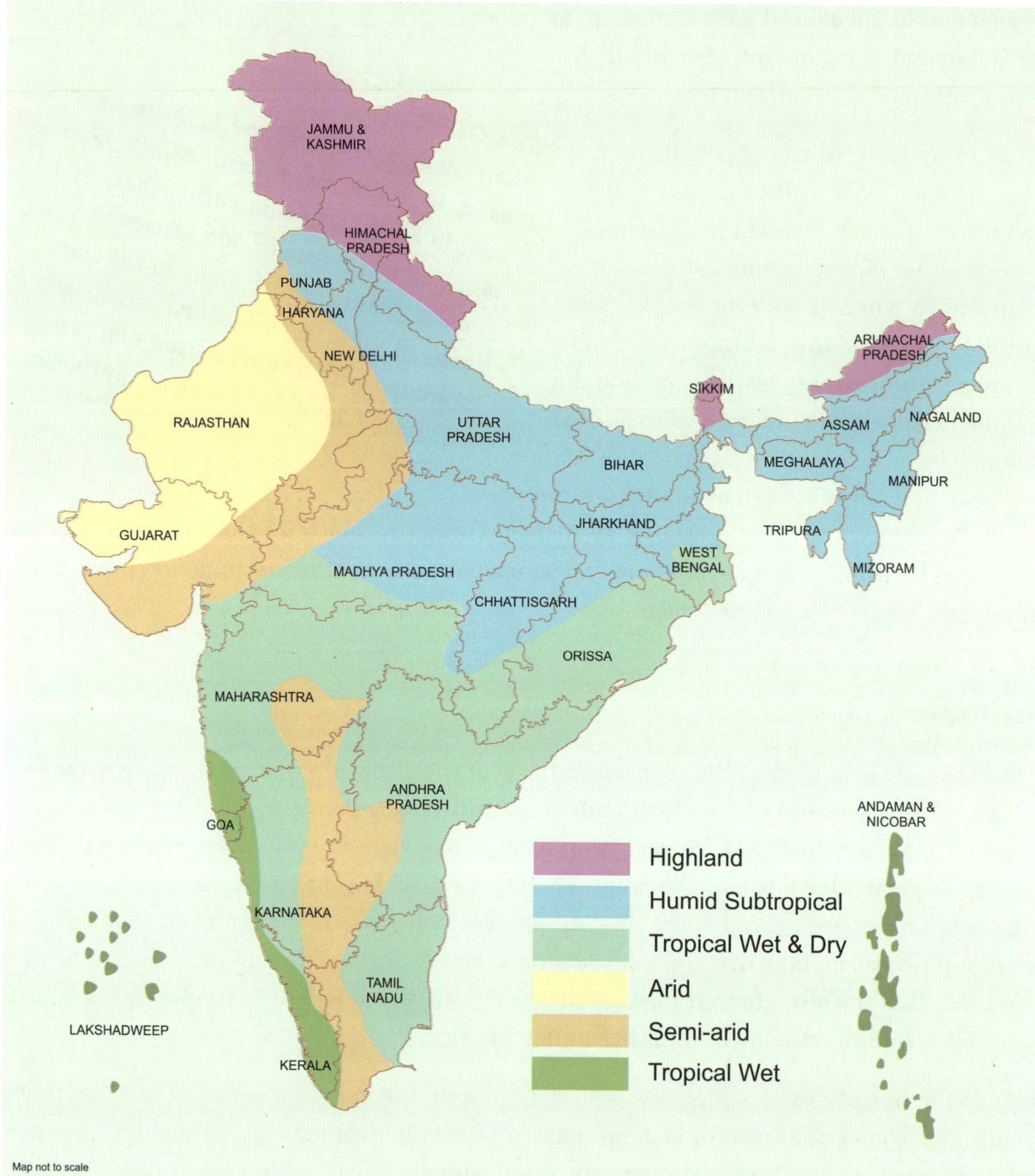

India Climatic Zone Map

The distance from the equator is not the only factor that decides the climate of a place. It also depends on several geographical features including the height above sea level, nearness to the sea or other large water bodies and the extent of vegetation cover.

It is usually cooler at higher altitudes. Thiruvananthapuram in Kerala is at sea level and very close to the equator. So the climate there is hot. But Srinagar, in Jammu and Kashmir, is not only far from the equator; it is also at a high altitude. So the climate in Srinagar is cooler. At places close to the equator, such as Chennai, in Tamil Nadu, the climate is typically tropical—quite hot and humid. But the climate at a hill station, such as Ooty, which is also in Tamil Nadu, is much cooler and quite pleasant. It is for this reason that people go to the hills of Mussoorie or Shimla to escape the scorching heat of Delhi in summer.

Hot deserts

Desert areas have a typical hot and dry climate. For example, in Rajasthan, the temperature is high during most parts of the year. But during winter, which lasts only for a few months, the temperature is quite low. This region receives very little rainfall. In contrast, the north-eastern parts of India receive rain for a major part of the year. The climate there can be described as wet.

Climate and adaptation

Unlike humans, animals cannot protect themselves from heat or cold by using air conditioners or woollen garments. But, nature has a provision for protecting animals by giving them the ability to adapt to the environments they live in. Of course, adaptation takes many generations and millions of years to happen. Animals living in different climatic regions have developed special features and habits that suit the surroundings they live in. Two common examples are animals living in the cold polar regions and those living in hot and humid tropical rainforests.

Polar regions

The polar regions are the areas around the two poles of the earth where the sun is visible for only about six months of the year. Even when the sun is visible, it shines very weakly. As a result, the polar regions remain extremely cold and covered with ice throughout the year, with temperatures dropping to as low as –37°C in winter. The animals living under such cold conditions usually have a thick layer of fat and fur to protect their bodies from the severe polar winter. Alaska in the United States, Canada, Finland, Greenland, Iceland, Norway, Sweden and the Siberian region of Russia are situated in the polar regions.

adaptation: adjustment to environmental conditions
polar region: the part of the earth's surface around the poles, characterised by icy climate

Polar bears live in the Arctic. They do not stay in one place. They travel across the snow looking for food. Sometimes they swim far out into the sea. The bear's large feet are like snowshoes. The hair on the soles of their feet help the bears walk on the slippery ice and snow. A polar bear can travel 30 km or more per day for several days, although some are capable of much more than that.

Polar bear

A polar bear has black skin, which aids its adjustment to the Arctic temperature, absorbing and holding heat from the sunlight. To conserve the heat, it has a thick layer of fat and dense white fur, which provide efficient insulation. The white fur not only protects the animal from the Arctic cold but also makes it almost invisible in the white snow. The animal swims well, using its broad forepaws as paddles. To help it remain under water for long durations, the polar bear keeps its nostrils closed and lays its small ears flat. The polar bear has a keen sense of smell. It can easily smell a whale carcass 32 km away or seals up to 2 m beneath the snow and ice.

Another well-known animal living in the polar region is the penguin. Most penguins live in the Antarctic, where it is extremely cold, and the water temperatures never rise above freezing point. Similar to polar bears, penguins that live in the polar regions also have a thick skin and a lot of fat to protect them from the cold. In severe winter, the emperor penguins use a novel method to keep warm; they huddle together. They keep their young ones warm by sheltering them between their furry feet. The bodies of penguins are streamlined and their feet have webs, making them good swimmers.

Penguin

Young one being sheltered

Some penguins live further north, but all penguins live in the southern hemisphere. All penguins are flightless. They cannot fly at all. Their wings are known as flippers.

Apart from polar bears and penguins, the polar region is also home to many other species of animals and birds including the musk ox, foxes, reindeers, whales fishes.

While fishes and whales can live in water, the other animals live on land during the polar winter; while birds migrate to warmer regions during winters.

Every year, during the winter in the north polar region, it is warmer in countries such as India. Hence, hundreds and thousands of migratory birds come to India for the winter months, to lakes and wetlands spread throughout the country. Bharatpur in Rajasthan, Kumarakom in Kottayam (Kerala), the Rann of Kutch in Gujarat and Sultanpur in Haryana are among the famous bird sanctuaries where these birds spend the winter.

Bird migration

Migratory birds fly thousands of kilometres to escape the extreme cold in their home territory. They exploit the winds in their favour so they can go the distance by spending the least amount of energy. Larger birds rely on thermals (hot air) rising from the ground in the mornings to gain altitude by simply soaring. These birds usually migrate during the day.

Studies suggest birds orient themselves to the compass points using the position of the sun during the day and the stars at night.

Siberian crane

Migratory birds in India: Yellow wagtail and blue throat

They can also sense the magnetic north. In addition, they use other clues such as the visual layout of the land, smell (of the sea), sound (waves) on shores and winds (through mountain passes). The most amazing aspect of bird migration is that the location, route and perhaps even the techniques are programmed into their brains. Many migrating birds abandon their young as soon as they fledge and a short time later, the young migrate on their own.

migration: the movement of birds and animals from one region to another according to the seasons

Tropical rainforests

Tropical rainforests are very dense, warm, wet forests that

are mostly found in the earth's tropical regions. They are located in a band around the equator, mostly in the area between the Tropic of Cancer (23.5°N latitude) and the Tropic of Capricorn (23.5°S latitude). The tropical region generally has hot climate and even in the coldest month, the temperature is generally higher than 15°C. During hot summers, the temperature often rises above 40°C. These regions get plenty of rainfall and the humidity level always remains high.

Factastic

The longest migration is undertaken by the Arctic Tern. It breeds in the Arctic North in the summer, then flies all the way to the other pole to spend winter on the Antarctic ice pack. The shortest distance between the two poles is 15,000 km, but the birds usually travel a more circuitous route and can cover up to 20,000 km, making a round trip of 30,000–40,000 km!

Tropical rainforests are found in South America, west Africa, Australia, southern India and Southeast Asia. These are home to millions of plants and animals. Rainforests are extremely important to the ecology of the earth as they generate much of the earth's oxygen. The plants found in the rainforests are also very important to people in other ways; many are used to make drugs that fight disease and illness. They are also home to a wide variety of animals. Some of the prominent animals living in the rainforests are monkeys, apes, gorillas, lions, tigers, elephants, leopards, lizards, snakes and a wide variety of birds and insects.

Factastic

Tropical rainforests cover only a small part of the earth's surface—only about 6%. Yet, they are home to over half the species of plants and animals in the world.

Rainforests are tremendously rich in animal life. They include microscopic animals, invertebrates (insects and worms), fish, reptiles, amphibians, birds and mammals. The different rainforests of the world support different populations of animals.

Different animals live in different layers of the rainforest to avoid competition for food. For example, birds live in the upper reaches of trees. Large animals, such as jaguars, generally live on the forest floor, but others, such as howler monkeys and sloths, live in tree branches. Insects are found almost everywhere.

tropical rainforest: a dense forest rich in animal and plant life, found typically in tropical areas with consistently heavy rainfall

Tropical rainforests are home to some of the strangest-looking and most beautiful, the largest and smallest, the most dangerous and least frightening, the loudest and quietest animals on earth. Among them is the antelope species the size of rabbits, frogs that can fly and a spider species that eats birds. Others include jaguars, gorillas, okapis, aye-ayes, toucans and parrots. In fact, there are so many fascinating animals in tropical rainforests that millions still remain unnamed or unidentified. Scientists estimate that there are more than 50 million different species of invertebrates living in rainforests. One scientist found fifty different species of ants on a single tree in Peru!

Jaguar

Crocodile

Orangutan

Each species living in the rainforest has evolved with its own set of unique adaptations, helping it to survive. Every animal has the ability to protect itself from being another's next meal. Camouflage is one of the most common adaptations.

The colouring of some animals protects them from their predators. For example, the stick insect or the 'walking stick' resembles leaves or twigs and is green or brown in colour. It can remain motionless and hang from plants or trees. Some butterflies, when they close their wings, look exactly like leaves. The three-toed sloth

camouflage: the natural colouring or shape of an animal which enables it to blend in with its surroundings

is born with brown fur, but is usually covered with green algae that helps it to blend in with trees tops, the canopy, where it makes its home. Camouflage also works in reverse, helping predators, such as boa constrictors, sneak up on unsuspecting animals. A coiled boa constrictor

Butterfly blending with a leaf

Anaconda

remains almost completely invisible on a pile of leaf litter on the forest floor and can pounce on a prey that comes too close. The black stripes of the tiger help it to blend in with the foliage in the forest.

Iguana

As there is stiff competition for food, many animals that live in rainforests adapt themselves to eating a specific food, which few other species are able to eat. For example,

Scarlet macaw

Gibbon

Green gecko

toucans and parrots have large beaks, which give them a great advantage over other birds with smaller beaks. With their large beaks, these birds can easily crack open the hard shell of fruits and nuts from many trees that other birds or animals cannot easily do.

Toucan and macaw

Many interesting animals are found in the tropical rainforests of India. The lion-tailed macaque, named for its lion-like tail, lives in the rainforests of the Western Ghats. This is the only species of macaque that prefers to spend its time on tree tops. It usually lives in evergreen trees in mature forests. Its most outstanding feature is the silver-white mane that surrounds its head and cheeks, running down to its chin. It feeds mainly on fruits, but also eats seeds, young leaves, stems, flowers and buds. Since it is able to get sufficient food on the trees, it rarely comes down on the ground.

Lion-tailed macaque

Factastic

The Amazon jungle in South America is home to the greatest variety of plants and animals on earth. About one-fifth of the world's plants and birds and one-tenth of all mammal species are found there.

The elephant is another well-known animal in Indian tropical rainforests that has adapted to the conditions of rainforests in many remarkable ways. To stay comfortable in the heat, an elephant has large ears which it flaps to create a cooling effect. Its tusks are modified teeth designed to tear the

Elephant herd

bark of trees that it loves to eat. The large molars in the elephant's mouth are used for chewing and grinding very fibrous plant materials, which are its diet. An elephant's trunk has many uses including picking up food, drinking water and communicating with other elephants. Elephants also have very low-pitched sounds that allow them to communicate with each other in dense forests.

Brainteaser

Eskimos are known to be very good hunters, but they never hunt penguins. Can you guess why?

Answer: The eskimos live in the North Pole while penguins live in the South Pole.

Revision Time

- Weather is what the atmosphere is like, with respect to the temperature, humidity, rainfall, wind-speed, in any one place at any one time.
- Even at one place, the weather does not remain the same throughout the day; it keeps changing all day.
- The various parameters, such as temperature, humidity, air pressure, which meteorologists use to forecast weather, are called elements of weather.
- It is the sun that drives the earth's weather engine; the sun's heat creates winds, clouds, cyclones and other weather phenomena.
- Generally, the highest temperature of the day occurs in the afternoon while the lowest temperature occurs early in the morning.
- The time of sunrise and sunset at a place depends not only on the month of year or the season but also on the latitude of the place.
- Climate is broadly the long-term weather of an area, taken over a period of at least 30 years.
- The latitude or the distance from the equator plays an important role in deciding the climate of a place. The climate also depends on several geographical features such as height above sea level, nearness to the sea or large water bodies and the extent of vegetation cover.
- Animals living in different climatic regions have developed features and habits that suit the surroundings they live in.

* The polar regions remain extremely cold and covered with ice throughout the year, with temperatures dropping to as low as –37°C in winter.
* Migratory birds fly thousands of kilometres to escape from the extreme cold in their home territory.
* Tropical rainforests are very dense, warm, wet forests that are mostly found in the earth's tropical regions.
* During hot summers, the temperature often rises above 40°C. These regions get plenty of rainfall and the humidity level always remains high.
* Rainforests are tremendously rich in animal life. They include microscopic animals, invertebrates (insects and worms), fish, reptiles, amphibians, birds and mammals.
* Many animals that live in tropical rainforests have sensitive hearing, sharp eyesight and natural covering that helps them blend in with their surroundings.

Quiz Time

1. Answer the questions.

a. Name the elements that determine the weather of a place.

b. What is the difference between weather and climate?

c. Why do the polar regions always remain freezing cold?

d. Is the climate cooler at high altitudes or in the plains at the same latitude?

e. What are the adaptations in the Indian elephant that help it to live in tropical rainforests?

2. Fill in the blanks.

a. On a single day, the ____________ at any one place may change significantly.

b. A rain gauge indirectly gives a measure of the ____________ of water falling as rain.

c. Climate is sometimes referred to as ____________ weather for a given area.

d. The thick fat layer and fur coat of polar bears are ____________ for life in the Arctic.

e. Rainforests are very dense, warm, wet forests that are mostly found in the earth's ____________ regions.

3. Match the following.

a.	polar bear	i.	Antarctica
b.	tiger	ii.	Western Ghats
c.	penguin	iii.	Arctic
d.	lion-tailed macaque	iv.	Assam
e.	rhinoceros	v.	Sunderbans

4. Indicate whether the statements are true or false.

a. Climate is what the atmosphere is like in any one place at a certain time. True False

b. Generally, the maximum temperature of the day occurs in the afternoon. True False

c. The distance from the equator is the only factor that decides the climate of a place. True False

d. Camouflage is one of the most common adaptations of animals to protect themselves from being eaten by predators. True False

e. Elephant tusks are modified teeth designed to kill its prey. True False

5. Project work

a. Collect information on the sunrise and sunset times, daily maximum and minimum temperatures, maximum and minimum humidity and rainfall for Srinagar, New Delhi, Kolkata, Mumbai, Chennai and Thiruvananthapuram for 7, 15, 22 and 30 December, March, June, and August for last year from the internet or the local met office. Enter the figures for each city in a separate table.

City:

Date	Sunrise	Sunset	Max. temp.	Min. temp.	Max. humidity	Min. humidity	Rainfall (mm)
7 Dec							
15 Dec							
22 Dec							
30 Dec							
7 Mar							
15 Mar							

22 Mar							
30 Mar							
7 Jun							
15 Jun							
22 Jun							
30 Jun							
7 Aug							
15 Aug							
22 Aug							
30 Aug							

From the table find out the following:

i. Which city has the longest day and when?

ii. Which city has the shortest day and when?

iii. Which city has the largest difference in the day length between summer and winter?

iv. Which city has the least difference in the day length between summer and winter?

v. Which city recorded the highest humidity?

vi. Which city recorded the lowest humidity?

vii. Can you explain your findings on the basis of the location of the cities?

Think it over

1. **Despite being near the equator, why is the climate at Ooty in Tamil Nadu cool and pleasant in summer?**
2. **How are thousands of species of animals able to live together in tropical rainforests without running out of food?**

8 Winds, Storms and Cyclones

Rain, snow and thunderstorms are common weather phenomena. Sometimes the rain continues for a few days or a severe thunderstorm lasts for a few hours. But occasionally, when a severe cyclonic storm hits the coast, it can bring torrential rain and deluge, inundating large areas and causing an extensive loss of life and property. In the central plains of the United States and in some parts of coastal India, violent whirlwinds known as tornadoes often strike, creating havoc within a matter of a few minutes. These weather phenomena are among the most violent seen in nature and cause extensive damage worldwide. However, they are nature's ways of maintaining the heat balance of our planet. Cyclones and hurricanes maintain equilibrium in the earth's troposphere and help maintain a relatively stable and warm temperature worldwide.

Air pressure

The earth's atmosphere extends up to a height of about 1,000 km. The total amount of gases in a column that is 1,000 km tall would be large. These gases press down on the earth's surface at ground level, exerting a force that we call atmospheric pressure or air pressure. Although we do not feel this pressure, it actually presses down very hard from all directions. Every square metre column of air at sea level weighs more than 10 tonnes—roughly equivalent to the force of an elephant balancing on a desk! Atmospheric pressure is measured with an instrument called a barometer.

atmospheric pressure: the pressure exerted by the atmosphere
barometer: an instrument to measure atmospheric pressure

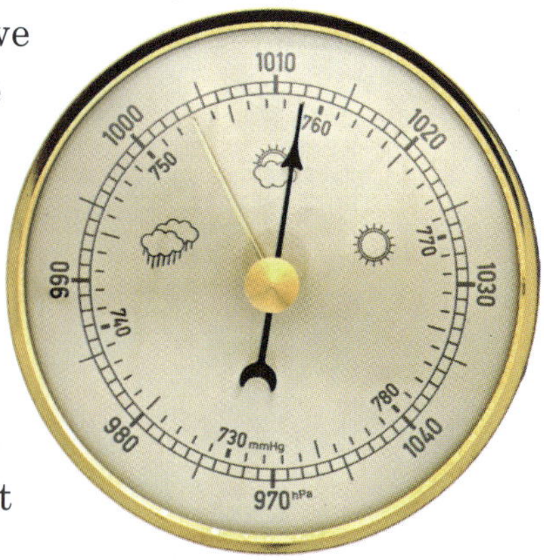

Barometer

Explore

Aim: To demonstrate the presence of atmospheric pressure.

Material required: a tin can with a screw-on cap, water and burner

Method:

1. Take the tin can and pour water in it.
2. Place the can on a tripod without its cap on and light the burner. Let the water boil for some time.
3. After you see steam coming out of the can, turn off the burner and immediately screw the cap on. Take care not to burn your fingers. Carefully take the can to the lab sink and place it there.
4. Pour cold water on the can and see what happens.

Does it give you the idea of the tremendous pressure that the atmosphere exerts on us?

(This activity should be done in the presence of a teacher.)

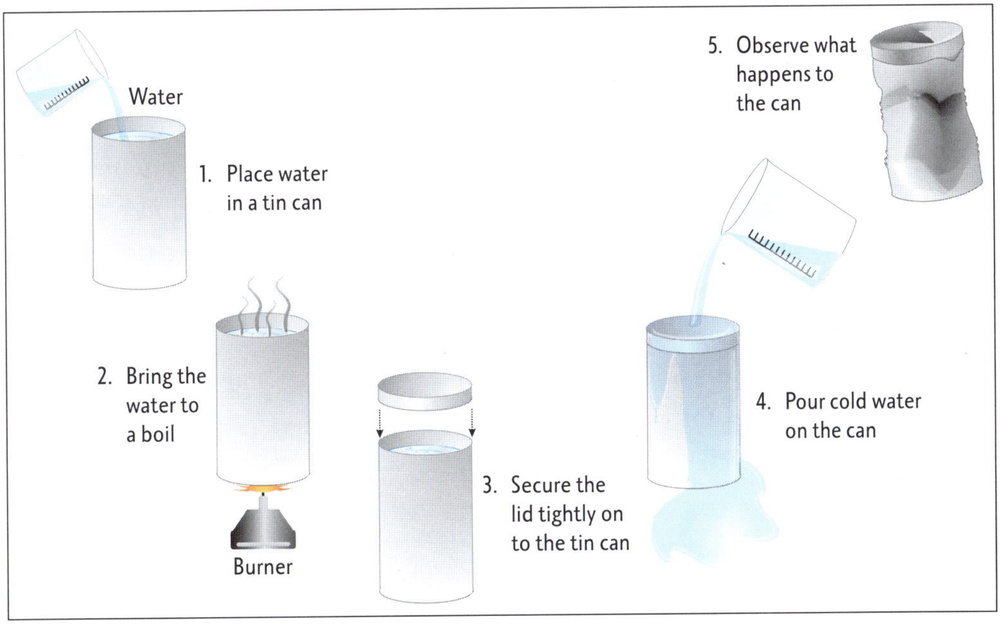

Tin can experiment

Air pressure changes over time and from place to place. It depends on many factors such as the height of a place, temperature and amount of moisture. With increasing height, the air pressure drops constantly. At greater heights, the air pressure is lower, because there is less air above that is weighing it down. The density of air reduces with height. So at higher altitudes, the amount of air weighing down on an area is much less than that weighing down on the same area at a lower altitude. This can be compared to the weight of a pile of blankets. If 1,000 blankets are piled up one above the other, the total weight at the bottom of the pile will be substantial.

The low density of air on high mountains with reduced amount of oxygen in it, makes breathing difficult. That is the reason why mountaineers have to carry oxygen cylinders when they go on high mountains.

Air pressure also depends on the amount of water vapour present in it. Moist air or humid air is lighter or less dense than dry air and hence exerts less pressure. This is because a water molecule (H_2O) weighs less than both, an oxygen molecule (O_2) and a nitrogen molecule (N_2). Thus, if nitrogen and oxygen are replaced with water vapour, it exerts less pressure. That is the reason why air rich in water vapour marks low pressure areas, which often brings unsettled weather and rain whereas regions of dry air mark fair weather areas and high pressure.

Air expands on heating

Atmospheric pressure also depends on temperature. Air expands on heating and becomes lighter. Being less dense, warm air exerts less pressure than cold air, which is denser and hence heavier. It is because air expands and becomes lighter on heating, smoke rises and hot air balloons rise. When warm air rises, it causes a region of low pressure below it. With low pressure, the weather is often wet and cloudy because as warm air rises, it cools and often condenses into clouds and causes rain. We often hear terms, such as low pressure and **deep** depression in weather bulletins, which is a forecast for heavy rainfall and bad weather.

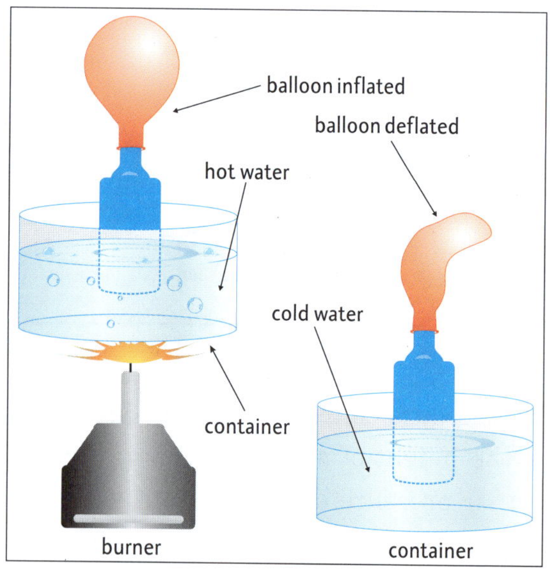

Hot air expands

Explore

Take a small empty glass bottle with a narrow mouth. Fix a small rubber balloon around the neck of the bottle with a thread. The balloon will stay limp. Now, immerse the bottle with the

depression: a region of lower atmospheric pressure, especially a cyclonic weather system

balloon in a container of hot water. Observe what happens. What happens if you immerse the bottle with the balloon in ice cold water? Can you explain what you observe?

When air moves, it is called wind. Air always moves from a higher pressure to a lower pressure area. The instrument used to measure wind speed is known as an **anemometer**.

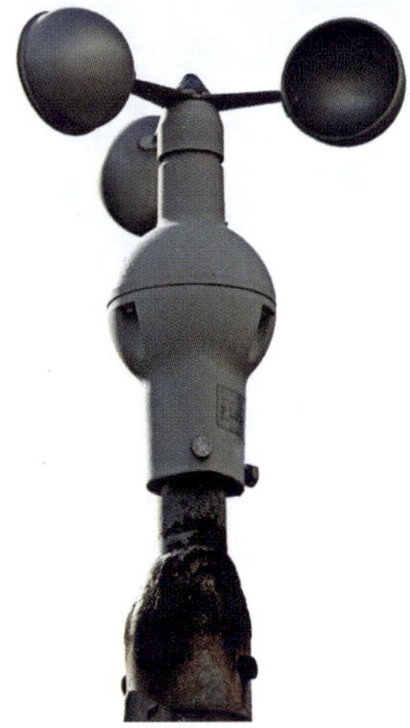

Anemometer

Air moves from cold areas to hot areas and dry air moves to places where there is moist air. If the pressure difference between two regions is considerably high, the wind blows with a greater speed.

When warm air rises, the air pressure at that place falls and cold air from the surrounding areas rushes in to fill its place. This sets up convection currents in air that play a major role in causing storms, rain and cyclones.

Air currents

If we take the earth as a whole, the region around the equator receives more heat from the sun than the poles. This uneven heating of the equator and the poles give rise to air currents. Warm air from the equator rises up and as it moves up, it becomes cool. As it cools at higher altitudes, it moves toward the poles. At the same time, cold and dense air at the poles sinks and starts to flow toward the equator, replacing the warm air rising in this region. As a result of this, a pattern of air circulation from the poles to the equator is set up in which wind from both the polar regions blows towards the equator in the north–south direction as well as the south–north direction. However, due to the rotation of the earth, the winds do not blow in a strictly north–south direction but turn westward near the equator.

Similar air currents are produced due to the uneven heating of land and water. In coastal areas, the rapid heating of the land during the day gives rise to sea breeze blowing from the sea, while the rapid cooling of the land after sunset gives rise to land breeze at night.

wind: the perceptible natural movement of the air
monsoon: a seasonal wind in the region of the Indian subcontinent, blowing from the south-west between May and September and bringing heavy rain

Monsoons in India are also caused by the uneven heating of land and sea surfaces but on a much larger scale. Summer heating of the Tibetan plateau and the Indian landmass

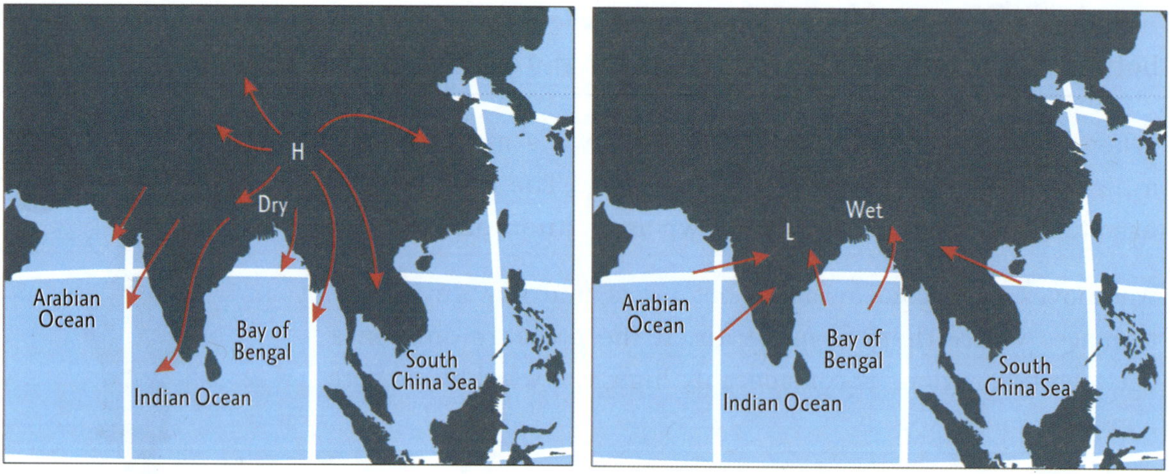

Winter conditions

Summer conditions

Winter and summer monsoon

makes moisture-laden air from the Indian Ocean move towards India, bringing plenty of rain during the monsoon months.

Factastic

The word monsoon is derived from the Arabic word *mausim*, which means 'the season of winds'. It was first used by Arab sailors to describe the annual alternating winds of the Arabian Sea.

Farmer planting rice

thunderstorm: a storm with thunder and lightning accompanied by heavy rain or hail
lightning: the occurrence of a natural electrical discharge between a cloud and the ground or within a cloud, accompanied by a bright flash and thunder
thunder: a loud rumbling or crashing noise heard after a lightning flash
thundercloud: a cloud with a towering or spreading top, charged with electricity and producing thunder and lightning

The monsoon rains are very important for India. Farmers depend on the rains to irrigate their land. Also, a great deal of electricity is generated by water power provided by the monsoon rains.

Thunderstorms and cyclones

A thunderstorm is a storm with lightning and thunder. It is produced by a type of cloud known as cumulonimbus cloud (from the word column), or thundercloud, usually producing gusty winds, heavy rain and sometimes

Thunderclouds

hail. A thunderstorm occurs when there is moisture and rising warm air. Moisture is needed to form clouds and rain. In a thundercloud, the moisture is carried to great heights by the rising air. As the moist air rises, it forms droplets of water that freeze and start falling. The up-and-down motion of the ice particles and water droplets within the cloud produces electric charge in the cloud, which causes lightning and thunder. Thunderstorms develop frequently in hot, humid tropical areas such as India.

Cyclones develop from thunderstorms over warm seas near the equator. The heat in the atmosphere causes water to vapourise. When warm air carrying water vapour rises from the seas and condenses to form clouds, massive amount of heat is released. The heat thus released into the atmosphere warms the air. This mixture of heat and moisture often produces thunderstorms from which a tropical cyclone can develop. As warm air rises, it produces low pressure, making cool air rush in to fill the void that is left. But the constant rotation of the earth on its axis, causes the air to bend inwards and then spirals upwards with great force, thus, creating a very low-pressure system. The swirling winds rotate faster and faster, forming a huge circle of clouds, which can be up to 2,000 km wide.

Factastic

A bolt of lightning can travel at speeds of more than 2,10,000 km/h and can reach temperatures approaching 30,000°C, that is, almost five times the temperature of the surface of the sun!

As the cyclone builds up, it begins to move, sustained by a steady flow of warm, moist air over the ocean. The strongest winds and heaviest rains are found in the towering clouds, which merge into a wall about 20–30 km from the storm's centre. The wind blows in a spiral direction around a relatively calm area known as the 'eye'. The eye of a cyclone is usually 30–50 km wide. At the centre of the eye there is no cloud or

cyclone: a very low-pressure system of clouds and rain with very high-speed winds revolving around it

Satellite picture of a cyclone

rain and the winds are fairly light. But winds around the eye can reach speeds of up to 200 km/h. The most violent activity takes place in the area immediately around the eye, called the 'eye wall'.

As the cyclone approaches the coast, the sky begins to darken and the wind gets stronger. As it nears lands, it may bring torrential rain and very high winds that cause widespread devastation. High-speed winds accompanying a cyclone can uproot trees, damage houses, telephone lines and other communication systems and cause tremendous loss of life and property.

Factastic

Cyclone is, in fact, one of the three names for rotating tropical storms with winds that have a speed of at least 110 km/h. These storms are called cyclones when they form over the Bay of Bengal and northern Indian Ocean. They are called **hurricanes** when they develop over the Atlantic or eastern Pacific oceans, and are known as **typhoons** when they develop in the western Pacific Ocean.

Tropical cyclones not only produce extremely powerful winds and torrential rain, they also produce high waves. The damaging storms surge in the oceans, with water rising to a height of 3–10 m, Appearing like a water-wall moving towards the shore. Coastal regions usually bear the brunt of a tropical cyclone, while inland regions are relatively safe from receiving strong winds. Heavy rains, however, can produce significant flooding inland, and storm surges can produce extensive coastal flooding even up to 50 km from the coastline. As a result, the seawater enters the low-lying coastal areas, causing severe loss of life and property. Inland flooding also reduces the fertility of the soil.

The whole coastline of India, particularly the east coast, is vulnerable to cyclones. On an average, more cyclones develop over the Bay of Bengal than over the Arabian Sea and they are more intense and cause extensive damage.

hurricane: a storm with a violent wind, in particular a tropical cyclone in the Caribbean
typhoon: a tropical storm in the region of the western Pacific Ocean

Cyclone warning

With satellites in orbit, it is now possible to track a developing cyclone round the clock and study its movement before it strikes the coast. It is also possible to issue advance warning to people in the coastal areas where the cyclone is likely to hit so that they can be evacuated well in advance. In India, a satellite-based disaster warning system has been established with over 250 disaster warning receivers installed in the cyclone-prone east and west coasts of the country. It makes use of the Indian National Satellite System (INSAT) for keeping track of developing cyclones and issue warnings to the vulnerable population. Cyclone shelters have also been constructed in vulnerable areas for accommodating people from nearby areas. Several thousands of lives have been saved by the INSAT disaster warning system because of timely evacuation.

Cyclone shelter

Pointers during a cyclone or storm

- Keep your radio or TV on and listen to the latest weather warnings.
- Avoid being misled by rumours and only pass official information that you receive from the radio or TV on to others.
- Stay in a safe place and do not go out.
- Get away from low-lying beaches or other locations that may be swept away by high tides or storm waves.
- Avoid going into the sea during a cyclone.
- Be alert since streams or rivers may flood due to heavy rains.
- Store extra food, especially those items that don't require cooking or require little preparation.
- Store extra drinking water in suitably covered vessels.

- When the authorities advise to evacuate, follow the instruction promptly and head to proper shelter or evacuation points indicated for your area and remain there till further notice.
- Keep calm at all times.

Tornadoes

A tornado

A tornado is yet another violent weather phenomenon that often strikes suddenly and leaves behind a trail of destruction. Tornadoes are one of nature's most destructive storms; they can destroy large buildings, uproot trees and hurl vehicles hundreds of metres. The word tornado comes from the Spanish word "tronada", meaning thunderstorm. A tornado is a violent rotating column of air extending from a thunderstorm to the ground. It may reach wind speeds of 160 km/h to over 480 km/h. Most tornadoes take on the appearance of a narrow funnel, a few hundred metres across, with a small cloud of debris near the ground. However, tornadoes can appear in many shapes and sizes.

The entire tornado moves across the ground at a speed of 30–65 km/h. Most tornadoes last less than 30 minutes, but can cause colossal destruction. The width of a tornado is usually not much larger than the size of a football field, but in some rare cases, it can be more than a kilometre wide. The funnel of a tornado sucks dust, debri and everything near its base, just like a vacuum cleaner, and throws them out near the top.

Tornadoes may strike at any time of the day, but are much more

Destruction caused by a tornado

tornado: localised and violently destructive windstorm occurring over land characterised by a funnel-shaped cloud extending towards the ground

frequent in the afternoon and evening. In the United States, which witnesses the most intense and devastating tornadoes, they are most common in what has come to be known as the 'Tornado Alley' that lies between the Rocky Mountains on the west and the Gulf of Mexico on the south.

Tornado shelter

In India, the states of Orissa and West Bengal are occasionally hit by tornadoes. In 1978, about 150 people were killed by a tornado in Orissa and again in 1998 more than 160 people were killed and more than 2,000 injured when a tornado passed through 20 coastal villages in West Bengal and Orissa. The tornado flattened 15,000 homes and left more than 10,000 people homeless. A tornado that hit the northern suburbs of New Delhi, near the Delhi University in 1978, killed twenty-eight people and injured 700. It had cut a path 5 km long and 50 m wide.

The safest protection from a tornado is a **tornado shelter**—a room situated underground having no windows. If there is no underground shelter available, it is better to shut the doors and windows and take shelter under a table or a bed.

Explore

The Great Pacific Garbage Patch stretches for hundreds of kilometres across the North Pacific Ocean, forming a floating junkyard of plastic waste on the high seas, stretching from California to the Sea of Japan. If this patch was pulled onto dry land, it would cover a territory that would equal twice the size of the entire United States of America. The garbage patch is formed by the North Pacific Tropical gyre. What is a gyre?

Revision Time

* The air around us exerts pressure.
* Air pressure depends on the amount of water vapour present. Moist air is lighter than dry air and hence exerts less pressure.
* Air expands on heating, and hot air being lighter, rises up.
* Moving air is called wind.
* The uneven heating of the equator and the poles gives rise to global air currents.
* Monsoons in India are caused by the uneven heating of land and sea surfaces.
* A thunderstorm is a storm with lightning and thunder.
* Cyclones develop from thunderstorms over warm seas near the equator.
* Tropical cyclones not only produce extremely powerful winds and torrential rain, they also produce high waves and damaging storm surges.
* In India, a satellite-based disaster warning system has been established with over 250 disaster warning receivers installed in the cyclone-prone east and west coasts of the country.
* A tornado is a violent rotating column of air extending from a thunderstorm to the ground, which may reach wind speeds of 160 km/h to over 480 km/h.
* The safest protection from a tornado is a tornado shelter—a room situated underground having no windows.

Quiz Time

1. Answer the questions.

a. Why do mountaineers need to carry oxygen cylinders while climbing high mountains?

b. What makes hot air balloons rise?

c. Why does a low-pressure region bring rain and storm?

d. Why do cyclones develop only over warm seas?

e. Which of the following places are unlikely to be hit by a cyclone and why?

i. Delhi ii. Chennai iii. Mumbai iv. Vishakhapatnam v. Bhopal

2. Fill in the blanks.

a. Moist air is ____________ than dry air.

b. Where warm air rises at a place, the air pressure at that place ____________.

c. Monsoons in India are caused by the ____________________ heating of land and sea surfaces.

d. Cyclones develop from ____________________ over warm seas near the equator.

e. A ____________________ is a violent rotating column of air extending from a thunderstorm to the ground.

3. Indicate whether the statements are true or false.

a.	At greater heights, the air pressure is lower, because the air is less dense.	True	False
b.	Moist air is heavier than dry air and hence exerts more pressure.	True	False
c.	A cyclone is formed by a very high-pressure system with very high-speed winds revolving around it.	True	False
d.	Air currents are produced due to the uneven heating of land and water.	True	False
e.	The strongest winds and heaviest rains are found at the centre of a cyclonic storm.	True	False

4. Project work

a. Using reference books or the internet find out how a barometer works and how many types of barometers are used. If there is a barometer in your school physics lab, find out from your science teacher how it works. Take readings of the barometer for a few days and see if there is any change in the atmospheric pressure. Compare the air pressure observed on stormy or rainy days with those of air pressure observed on a clear day.

b. Fix a 30-cm long ribbon on the top of a 1-m vertical pole and set the pole on the terrace of your school or home. Using a magnetic compass, mark the east, west, north and south directions on the terrace below the pole. When the wind blows, you can tell the direction of the wind by looking at the ribbon, which will point in the opposite direction. For example, if the wind is blowing from the east, the ribbon will point to the west. Observe the wind direction during the different seasons and record your observations. Note the change particularly during the monsoon months. Do you observe anything different?

Think it over

1. Why do most parts of India receive heavy rains only after a hot summer?

2. If there is a nuclear explosion in the path of a cyclone, would it be strong enough to deflect the storm?

9 Soil

Soil covers a large part of the land surface and is an important component of the earth's resources that supports most of the planet's life. Soil is essential for agriculture. Directly or indirectly, agriculture provides food, clothing and shelter for all. Soil is, thus, an inseparable part of our life. Animals are dependent on plants or other animals that eat plants for their food. Soil is home to several animals and provides shelter to many of them. The breakdown of dead organisms by microbes in the soil adds more nutrients to the soil.

Farmer tilling soil

Soil is a mixture of different things including rocks, minerals, dead and decaying plants as well as animals. Soil may vary from one location to another, but it generally consists of a mixture of organic and inorganic materials, water and air. The inorganic materials comprise rocks that have broken down into smaller pieces. The size of the pieces varies. They may appear as pebbles, gravel or small particles of sand or clay. The organic material includes decaying plants or animals. The amount of water in the soil is closely linked to the climate and other characteristics of the region. The composition of the soil affects the plants and, therefore, the animals that can live there.

soil: the upper layer of earth in which plants grow

Circle Time

With your classmates, collect samples of soil from different areas in your school compound and outside—the school garden, football ground, playground, behind the canteen, under a large tree or any other place you like. Label each sample carefully. Study the samples under a magnifying glass to see what plants and animals, such as insects or worms, each sample contains. Record your observations in a table.

What do you find from your observations? Are all soil samples composed of similar matter?

Soil profile

A vertical section of soil from the ground surface to the bedrock showing the layers of soil, called horizons, is called the **soil profile**. **Horizon A** refers to the uppermost layer of soil that is nearest to the surface. It is commonly known as topsoil. In the woods or other areas that have not been ploughed or tilled, this layer would probably include organic litter such as fallen leaves and twigs. The litter helps prevent erosion, holds moisture and decays to form a very rich soil known as humus. Horizon A is generally dark in colour as it is rich in humus and minerals. This layer is generally soft, porous and can retain water. It provides plants with the nutrients they need for a healthy life. The topsoil also provides shelter for many living organisms such as worms, rodents, moles and beetles. Small plants have their roots embedded entirely in the topsoil.

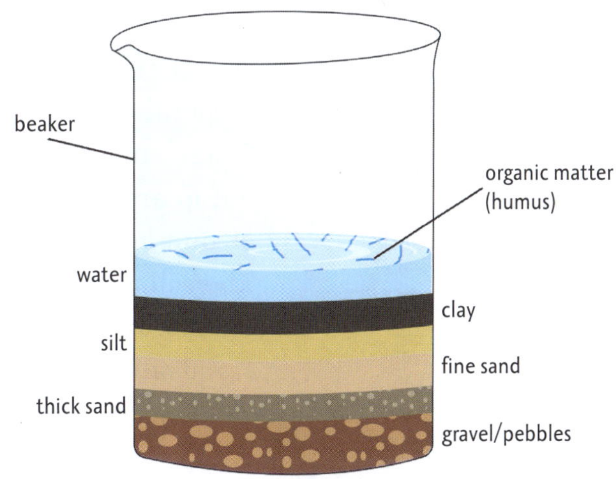

Composition of soil

topsoil: the topmost layer of soil
humus: the organic component of soil, formed by the decomposition of leaves and other plant material by soil micro-organisms

The second layer is called **Horizon B**. Litter is not present in this layer and, therefore, there is much less humus. Horizon B is generally harder and more compact.

Soil profile showing three horizons

Below Horizon B is the third layer called **Horizon C**. It is mostly made up of small lumps of rocks with cracks and crevices. Below this layer is the bedrock, which is hard and difficult to dig with a spade.

Soil profiles vary in different areas of the world.

Soil types

Soil is a mixture of particles formed by the weathering of rocks and decaying plants and animals. But the composition of soil differs from place to place. Different-sized mineral particles, such as sand, silt, clay and humus, give soil its texture or feel. Living organisms, such as bacteria, plant roots and earthworms, are also important components of any soil.

Factastic

Soil composite 49% oxygen, 33% silicon, 7% aluminium, 4% iron and 2% carbon. Air and water make up 50% of the soil. Minerals and organic matter make up the rest.

Soil can be broadly classified into three types based on the size of the particles it contains—sandy, clayey and loamy. Sandy soil contains the biggest-sized particles. It contains less than 10 per cent of clay and mainly consists of particles of silica and quartz. Therefore, the texture is gritty. The amount of humus present decides the colour and the texture of the soil. Clayey soil, on the other hand, contains a larger proportion of very fine-grained particles, and is smooth and silky to touch. If the ratio of large to fine particles is about the same, then the soil is called **loamy**.

bedrock: solid unweathered rock lying beneath surface deposits of soil
weathering: wearing away or change in the appearance or texture of something due to prolonged exposure to the atmosphere
texture: the feel, appearance, or consistency of a surface or a substance
sandy soil: soil containing large amounts of sand
clayey soil: sticky fine-grained soil that can be moulded when wet, and is dried and baked to make bricks and pottery

Soil samples—clayey, sandy and loamy

Explore

Collect samples of different types of soil. Dry them completely and sieve the samples to remove rocks, pebble and grass blades. Take a fistful of the sieved soil from one of the samples. Add water drop by drop and knead the soil. Add just enough water to make dough. Use the dough to make a ball, then roll the ball into a cylindrical shape and make a doughnut-shape from the rolled cylinder.

Repeat this activity with the other samples. Can you make the cylindrical and doughnut shape with all the soil samples? Which type of soil was most difficult to work with and which was the easiest to work with? Can you tell the clayey soil from the others from this activity?

Since sandy soil contains large particles, it is quite porous. It contains a lot of air and hence is quite light. Water can flow easily through the spaces between the sand particles; so sandy soil does not retain moisture and dries up quite fast. In contrast, clayey soil consists of very fine-grained material. Since the smaller particles pack together tightly, clayey soil contains very little air spaces. So it is heavier than sandy soil. Water cannot percolate

percolate: filter gradually through a porous surface or substance

through clayey soil particles easily, so this type of soil can retain water and remain wet for a long time. Clayey soil is considered ideal for making earthen pottery and sculptures.

Loamy soil consists of a mixture of sand, clay and silt and is considered to be the perfect soil for growing plants. Silt is found in river beds and has a particle size between that of sand and clay. The texture of loamy soil is gritty. It retains water, yet the water can also flow through it easily. It also contains humus. There are various varieties of loamy soil, ranging from fertile to very muddy. Out of all the different kinds of soil, loamy soil is considered to be ideal for cultivation.

Explore

Take a little soil from three different places—a garden, playground and the bank of a nearby pond or lake. Break the clumps with your hand to powder it. Take three identical glass tumblers and fill each up to about three-quarters with water. Add a handful of the three samples to the three glasses and stir them well. Let the glasses stand undisturbed for some time. If you observe the three glasses you will see layers formed of different sized particles.

Is the layer separation the same in all the three glasses? Which glass has more particles of large size? Which one has more particles of smaller size? Which glass has the largest amount of floating dead matter? From your observations, what can you deduce about the types of soil you had collected?

Properties of soil

The soil in one location can be very different from the soil in another location because soils develop under a variety of conditions. In order to understand soil and how one soil differs from another, geologists look at certain properties of soil.

Colour

The colour of soil can tell a lot about it its qualities. Most soils appear in shades of black, brown, red, grey and white. Generally speaking, darker soils are considered more nutrient rich because the darker colour often indicates that a large amount of decomposed organic matter, or humus, is present in the soil. Grey colour often indicates clayey soil with poor drainage, while red soils indicate that the soil is very poor in nutrients.

loamy soil: a fertile soil made of clay and sand containing humus

Texture

Another important property of soil is its texture. Some soils have more large particles and fewer small particles and feel gritty, while other soils have an abundance of small particles with few large particles and feel smooth. Some other soils have an equal balance between small and large particles and are the best kind of soils for plants to grow in.

Moisture content

Some moisture is always present in soil although the amount may differ depending on the season and location. It is the moisture in the soil that plant roots take up. In the absence of any moisture in the soil, most plants would die.

The presence of moisture in the soil can be tested simply by heating a small amount of soil in a test tube. On heating the soil, tiny droplets of water can be seen condensing near the mouth of the test tube. Water present in the soil sample is released as vapour on heating the soil sample.

Structure

The structure of the soil is also an important property. Porous soil allows easy percolation of water but soil that is too tightly packed will not allow water to pass through easily. For example, sandy soils are porous while clayey soils are compact and become hard when dry.

Circle Time

Whether the soil in a certain location is porous or not can be easily found out by a simple activity. For this, you will need a few hollow cylinders or pipes that are 8 cm in diameter and 25 cm long. You can use PVC or metal pipes. You would also need a stopwatch or a wrist watch.

This activity should be done in small groups. One group may test the soil at a single location. At the location where you want to test the soil, dig a small pit and place the pipe upright, about 1 cm deep in the ground. Make sure that the soil is dry. Now pour 200 ml of water in the pipe slowly. Hold the pipe firmly pressed to the ground so that no water flows out from the bottom of the pipe. Also make sure that water does not spill over from the top. Note the time when you start pouring water. Note the time again when all the water has soaked into the soil, leaving the pipe empty.

1. **Start the stopwatch when 200 ml water is poured evenly on the dry soil in the pipe.**

2. **Stop the stopwatch when all the poured water has been absorbed.**
3. **Note the time.**
4. **Repeat the experiment for different soil types.**
5. **Compare the time of percolation in different soil types.**

From the time taken for 200 ml water to soak in, the rate of percolation can be calculated easily in terms of ml/minute. Compare your findings with the other groups. Do all the groups get the same result? Percolation of water was fastest at which location? What type of soil would it be?

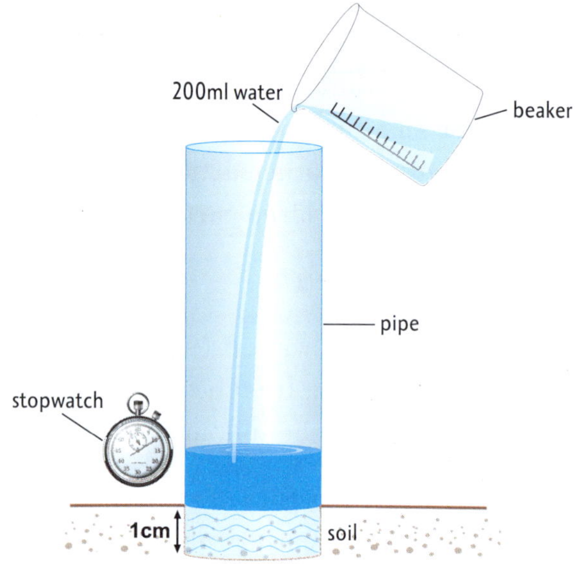

Water absorption test

Water absorption

Water absorption by soil is important for growing any crop because it is from soil that plants get water through their roots. If the soil is too porous, water drains away easily and not much is held within. Such soil dries up quickly and needs frequent watering. The presence of organic matter, such as humus, helps to hold more water.

Explore

Take a glass or plastic funnel. Fold a filter paper into a cone and place it within the funnel. Place the funnel over the mouth of a bottle or a conical flask. Put 50 gm of dry, powdered soil in the folded filter paper. Take a measured amount of water in a measuring cylinder and pour it drop by drop on the soil so that it falls uniformly all over the soil. Keep pouring water till the entire soil is wet and a few drops come out of the funnel. From the water remaining in the measuring cylinder, the amount of water absorbed by the soil can be calculated easily.

1. **Have equal weight of dry soil samples ready.**
2. **Fold a filter paper, put it in the funnel and put one soil sample evenly in the funnel.**
3. **Pour a measured amount of water evenly on the soil.**
4. **When the water stops dripping into the beaker, measure water volume filtered out.**
5. **Calculate the water absorbed by the soil.**

6. Repeat the experiment for all the soil types using the same measure of water and soil. Change the filter paper each time.
7. Compare your results to see which soil absorbs the maximum amount of water.

Which type of soil absorbs the largest amount of water and which absorbs the least?

Testing water absorption using funnel and filter paper

Soil type and crops

Soil is affected by climatic factors such as wind, rainfall, temperature, light and humidity. Hence, just as different parts of India have different climates, similarly the soil types found in different parts also vary. For example, the type of soil found in the plains of Uttar Pradesh, Bihar and West Bengal is different from the type of soil found in the southern states of Tamil Nadu and Karnataka, and that found in Rajasthan and Gujarat. In some parts, the soil is clayey, in others it is loamy, while in some other parts it is sandy.

Factastic

Soil holds 0.01% of the earth's water. It holds 3,750 tonnes of water per hectare, thus reducing the risk of floods. It holds pollutants to a certain extent. Soil stores around 10% of the emissions of carbon dioxide.

Paddy plants

The type of crops that can be grown in a particular area depends on climatic factors, as well as the type of soil found there. For example, cereals, such as wheat and gram, grow well in clayey and loamy soils, which are rich in humus and retain water well. Soils rich in clay and organic matter have a good capacity to retain water and are ideal for growing paddy because paddy cultivation needs standing water in the field. Loamy soils, that drain water easily, are good for growing pulses. Sandy loam or loam that drains water easily and can hold plenty of air is suitable for growing cotton.

Soil erosion

Soil erosion caused due to deforestation

The earth's surface is being worn away continuously by the action of water and wind, a process known as erosion. Soil erosion takes place only when the soil is bare and exposed and has no vegetation cover on it. Plant roots firmly bind the soil. In the absence of plants, soil becomes loose and is easily blown away by wind or washed away by water. When trees and forests are cut, especially on hillsides, the bare land is susceptible to soil erosion. During rains, soil from the bare hillsides is washed down into the rivers below, which silt up and cause floods downstream. That is why it is important that forests are not cut and more trees are planted wherever possible. Damage to the soil can disturb nature's balance and can be life threatening.

Planting of saplings

erosion: the process of wearing away of the earth's surface by the action of water and wind

Revision Time

- ✶ Soil covers a major portion of the earth's land surface and is an inseparable part of our life.
- ✶ Soil is a mixture of particles formed by the weathering of rocks and decaying plants and animals.
- ✶ Soil profile is a section through the different layers of the soil known as horizons.
- ✶ Soil can be broadly classified into three types based on the size of the particles it contains—sandy, clayey and loamy.
- ✶ Sandy soil is the most porous and allows water to percolate freely; clayey soil is the least porous and retains the most water.
- ✶ Because soils develop under a variety of conditions, the soil in one location can be very different from the soil in another location.
- ✶ Water absorption by soil is important for growing any crop because it is from the soil that plants take in water through their roots.
- ✶ The type of crop that can be grown in a particular type of soil depends on the climatic factors as well as the components of the soil.
- ✶ Soil erosion is a major environmental problem.
- ✶ Plant roots firmly bind the soil; in the absence of plants, soil becomes loose and is easily blown away by wind or washed away by water.
- ✶ It is important that forests are not cut and more trees are planted wherever possible.

Quiz Time

1. Answer the questions.

a. What are the main constituents of soil?

b. What is the role of microbes in the soil?

c. What is soil profile?

d. What type of soil is good for making pottery and sculptures?

e. Why is planting of more trees important for the conservation of soil?

2. Fill in the blanks.

a. Organic material is mainly ________________ living matter.

b. The uppermost layer of soil is commonly known as ________________.

c. Soil is a mixture of particles formed by ____________ of rocks and decaying plants and animals.

d. Sandy soil contains more ____________ particles while clayey soil contains more ____________ particles.

e. Loamy soil consists of a mixture of sand, clay and silt and is considered to be the ____________ for growing plants.

3. Indicate whether the statements are true or false.

a.	The humus layer is generally soft, porous and cannot retain water.	True	False
b.	Different-sized mineral particles, such as sand, silt and clay as well as humus, give soil its texture.	True	False
c.	Silt is found in river beds and the size of silt particles is larger than that of sand.	True	False
d.	The presence of moisture in soil can be tested simply by heating a small amount of soil.	True	False
e.	Soils rich in clay and organic matter and having a good capacity to retain water are ideal for growing pulses.	True	False

4. Match the following.

a. humus	i. topsoil
b. clayey soil	ii. soil erosion
c. deforestation	iii. decaying organisms
d. Horizon A	iv. solid rock below soil
e. bedrock	v. fine particles

5. Project work

a. List the major crops grown in the different states of India and the kind of soil in those regions. On a political map of India, mark the soil type and crops grown in each state. You may use pictures of the crops and paste them in the appropriate places.

b. Why does the use of chemical fertilisers damage the quality of soil and why should organic fertilisers be used. Prepare a brief report outlining the major points.

Think it over

1. **Why does the water of a pond not percolate through the soil making the pond dry?**
2. **Where does the water in mountain springs come from?**

10 Respiration for Energy

Most living organisms including humans need oxygen to live. This oxygen is usually taken from the air. After we breathe in the oxygen, it is carried by blood to all parts of the body and finally to each individual cell where it is used to break down the glucose obtained from food and produce energy. This process of the breakdown of food chemicals with the release of energy using oxygen is called cellular respiration and occurs in every cell of living organisms. It is a process of releasing energy from the food we consume. During the process, carbon dioxide is produced as a by-product, which is carried to the lungs by blood and is expelled when we breathe out. Different organisms use different organs for respiration. Mammals, such as humans, use lungs for respiration. Fish that live under water, use gills to extract oxygen from water; earthworms use their skin to absorb oxygen; while amoeba use their cell surface for the same purpose.

Energy for cells

Cells, which are the building blocks of all living organisms, carry out a variety of functions to keep the organism alive. In order to perform these functions, cells need energy, which they get from food. In cellular respiration, glucose obtained from the consumed food is broken down into carbon dioxide and water using oxygen while releasing energy that keeps the cells going. In fact, the energy stored in food is released during respiration that enables the organism to perform various activities. In humans, for example, activities, such as eating, moving, talking, sleeping and reading require energy, which comes from food. It is for this reason that all organisms need to consume food regularly to live and grow.

cellular respiration: the process of the breakdown of glucose with the release of energy in cells using oxygen

In the cell, respiration or the breakdown of food may occur

in two ways. When the chemical breakdown of glucose obtained from food into carbon dioxide and water takes place in the presence of oxygen it is called aerobic respiration. This, in simple terms, translates into respiration in the presence of air.

Aerobic respiration: **glucose + oxygen (O_2) → carbon dioxide (CO_2) + water (H_2O) + energy**

There are some organisms that can break down glucose even without using oxygen. This process is called anaerobic respiration and here alcohol is produced as a by-product instead of water. Anaerobic indicates that the process happens in the absence of air. The amount of energy released in this process is, however, much less than that released during aerobic respiration.

Anaerobic respiration: **glucose → carbon dioxide (CO_2) + alcohol + energy**

The anaerobic breakdown of sugar into alcohol is also known as fermentation. Organisms that undergo anaerobic respiration can live in the absence of air and are known as anaerobes. A common example is yeast, that is used in making alcoholic drinks such as wine and beer. For some anaerobes, oxygen acts as poison as they cannot live in its presence.

Weightlifter

Human muscle cells undergo anaerobic respiration when they are not able to meet the increased demand for oxygen, for example during vigorous physical activities such as running, cycling, weightlifting or walking at a stretch for a long time.

During strenuous activities, the cells require much more energy than at other times and they have to produce this extra energy through anaerobic respiration, since enough oxygen is not available. In such a situation, the breakdown of glucose takes place in the presence of insufficient oxygen which leads to the production of lactic acid (the same acid present in curd or *dahi*) instead of carbon dioxide and water.

But anaerobic respiration in muscle cells cannot go on for a long time. When lactic acid accumulates in the muscle

aerobic respiration: chemical break down of glucose into carbon dioxide and water in the presence of oxygen
anaerobic respiration: chemical break down of glucose into carbon dioxide and alcohol or lactic acid in the absence of oxygen
fermentation: chemical breakdown of sugar into alcohol in the absence of oxygen
anaerobe: a micro-organism that can live in the absence of oxygen

cells, muscles cramp, making it difficult for one to move one's muscles. Relaxation or a hot bath usually relieves the cramps because as blood circulation improves, the normal supply of oxygen to the cells is restored, which causes the final breakdown of lactic acid into carbon dioxide and water, similar to that in aerobic respiration. Thus, although the cells in the human body normally undergo aerobic respiration, sometimes they also undergo anaerobic respiration to meet the demand for extra energy.

Breathing

Breathing is a natural process of inhalation and exhalation that helps the body take in oxygen-rich air for aerobic respiration and give off carbon dioxide and water vapour—the by-products formed in the process. It is an ongoing process occuring throughout the life of an organism. Most of the time we do not even notice our breathing; it happens almost automatically.

One inhalation and one exhalation make one breath. The number of times a person inhales or exhales in a minute is called the breathing rate. The breathing rate depends on many factors such as age and physical activity. For example, children usually have a breathing rate of 16 to 25 breaths per minute whereas adults have a breathing rate of 14 to 18 breaths per minute. However, after strenuous activities, such as brisk walking or running, the breathing rate increases and the breaths need to be deeper to inhale more oxygen because the body cells demand more oxygen.

cramp: the painful contraction of a muscle, typically caused by strenuous physical activity
inhalation: the action of breathing in
exhalation: the action of breathing out
breathing rate: the number of times a person inhales or exhales in a minute

Muscle cells die if the supply of oxygen is not constant or adequate. That is why if we try to hold our breath for long, we feel breathless and dizzy, and may even faint. Some swimmers are able to hold their breath under water for as long as two minutes, but they can do it only after long training.

The mechanism of breathing

The process of breathing begins in the nose. When we take in or inhale through our nose, air passes through the nostrils into the nasal cavity. Any dust particle in the inhaled air is filtered out by the fine hair that line the nasal cavity. From the nasal cavity, the filtered air passes through the wind pipe and reaches the lungs in the chest cavity. A bony cage called the ribcage surrounds and protects the lungs in the chest cavity. At the floor of the chest cavity is a thin muscular sheet called diaphragm that plays a key role along with the ribcage in the breathing process. During breathing, the chest or the abdomen expands and contracts alternately, which can be counted to determine the breathing rate.

During inhalation, the diaphragm moves down and the ribcage expands, thereby increasing the space in the chest cavity, which causes the pressure in the chest cavity to drop. As a result air rushes into the lungs, filling them with air and making them expand. During exhalation, just the opposite happens. The ribcage shrinks and the diaphragm moves up, reducing the space and increasing the pressure in the chest cavity. As a result, air is now pushed out of the lungs. The change in the size of the ribcage during inhalation and exhalation can be measured with a measuring tape and can give an idea of the lung capacity of an individual.

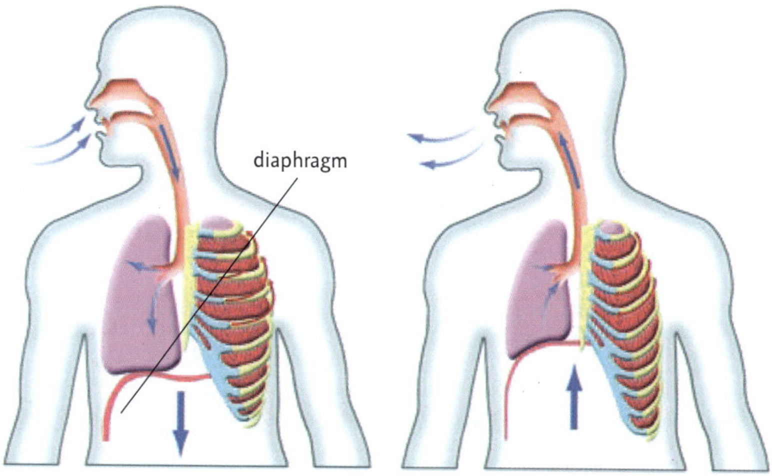

Breathing in   Breathing out

nasal cavity: the space above and inside the nose
lungs: each of the pair of organs situated within the ribcage, used for breathing
ribcage: the bony frame formed by the ribs around the chest that encloses the lungs and the heart
diaphragm: a muscular partition separating the abdominal and chest cavities that takes part in respiration
lung capacity: the maximum amount of air a person's lungs can hold

Factastic

If a particle of dust or ground pepper gets past the hair lining the nasal cavity, it can cause irritation inside the nose and we sneeze. Sneezing can send tiny particles speeding out of the nose at up to 160 km/h!

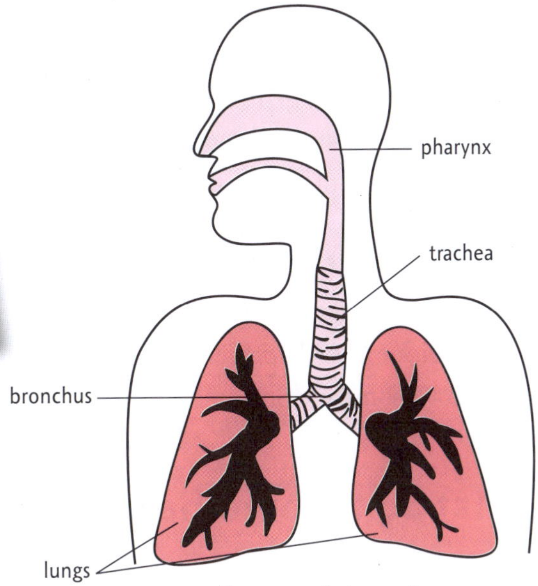

Human respiratory system

Explore

Aim: To observe the breathing mechanism in humans.

Material required: a plastic bottle, a Y-shaped tube, balloons, a rubber sheet and a stopper

Method: Take a wide plastic bottle with stiff walls and cut out the bottom. Get a Y-shaped glass or plastic tube. On the two forked ends of the tube, fix two small inflatable balloons. Fit a large cork or rubber stopper with a hole in the mouth of the bottle. Now push the tube with balloons into the hole in the stopper from the bottom so that the forked end is inside the bottle. Make sure that the stopper and tube in it fit tightly so that air cannot pass. Cover the open bottom end of the bottle with a thin rubber sheet (cut out from a large balloon), by tying it with a large rubber band. The tied rubber sheet should be loose enough to be easily pushed in and pulled out.

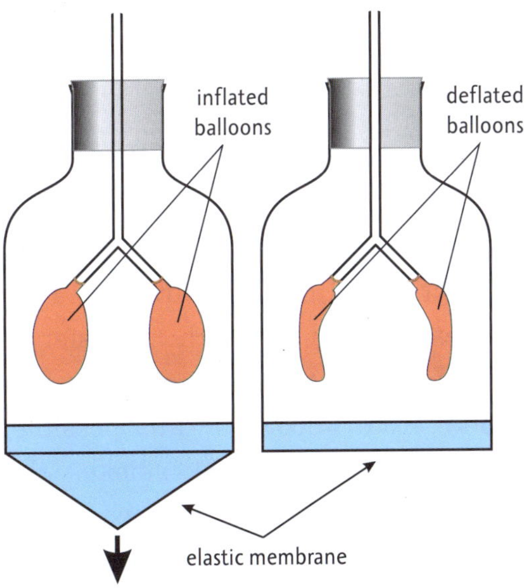

When the membrane is pulled down, air is sucked into the balloons attached to the forked tube. When the membrane is released, the air is pushed out of the balloon.

Mechanism of breathing in humans

Observe what happens to the balloons when the rubber sheet is pulled down. What happens when the rubber sheet is pushed in by pressing it at the middle? Does it explain the mechanism of breathing? What does the rubber sheet represent in this model?

Lung capacity is the maximum amount of air a person's lungs can hold at any point of time. A large lung capacity is considered a sign of good health. While the size of the lungs cannot be increased, there are breathing exercises that if practised daily can help increase the lung capacity and the efficiency with which they hold oxygen to some extent.

Factastic

Only a third of the total lung capacity of about 4–6 litres for the average human is used during normal activity, but this fraction increases during strenuous activity when the body requires more oxygen. On an average, males have a 20-25% larger lung capacity than females and tall individuals have a greater capacity than short people.

What do we breathe out?

The composition of air entering the lungs is quite different from that released from the lungs. The inhaled air is rich in oxygen while the exhaled air has a higher percentage of carbon dioxide and water vapour in it.

To check for the presence of carbon dioxide in exhaled air, one can blow through a straw into freshly prepared limewater kept in a glass or a test tube. The carbon dioxide in the exhaled air turns lime water milky due to the formation of insoluble calcium carbonate. If you exhale on a cold glass or mirror, you will observe that water vapour condenses on the surface indicating the presence of water vapour in exhaled air. Similarly one can also see the moisture condense in air when one exhales in very cold weather.

Factastic

More than half a litre of water is lost each day through breathing!

Our lungs are very delicate organs and have millions of tiny structures and thin blood vessels that make the transfer of oxygen from air to blood and of carbon dioxide from blood to air possible. However, when people smoke, the chemicals contained in tobacco smoke damage these delicate structures and reduce the efficiency of the lungs. Tobacco smoking could also result in lung cancer.

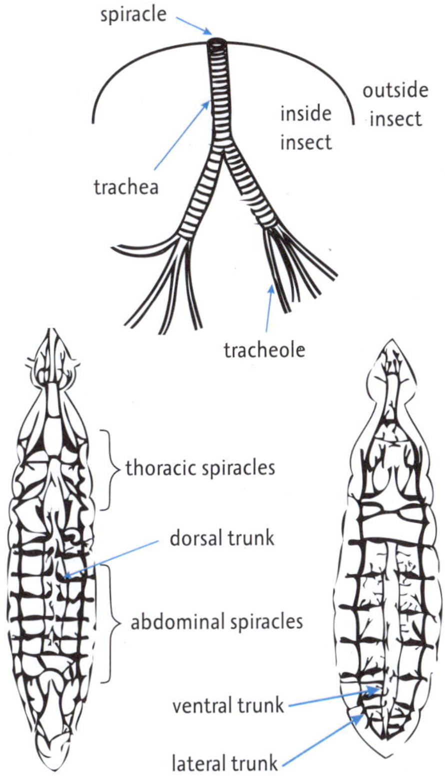

Respiratory system of a cockroach

How other animals breathe

Apart from humans, most animals, such as cows, buffaloes, deer, dogs, cats, other mammals, snakes and other reptiles, breathe using lungs. But there are many organisms and insects that do not have lungs and breathe with other organs.

Cockroach

Cockroaches and some other insects have breathing pores called spiracles on their body, which are part of their respiratory systems. Insects also have a network of tubes called tracheae, which carry air from spiracles direct to the tissues. During breathing, oxygen-rich air is drawn in through the spiracles and carried to every cell of the insect body through the tracheae. In the same way, the carbon dioxide formed in the cells is carried by the tracheae to the spiracles and expelled out.

Earthworm

An earthworm has no lungs. It uses its moist outer skin as a respiratory organ from where oxygen enters the earthworm's bloodstream and is carried to the body cells. Similarly, the carbon dioxide produced in the cells is similarly transported to the skin from where it passes out of the body.

Interestingly, although frogs have lungs like human beings, they can also breathe through their moist and slippery skin. They have tiny blood vessels beneath the outer skin layers which assist in breathing.

spiracles: breathing pores found in insects and used for respiration
tracheae: a network of tubes found in insects and used to carry oxygen to the tissues

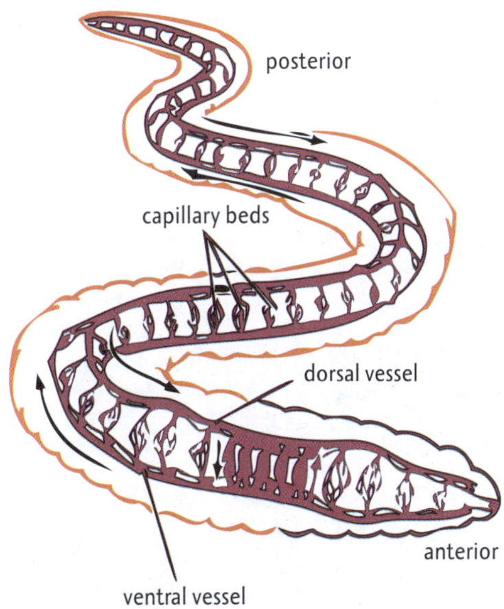

Respiratory system of an earthworm

Breathing under water

Organisms that live on land usually take in oxygen from the air. But organisms that live under water have specialised organs that enable them to extract the oxygen dissolved in water. However, some animals, such as whales and dolphins, which live in water come up to the surface at regular intervals for breathing air.

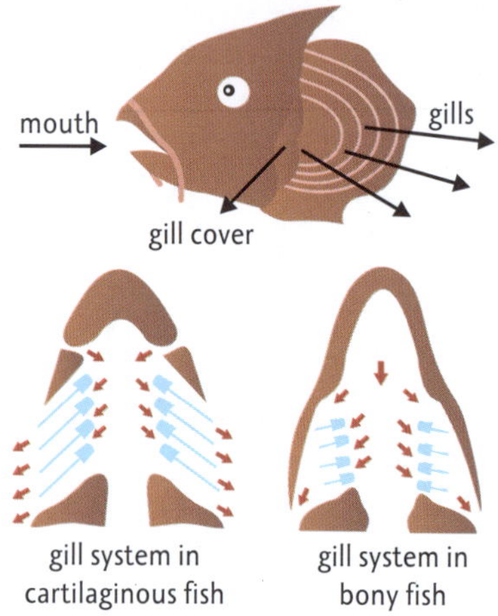

Fish gills

Fish take in the dissolved oxygen from the water using their gills. Gills have a dense network of blood vessels that absorb oxygen from water as it flows past them. The very fine structure of the gills greatly increases their surface area, making them absorb oxygen more efficiently from water.

Respiration in plants

Factastic

Water contains only about one-thirtieth as much oxygen per volume as air. If we were somehow able to 'breathe' water, we would need to take about 450 'breaths' per minute just to get enough oxygen from water into our lungs!

Like any organism, plants also require oxygen for respiration, but they do not have respiratory organs. They use stomata present in leaves to take in oxygen from the air. The root cells in plants also need oxygen to produce energy, which they get from the air spaces available between soil particles. Plants do not need much oxygen for respiration, hence, the rates of respiration in plants are far lower than in animals.

During the process of respiration, plants use oxygen, and release carbon dioxide, water and energy as products.

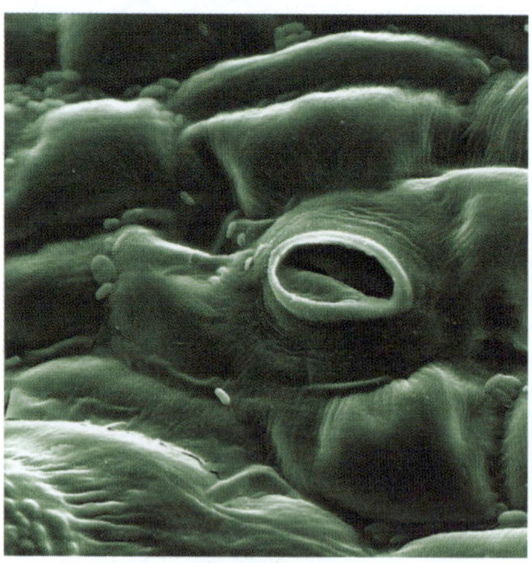
Stomata in leaves

Roots take in oxygen

Brainteaser

A lady has a match. She enters a dark room and wants some light. She has a gas stove and a candle. What would she light first?

Answer: She would first light the match!

Revision Time

- Respiration is the process of releasing energy from food and this occurs in each cell of all living organisms.
- The oxygen we inhale is carried by the blood to each individual cell of the body where it is used to breakdown the glucose into carbon dioxide and water to produce energy.
- When glucose breaks down to form carbon dioxide and water in the presence of oxygen, it is called aerobic respiration.
- When the breakdown of glucose takes place in the absence of oxygen, the process is called anaerobic respiration. Here, alcohol is produced instead of water.
- Human muscle cells undergo anaerobic respiration when they do not receive enough oxygen such as during vigorous physical activities like running, cycling, weightlifting or walking at a stretch for a long time.
- Breathing is a natural process of inhalation and exhalation that helps the body take in oxygen-rich air for aerobic respiration and give off carbon dioxide and water vapour—the by-products formed during the process.
- During inhalation, the diaphragm moves down and the ribcage expands, making air rush into the lungs, filling them and making them expand. During exhalation the lungs shrink back to their normal size.
- The change in the size of the ribcage during inhalation and exhalation gives an idea of the lung capacity of an individual.
- Insects have breathing pores called spiracles, which are part of their respiratory system.
- Earthworms use their moist skin for respiration.
- Fish have gills that can extract oxygen dissolved in water for respiration.
- Plants use leaves and roots to take in oxygen from the air and give off carbon dioxide during respiration.

Quiz Time

1. Answer the questions.

a. Why do all living organisms need to respire?

b. What are the products formed during anaerobic respiration?

c. Why do muscles cramp during strenuous exercise?

d. Why does the breathing rate change during physical activities like running or cycling?

e. What is the role of the diaphragm in the process of breathing?

2. Match the columns.

a. cockroach	i. stomata
b. earthworm	ii. lungs
c. snake	iii. gills
d. fish	iv. skin
e. plants	v. spiracles

3. Fill in the blanks.

a. The process of the breakdown of food chemicals into carbon dioxide and water with the release of energy in the presence of oxygen is called ________________ respiration.

b. Anaerobic respiration in muscle cells produces ________________ acid, the accumulation of which causes muscles to cramp.

c. Along with the ribcage, the ________________ plays a key role in the breathing process.

d. Lung capacity is the ________________ amount of air a person's lungs can hold.

e. Cockroaches and other insects respire through breathing pores called ________________.

4. Indicate whether the statements are true or false.

a. In cellular respiration, lactose obtained from food in the cells is broken down into carbon dioxide and water using oxygen. True False

b. In anaerobic respiration, alcohol is produced instead of water. True False

c. The number of times a person inhales or exhales in a second is called the breathing rate. True False

d. During inhalation, the diaphragm moves down and the ribcage shrinks. True False

e. The earthworm breathes through its moist outer skin. True False

5. Project work

a. Use a stop watch to count how many breaths you take in a minute when you are resting. Remember, one inhalation and one exhalation together are counted as one breath. Walk for 10 minutes and immediately count the number of breaths you take in a minute. Next, run 100 m and record your breathing rate again. Record your observations in the table given below. Do the same for your classmates.

Name	Breathing rate		
	At rest	After a 10-minute brisk walk	After a 100 m run

From the table do you notice that the breathing rate becomes faster after physical activity? Why do you think you need to breathe faster after a physical activity?

b. Find out from a doctor or a paramedic under what conditions a person needs artificial respiration and how it is given. Also find out how a ventilator used in hospitals helps a person breathe.

Think it over

1. **How is the mudskipper, which is a fish and breathes through gills, able to spend a substantial amount of time out of water?**
2. **Why do some people sneeze when they are exposed to bright light?**

11 Transportation of Materials in Animals and Plants

Animals and plants are made up of a large number of cells of different types, hence are called multicellular organisms. These organisms have different organs that carry out different functions to remain alive. For example, in the human body, the heart, the brain, the kidney, the lungs and other organs need nutrition, water and oxygen to function. Thus, there has to be a transport system to carry all these substances to the different organs. In addition, all organisms also need a system to transport wastes to organs from where they can be removed. In the human body, the circulatory system takes care of transporting food, water and oxygen to different organs while the excretory system functions to dispose off the wastes.

The human circulatory system

The circulatory system is essentially a pumping system comprising a muscular pump and several networks of vessels that control the movement of blood around the body. The main parts of the system are: blood, the vital fluid that keeps us alive; the heart, which pumps the blood; and different types of blood vessels called arteries, capillaries and veins, that carry the blood to and from different organs of the body.

circulatory system: essentially a pumping system comprising the heart and networks of vessels that control the flow of blood around the body

Blood

We are all familiar with blood—the red-coloured fluid that flows out whenever we have a cut in our body. Blood is

Factastic
It was the English physician, William Harvey, who discovered the circulation of blood in 1628. The popular belief at that time was that blood was circulated by a sort of pulsing action of the arteries.

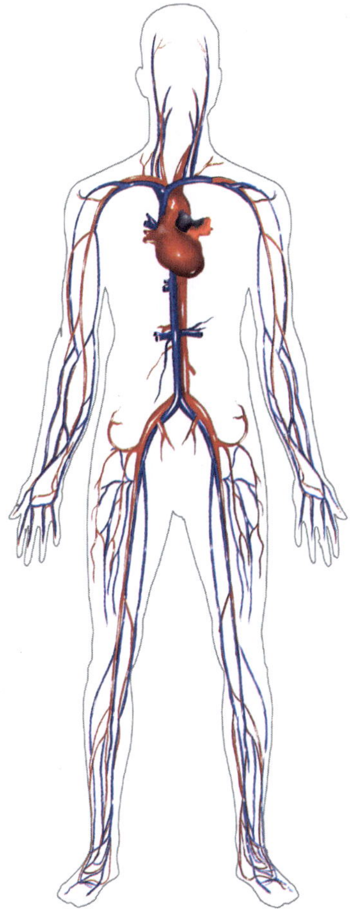
Circulatory system

vital for life as it transports substances, such as digested food, oxygen, proteins and hormones, around the body. It carries oxygen from the lungs to the body cells and also transports carbon dioxide back to the lungs to be expelled as waste. Substances from digested food, such as proteins and carbohydrates, are carried from the small intestine to other parts of the body and hormones released by different glands are carried to various organs. Blood also has substances that act and seal damaged blood vessels to prevent excessive blood loss in case of an injury and other substances that help fight infection.

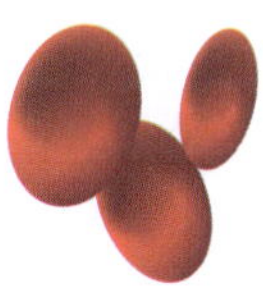
Erythrocytes (RBC)

Blood is made up of a transparent yellowish fluid called plasma in which various types of cells are suspended. The red colour of blood comes from the red blood cells (RBCs) which contain a red substance called haemoglobin. Haemoglobin binds with oxygen taken from air by the lungs and transports it to cells in every part of the body. It also carries carbon dioxide from the cells back to the lungs.

plasma: the colourless fluid part of blood
red blood cells: blood cells that contain the pigment haemoglobin and transport oxygen and carbon dioxide to and from the tissues
haemoglobin: a red protein that transports oxygen in the blood of vertebrates
white blood cells: blood cells that engulf and digest bacteria and fungi and are an important part of the body's defence system

Blood also has white blood cells (WBCs) that are larger than

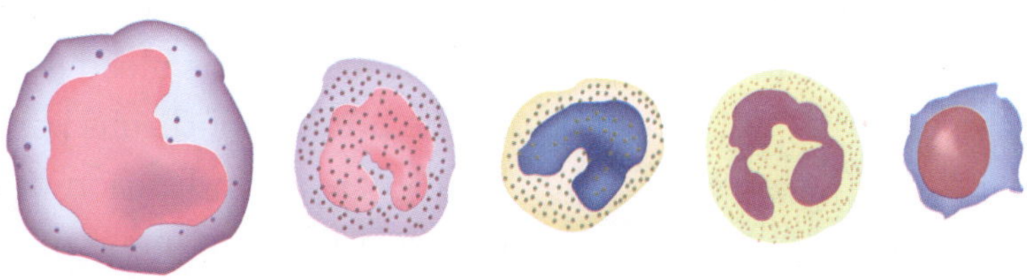

Leucocytes (WBC)

RBCs but are much less in number. The main role of WBCs is to fight against germs entering the body. A high WBC count often indicates the presence of some infection in the body.

The third type of cells present in blood are called platelets. These are very tiny cells, much smaller than RBCs, which stick together and form a clot when a blood vessel is torn or cut and blood starts flowing out. Clotting helps to prevent excessive blood loss.

Thrombocytes (platelets)

Blood vessels

Two types of blood vessels, known as arteries and veins, carry blood throughout the body. Arteries are very thick-walled, strong and elastic blood vessels that carry oxygen-rich blood from the heart to other parts of the body and also carry blood rich in carbon dioxide from the heart to the lungs. Arteries have to be strong because they carry blood at quite a high pressure. Blood flowing through the arteries (except the pulmonary artery) looks bright red as it is rich in oxygen.

Veins are thin-walled blood vessels that carry carbon dioxide-rich blood from different parts of the body to the heart. Veins have valves that allow blood to flow only in one direction towards the heart. Blood flowing through the veins (except the pulmonary vein) looks dark red because it does not carry much oxygen.

When an artery reaches an organ, it branches out into smaller vessels. These vessels finally branch into extremely thin tubes called capillaries that ultimately join the veins. In the capillaries, red blood cells give oxygen to the cells and take in carbon dioxide back to the heart and then to the lungs.

Since blood from the heart goes directly into arteries, the beating of the heart can be felt as a pulse in arteries. The simplest way to feel the pulse is to place the middle and index finger of the right hand on the inner side of the left wrist, where a regular throbbing sensation can be felt. The pulse is produced by a rhythmic expansion and contraction of the arteries as blood is forced through them by the heart. The number of throbs per minute is called the **pulse rate**. It gives an indication of the number of times a person's heart beats in one minute.

platelets: tiny cells present in blood that cause blood to clot
blood vessels: tube-like muscular structures through which blood flows
arteries: blood vessels that carry blood from the heart to the rest of the body
veins: blood vessels that carry blood from other parts of the body to the heart
capillaries: any of the fine branching blood vessels that form a network between the arteries and veins
pulse: a rhythmical throbbing of the arteries, as blood is forced through them

The pulse rate depends on age as well as the physical fitness of an individual. For example, a child of age 14 will have an average pulse rate of 84, while a physically fit adult has a pulse rate of 72 per minute. But the pulse rate could go up in case of fever and some diseases. That is why doctors first check the pulse when doing a medical examination.

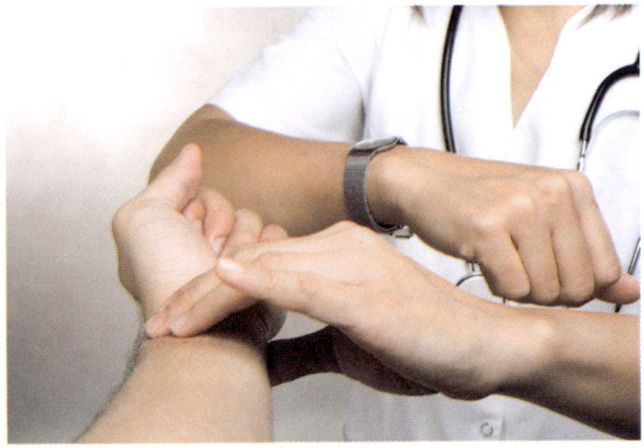

Checking of pulse

The heart

The heart is nothing but a hard-working pump made of a special type of muscle, which works non-stop for years and as long as a person lives. The heart is roughly the size of a person's fist and is located in the chest cavity almost in the middle, with its lower tip slightly tilted towards the left.

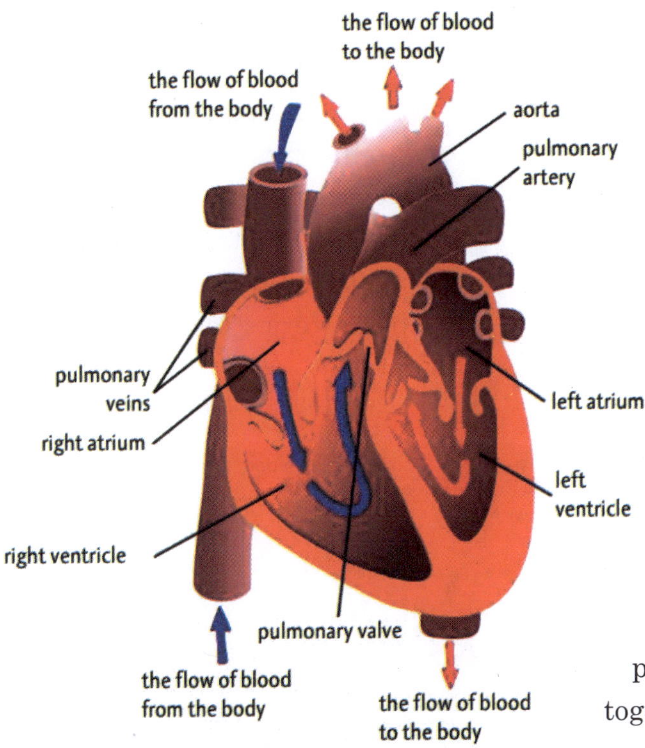

Working of the human heart

The heart actually works as two pumps in one. It is vertically divided into two sides—right and left. Each side has one upper chamber called the atrium and a lower chamber called the ventricle. On each side, the upper and lower chambers are linked through valves, each forming a separate pump. However, the two pumps do not work independently, but together as a team.

The right side of the heart receives blood rich in carbon dioxide from the rest of the body and sends it to the lungs for oxygenation. The left side of the heart receives oxygen-rich blood from the lungs and sends it to the rest of the body. At no point do the two types of blood mix in the heart. They remain separate from each other.

atrium: each of the two upper chambers of heart from which blood is passed to the ventricles
ventricle: each of the two lower chambers of the heart from which blood is pumped out of the heart

Blood enters the right side of the heart through the right atrium and from there it flows into the right ventricle through a valve, which allows the blood to flow only in one direction. From the right ventricle, the carbon dioxide-rich blood is pushed out toward the lungs through the pulmonary artery for oxygenation.

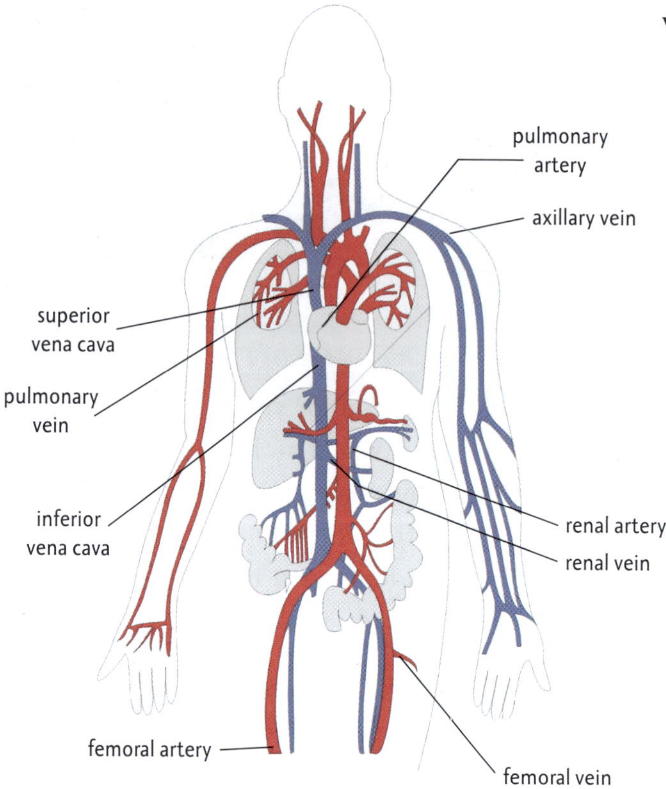

Blood circulation: veins and arteries

The left side of the heart is more powerful than the right side because it has to push oxygenated blood to all parts of the body. Oxygenated blood from the lungs enters the left atrium through the pulmonary vein. From there it passes through a valve into the left ventricle, which then pushes it through the aorta and other arteries to the rest of the body.

Overall, the rhythmic and coordinated beating of the four chambers of the heart maintains the circulation of blood and transportation of substances to the different parts of the body.

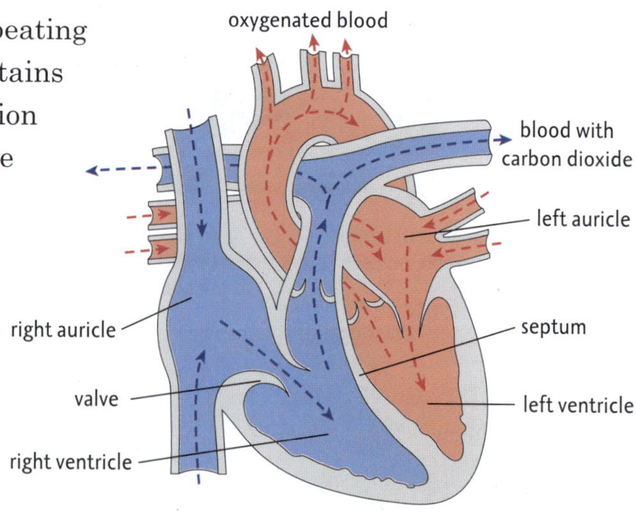

Cross section of the heart

pulmonary artery: one of two arteries that carry blood depleted in oxygen from the right ventricle of the heart to the lungs
oxygenated: enriched with oxygen
pulmonary vein: a vein carrying oxygenated blood from the lungs to the left atrium of the heart

Heartbeat

The walls of the chambers of the heart are made up of special type of muscles called cardiac muscles, which never get tired. For pumping blood, these muscles contract and relax in a rhythmic manner, which can be detected as heartbeats. The beating of the heart can be felt indirectly by feeling the pulse, but the sound of heartbeats can be heard directly by using an instrument called a stethoscope. It consists of a Y-shaped flexible plastic tube with an earpiece attached to each end of the Y and a sound-detecting device at the other end. The sound-detecting device has a thin plastic diaphragm on one side that is kept in contact with the skin for receiving the sounds of the heartbeat. If a stethoscope is placed on the chest directly over the region of the heart, it amplifies the sound of the beating heart, which the doctor can hear. In healthy adults, there are two normal heart sounds often described as a 'lub' and a 'dub' that occur in sequence with each heart beat. From the sounds of the beating heart, a doctor may get clues about the condition of the heart.

Factastic

The heart is made up of the strongest muscles in the body. The heart works non-stop day and night to circulate the entire blood in the body more than 1,000 times per day, pumping a total of about 6,000 litres of blood every day.

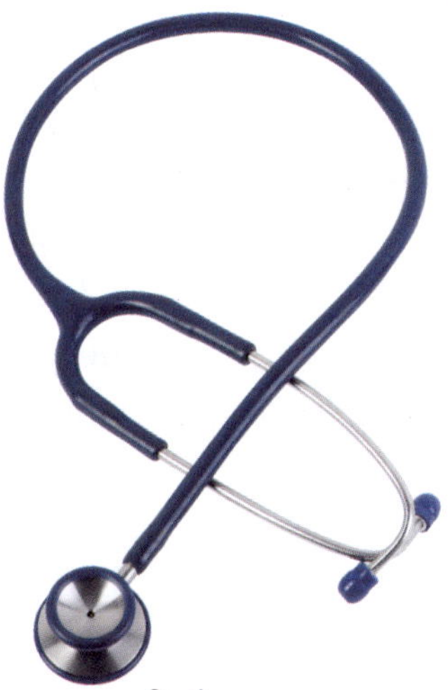

Stethoscope

Explore

Make a model stethoscope by taking a small plastic funnel about 5 cm in diameter and a rubber tube that fits tightly over the stem of the funnel. Stretch a thin rubber sheet, for example, a piece of a large balloon, over the mouth of the funnel and fix it with tape or a thick rubber band.

Place the open end of the rubber tube in one ear and the rubber sheet

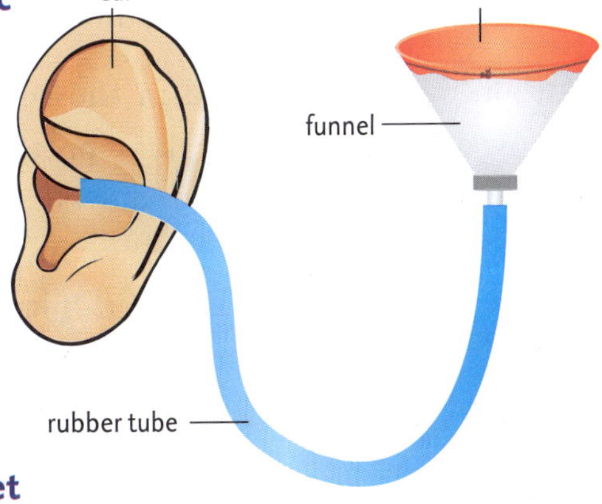

Model stethoscope

cardiac muscle: a type of muscle found only in the walls of the heart

stethoscope: a medical instrument for listening to the sounds of the heart

covered mouth of the funnel on the chest near the heart. Listen carefully. Can you hear the lub–dub sounds of your heartbeat? Count the number of lub–dub sounds in a minute. Is it the same as your pulse rate?

Organisms without a circulatory system

Sponges and hydra

All organisms do not have a circulatory system. For example, sponges and hydra get their food and oxygen directly from the water in which they live. Sponges are the simplest form of multi-cellular organisms. They do not have internal organs, muscles, a nervous system or a circulatory system. Their walls are lined with many small pores that allow water to flow into the sponge and provide food and oxygen. The water also carries away waste material and carbon dioxide as it flows out of the organism. Tube-like microscopic freshwater organisms called hydra also take in food and oxygen and get rid of waste in a similar manner. They do not need a circulatory system or a fluid like blood to tranport nutrients and waste products.

Human excretory system

Humans need food for energy. When food is used by body cells, carbon dioxide and other waste products are formed, which need to be removed from the body. The process of removal of wastes produced in the cells of living organisms is called excretion, and the organs involved in the excretion process form the excretory system.

Carbon dioxide produced in the cells is carried by blood to the lungs from where it is removed by exhalation. But apart from carbon dioxide, blood also carries other waste products that need to be removed. This is done by a filtering mechanism present in the kidneys. The kidneys contain very fine capillaries that carry out filtration and separate out water-soluble wastes from blood.

excretory system: the organs involved in the excretion of waste products from the body
kidneys: either of two bean-shaped organs that filter wastes from the blood and produce urine

Blood contains both useful and harmful substances. So, after filtration, the useful substances, including salt, are again absorbed in the blood and the harmful substances are removed from the body as urine. From the kidneys, the urine goes into the urinary bladder through a pair of tubes called ureters and is stored there. The urine is finally passed out through the urinary opening at the end of a muscular tube called the urethra. Together the kidneys, ureters, bladder and urethra make up the human excretory system.

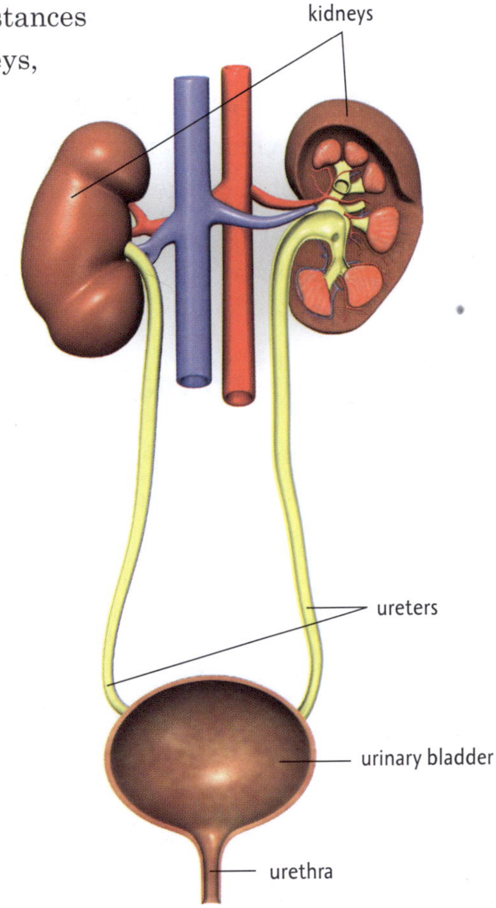

Human excretory system

Factastic

A healthy adult normally passes from 1 to 1.8 litres of urine in 24 hours. Urine is 95% water, with dissolved substances such as urea, creatinine, uric acid and chloride salts of sodium, potassium, magnesium and calcium. The precise proportions of any of these depend on a person's diet, hormones and level of hydration.

If the kidneys stop working due to infection or injury, waste products start accumulating in the blood. In such a case, the affected persons cannot survive unless their blood is filtered periodically through an artificial kidney. This process is called **dialysis**. With regular dialysis, patients with kidney failure can live for many years.

bladder: a membranous bag-like organ that temporarily holds urine before excretion
ureters: tubes through which urine passes from the kidneys to the bladder
urethra: the muscular duct through which urine is passed out
urea: the main solid component of urine
uric acid: a white, tasteless and odourless crystalline product found in blood and urine

Sweating

In humans, sweating is primarily a means of controlling body temperature. The evaporation of sweat from the skin surface has a cooling effect because evaporation of water takes away a lot of heat. Water in earthen pots also remains cool in summer for the same reason.

In hot weather, or if the muscles heat up due to exertion, more sweat is produced. Sweat consists primarily of water with dissolved salts, mainly sodium chloride and a little urea, which are excreted by the sweat glands in the skin. The presence of sodium chloride gives sweat a salty taste.

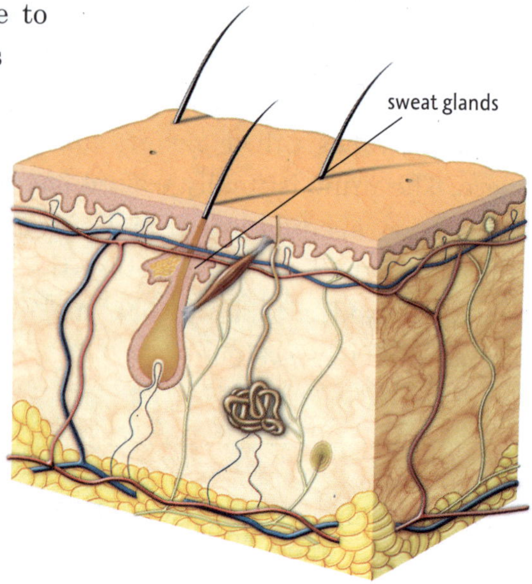

Skin showing sweat glands, root cell and hair

Excretion in animals

Nitrogenous waste materials, such as ammonia and urea, produced in the body of an animal are of no use to the cells, and are harmful to the body. These waste materials are usually poisonous and, therefore, need to be removed from the body. The process of elimination of these waste materials depends on the availability of water. In humans and most mammals, urea dissolved in water is excreted as urine. But animals that live in water, such as fishes and sponges, excrete nitrogenous waste in the form of ammonia gas, which directly dissolves in water. Animals that have limited access to water, such as birds, lizards and snakes, excrete waste in the form of a white, semi-solid compound, which is mainly uric acid.

Transportation in plants

Unlike other organisms, which depend on food taken from other sources, plants make their own food by the process of photosynthesis. For photosynthesis, plants require carbon dioxide and water. The roots of plants take in water and minerals from the soil, and carbon dioxide is taken from air by the leaves. After photosynthesis, the products—mainly sugars and other food molecules, which provide food for the cells—are carried from leaves to different parts of the plant for producing energy. Plants store the extra amount of food that is produced in various forms in their fruits, stem and roots.

sweat glands: any of the glands in the skin that secrete sweat
ammonia: a colourless gas with a characteristic pungent smell, which dissolves in water

Plants take up water and minerals from the soil through roots, which have fine hair for better absorption. These root hair remain in constant contact with the moist soil particles.

After absorption, the water with minerals dissolved in it is carried upwards from the roots through pipe-like vessels called xylem, which are made of special type of cells that form the vascular tissue. The xylem forms a continuous network of channels that connects the roots to the leaves through the stem and branches, transporting water and minerals to the entire plant. Food substances, such as sugars and other molecules, synthesised in the leaves are transported to other parts of the plant through another type of vascular tissue called the phloem. Thus, water, minerals and food products in a plant are carried to the various parts of a plant with the help of the xylem and phloem.

Explore

Take two small potted plants. Any flowering or ornamental plant will do (but not those plants that can be grown from cuttings). Take out both the plants from the pots and keep them in the shade. Replant one of them with its roots intact in the same pot. Cut off the roots from the other plant and plant it back in the pot. Pack the soil well in both the pots and water them lightly.

Healthy plant

Root removed and replanted

Plant dies

Water both the plants regularly. Watch the plants for a few days. Do you find any change? What happened to the plant without roots? Can you explain why a plant dies if its roots are cut off? Can a plant absorb water from the soil without roots?

xylem: tubes that carry water and minerals from the roots to other parts of a plant
vascular tissue: tissue that carries water and nutrients through the plant body
phloem: tubes that carry synthesised food substances from the leaves to other parts of plants
ascent of sap: the upward movement of water from the root to the top of the plant

Transpiration

The rise of water and dissolved minerals in the xylem vessels against the force of gravity is known as the ascent of sap. This process is greatly helped by **transpiration**, the process by which water vapour escapes from the stomata in the leaves of living plants. A lot of water is lost by plants during transpiration. The evaporation of water from leaves generates an upward pull that helps water and minerals reach the upper parts of trees. This is similar to the upward pull produced when water or a soft drink is sucked through a straw. Transpiration also cools the plant.

Factastic

The volume of water lost by plants in transpiration can be very high. For a tree, about 10% of the water it takes up from the soil is used for photosynthesis, while 90% is lost by transpiration.

Brainteaser

Which is the only part of the body that has no blood supply?

Answer: The cornea of the eye.

Revision Time

- In most animals, the transport of nutrients, water and oxygen to the cells and the transport of waste products to different parts of the body for excretion are carried out by blood.
- The circulatory system is essentially a pumping system comprising a muscular pump and networks of vessels that control the flow of blood around the body.
- In the human body, blood is pumped by the heart and circulated through arteries and veins.
- Blood is made up of a transparent, yellowish fluid called plasma in which red and white blood cells and platelets are suspended.
- The red colour of blood is due to the presence of a red pigment called haemoglobin in it.
- The human heart beats about 72–80 times per minute that can be felt as the pulse. The number of times the pulse is felt throbbing per minute is called the pulse rate.
- Arteries carry blood from the heart to the rest of the body.
- Veins carry blood from all parts of the body to the heart.
- The excretory system removes waste and toxic products from the body.
- The human excretory system consists of two kidneys, two ureters, a urinary bladder and a urethra.
- Sweat consists primarily of water with dissolved salts, mainly sodium chloride, and a little urea, which are excreted by the sweat glands in the skin.
- Fish and other aquatic animals excrete nitrogenous waste in the form of ammonia gas, which directly dissolves in water.
- Animals that have limited access to water, such as birds, lizards and snakes, excrete waste in the form of a white, semi-solid compound, which is composed mainly of uric acid.

* Plants take up water and minerals from the soil through their roots, which have fine hair for better absorption.
* In plants, vascular tissues called xylem and phloem transport water, minerals and food to different parts of the plant body.
* Food substances, such as sugars and other molecules synthesised in the leaves are transported to other parts of the plant through the phloem.
* Water and minerals are transported from the roots to the leaves through the xylem.
* The rise of water and dissolved minerals in the xylem against the force of gravity is greatly helped by transpiration.

Quiz Time

1. Answer the questions.

a. Which system in the human body takes care of transporting food, water and oxygen to different organs?

b. Which component of red blood cells binds with oxygen taken from the air by the lungs and transports it to cells in every corner of the body?

c. What is the role of platelets in blood?

d. How many chambers does the human heart have?

e. In what form do animals that live in water, such as fishes and sponges, excrete nitrogenous waste?

2. Fill in the blanks.

a. The ____________________ system is essentially a pumping system comprising a muscular pump and networks of vessels that control the flow of blood around the body.

b. Red blood cells contain a red substance called ____________________ .

c. Since blood from the heart goes directly into arteries, the beating of the heart can be felt as ____________________ in arteries.

d. The main job of the ____________________ side of the heart is to receive blood from other parts of the body and send it to the lungs.

e. The filtration of blood in the human body to remove waste products is done by the ____________________ .

3. **Indicate whether the statements are true or false.**

a. All veins carry blood rich in carbon dioxide. True False

b. A high count of white blood cells often indicates the presence of some infection in the body. True False

c. Each side of the human heart has one upper chamber called the ventricle and a lower chamber called the atrium. True False

d. In plants, water and minerals taken up from the soil are carried upwards through pipe-like vessels called phloem. True False

e. Transpiration is a process by which water vapour escapes from the stomata in the leaves of living plants. True False

4. **Match the columns.**

a. photosynthesis	i. stomata
b. transpiration	ii. transport of water
c. phloem	iii. leaf
d. artery	iv. blood to heart
e. vein	v. blood from heart

5. **Project work**

a. What are blood groups? Can blood be transfused without knowing the blood groups of both the recepient and the donor?

b. Check your heartbeat and that of your friends using a model stethoscope and also the pulse rate at the wrist, while resting and after running for 5 minutes. Record your observations in the table given below.

Name	At rest		After running	
	Heart rate	Pulse rate	Heart rate	Pulse rate

From the table do you find any link between the heart rate and the pulse rate? Can you explain how the two are linked?

Think it over

Why is blood for testing always drawn from a vein?

12 Reproduction in Plants

Like all living organisms, plants also reproduce or multiply. A mango tree will produce more mango plants; a banana plant will produce more banana plants, and so on.

Modes of reproduction

Plants can be classified in several ways—according to the size of the plant, the area where it is grown, etc. One way of classifying plants is on the basis of whether they are flowering or non-flowering plants. Most plants have roots, stems or trunks and leaves; which do not take part in reproduction and are known as the **vegetative parts**. After they reach maturity, most flowering plants produce flowers, which in turn produce seeds from which new plants grow. Flowers, thus, perform the function of reproduction in plants and are known as the **reproductive parts** of a plant. Flowers are usually of three types—those possessing the male part only, those possessing the female part only, and those with both male and female parts.

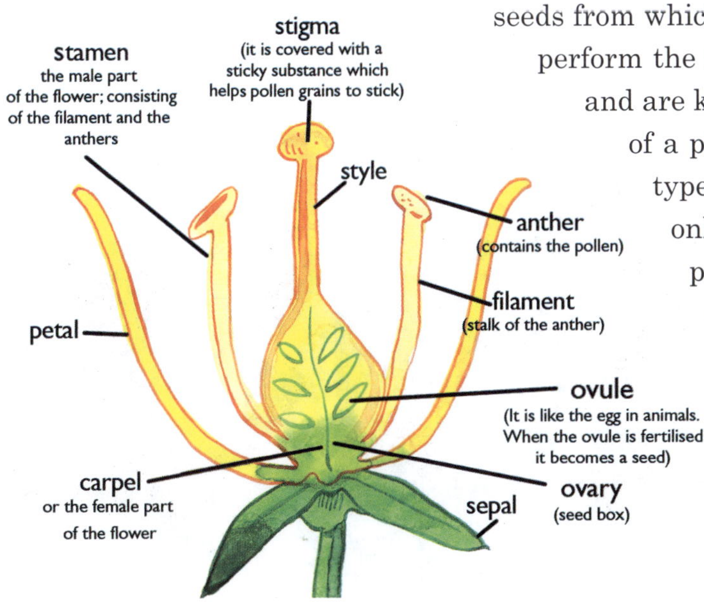

Parts of a flower

All flowering plants produce fruits, some of which are edible while others cannot be eaten by humans. Mango, guava and berries are common fruits, while the fruits of some plants, such as *datura*, are poisonous. After eating the fruit, the seeds are usually thrown away. However, if planted under suitable conditions, new plants can be grown from the seeds.

Plants can reproduce in two ways: asexual reproduction or sexual reproduction. In asexual reproduction, a plant can produce new plants without forming seeds, while in sexual reproduction new plants can grow only from seeds. Yet, even plants that produce flowers and seeds can multiply by asexual reproduction.

Asexual reproduction

The ability to produce new individuals asexually is common in plants. The various ways in which the parts of plants are involved in asexual reproduction are discussed in detail next.

Vegetative propagation

Vegetative propagation is a type of asexual reproduction in which new plants can be grown from roots, stems, leaves or buds without the need for seeds. New plants are usually grown from leaves or vegetative buds in stems, or shoots called 'eyes' in tubers or roots. Vegetative buds are similar to flower buds. The only difference is that, while a flower bud opens into a flower, a vegetative bud grows into a stem with leaves. Most plants have vegetative buds at every node in their stem.

Potato tubers with eyes

asexual reproduction: reproduction without involving the fusion of the male and female gametes
sexual reproduction: reproduction involving the fusion of the male and female gametes
vegetative propagation: a type of asexual reproduction in which new plants can be grown from roots, stems, leaves or buds without the need for seeds
node: the part of a plant stem from which one or more leaves emerge

Stem cutting of a rose plant

Money plant

Rose plants can be grown from stem cuttings with vegetative buds; money plant can be grown from a cut stem; potato and ginger plants can be grown from 'eyes' growing on a potato or a piece of ginger.

Plants belonging to the *Bryophyllum* group (sprout leaf plant) are notable for having small plantlets on the edges of the leaves, which eventually drop off and form roots. So, if a *Bryophyllum* leaf or even a piece of it is planted in soil, new *Bryophyllum* plants would grow from it. The roots or tubers of some plants can also give rise to new plants, as is seen in the case of *Dahlia* and sweet potatoes.

Bryophyllum leaf

Explore

Take a whole potato. You can see the 'eyes' on the potato as indents or pits on the surface. Cut out chunks of the potato with an 'eye' in each piece. Now take a shallow dish or a petri dish and pour a mixture of water with a bit of salt in it. Place the chunks of potato with 'eyes' in the water. Keep the petri dish in a well-lit place. Observe the 'eyes' after a few days. Do you find any change? What do you see coming out of the 'eyes'? Do you see any roots at the bottom of the potato pieces?

Plant the sprouted potato pieces in soil in a pot and water them regularly. Cover the stems with more soil as they grow because potatoes are formed on the stem, not roots.

Asexual reproduction in plants has many advantages. For example, vegetative propagation take less time and the plants bear flowers and fruits earlier than those produced from seeds. Besides, the new plants are exact copies of the parent plant, as they are all produced from a single parent. So a large number of almost identical disease-and virus-free plants can be grown from a single healthy plant.

Budding

budding: reproduction by growth and division of the parent cell into daughter cells

Yeast is a type of single-celled fungus that has many uses, but is most commonly used in baking and brewing. Yeast reproduces asexually, by splitting, or budding. In this process, the parent cell grows and divides to form a new cell, which is the "daughter" cell. The new cell stays attached to the parent cell while it grows and only when it is fully grown does it detach from the parent cell.

When a yeast cell divides, the small bulb-like projection coming out from the cell is called a **bud**, which grows and ultimately gets detached from the parent cell, forming a new yeast cell. After some time, a chain of new yeast cells can be seen. The new yeast cells grow, mature and produce more yeast cells. A large number of yeast cells can be produced in a short time in this way. Yeast cells can be grown in a sugar solution and the process of budding can be observed by placing a drop of the culture on a glass slide under a microscope.

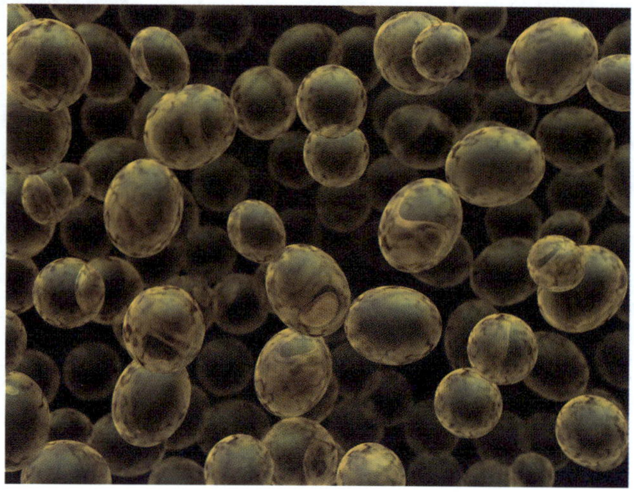

Budding yeast cells under a microscope

Fragmentation

Fragmentation is another form of asexual reproduction where an organism splits into fragments when adequate water and nutrients are available. Each of the fragments formed develops into a mature, fully grown individual that is a clone of the original organism. If the organism divides any further, the process is repeated and in the course of time a large number of identical organisms are produced. The common algae, often seen as slimy green patches in ponds or other stagnant water bodies, multiply rapidly by fragmentation and can spread over a large area in a short period of time.

Algae in a pond

Spore formation

A spore is a reproductive structure that can survive for a long time and can be dispersed widely. Being covered by a hard protective coat, spores are able to withstand high

fragmentation: reproduction by splitting of a single organism
spore: a minute, typically one-celled reproductive unit capable of giving rise to a new individual plant

temperature and low humidity conditions and hence, they can survive for a long time. Spores can reproduce asexually and a single spore can develop into a new organism. Spores form part of the life cycles of many bacteria, plants, algae and fungi.

When spores are released, they keep floating in the air. Being very light they can cover long distances. When favourable conditions are available, a spore germinates and develops into a new plant. Plants such as mosses and ferns also reproduce by means of spores.

Sexual reproduction

Flowering plants usually multiply by sexual reproduction. Flowers carry the reproductive parts of a plant. The male reproductive part of a flower is called the **stamen** and the female part is called the **pistil**.

Not all flowers, however, carry both the male and female reproductive parts. Some flowers carry either the male or the female reproductive part. Such flowers are known as unisexual flowers. Usually different plants produce unisexual flowers with male or female reproductive parts, but the same plant may also have both the male and the female unisexual flowers. Flowers that carry both the male and female reproductive parts are known as bisexual flowers.

Explore

Bisexual flowers

unisexual flower: a flower in which either the stamen or the pistil is present
bisexual flower: a flower in which both stamen and pistil are present

Collect flowers of hibiscus, petunia and papaya from different plants. Cut the flowers and carefully separate their reproductive parts. Identify each part. Do all the collected flowers have both male and female reproductive parts? Do some flowers have

only male parts and some only female parts? Which plants carrying unisexual flowers would bear fruit; those carrying male flowers or those carrying female flowers? Can you tell why?

Stamens usually consist of a long slender stalk that is made up of the filament, with saclike structures called anthers at the tip. Anthers contain pollen—a fine powdery substance, which consists of microscopic grains. Pollen grains produce **male** gametes, which take part in sexual reproduction.

A pistil consists of the stigma, style and **ovary**, which ultimately grows into a fruit. The ovary contains one or more ovules that contain the **female gamete** or the **egg**. The male and female gametes come together after pollination and fuse to form a zygote. The process of fusion of the male and female gametes to form a zygote is called fertilisation. After fertilisation, the zygote develops into an embryo, which ultimately grows into a fruit.

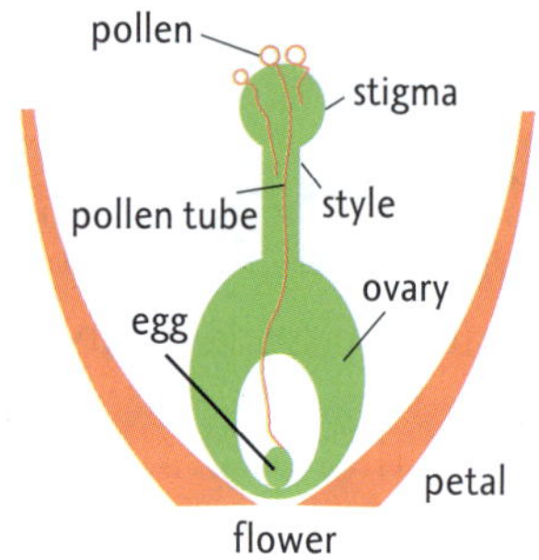

Pollen tube formation

Pollination

Pollination involves transporting pollen grains from the anthers and depositing them on the stigma for fertilisation. Generally, pollen grains have a tough protective coat, which prevents them from drying up. Being light, pollen grains can be carried by the wind or water. Insects feeding on nectar also carry away pollen on their bodies. Pollination takes

anthers: the part of a flower that contains the pollen
pollen: a fine powdery substance, consisting of microscopic grains discharged from the male part of a flower
gametes: reproductive cells
ovule: a small body that contains the female germ cell of a plant
pollination: transfer of pollen from the anther to the stigma of a plant
zygote: a cell formed by the fusion of male and female gametes
fertilisation: fusion of male and female gametes after pollination
embryo: the part of a seed which develops into a plant
fruit: the seed-bearing structure of a plant, which can be fleshy and edible

Factastic

Conifers, such as pine trees, do not produce flowers. But they produce two types of cones on the same tree. One of them gives off pollen and the other catches the pollen. If the wind is blowing in the right direction then the pollen might reach the cone of another conifer of the same species.

place when pollen lands on the stigma of a flower of the same kind. If the pollen lands on the stigma of the same flower, which can happen only with bisexual flowers, it is called **self-pollination**. When the pollen of a flower lands on the stigma of another flower on the same plant, or lands on another flower of a different plant of the same species, it is called **cross-pollination**.

Activity

Aim: To observe the pollination process in flowers.

Material required: seeds of the nasturtium plant, pot with soil and a nylon net

Method: Get some seeds of nasturtium and plant them in two pots filled with soil. Water the pots regularly so that the soil remains moist. Keep a watch on the pots and notice how the first shoots and leaves emerge. Note the shape of the leaves. Keep a record of the changes taking place as the plants grow. Note when the first flower buds appear.

At this point cover one pot completely with a nylon net so that no insect can reach the flowers. Take care that the pots are not exposed to strong gusts of wind.

Let the flowers bloom in both the pots. Keep both the pots in the open. When a few flowers dry up after a few days, watch closely. Do you see seeds developing? Do you find seeds developing in the pot covered with nylon net? What is missing there? Observe for a few weeks. Record the number of seeds produced in each of the two pots. Which pot has less? Why?

Let the seeds remain on the plant till they are completely dry. Take the dry seeds formed and plant them in soil. Do you find new plants growing from the seeds?

What have you learnt about pollination and the life cycle of the nasturtium plant?

Fruit and seed formation

After fertilisation, the ovary grows into a fruit and other parts of the flower fall off. The fruit of a flowering plant is actually the mature ovary—a structure of a plant that contains its seeds. As seeds mature, the surrounding ovary wall forms a protective structure that may aid in dispersal. The seeds of most plants contain an embryo enclosed

Factastic

The jackfruit is the largest seed-bearing fruit that grows on a tree. Jackfruits may reach 90 cm in length and weigh up to 34 kg. But the undisputed record for the world's largest fruit is a 670 kg pumpkin.

in a protective seed coat, which is capable of developing into another similar plant.

Seeds of some fleshy fruits, such as mango, apple and *jamun*, are thrown away. The fruits of almond and walnut are non-edible; the edible nuts are actually the seeds of these plants.

Seeds in apple, peach and walnut

Seed dispersal

Before they can grow into new plants, seeds need to be dispersed or scattered over a wide area. Plants benefit by seed dispersal because it prevents overcrowding at one place, thus, avoiding competition between the parent plant and its own seedlings for sunlight, water and minerals. It also makes it possible for the plants to spread into new areas for wider distribution. The various methods of seed dispersal ensure that a large number of seeds have a good chance of growing up to produce seeds of their own.

Dandelion

There are many ways in which seeds are dispersed. Some seeds are light and are easily carried to a new place by the wind. For example, the seeds of the orchid plant are almost as fine as dust and can be carried long distances by the wind. Some seeds, such as those of silk cotton and dandelion, have hairy growths, which act like little parachutes and carry the seeds far away with the wind. The seeds of the sycamore tree have wings that help them fly in the wind and hence get dispersed far away from the parent plant.

Cotton

seed dispersal: the scattering or distribution of seeds over a wide area through various agents

Fruits that float, such as those of the water lily and the coconut palm, are carried by

Coconut seed

water. The coconut seed has a fibrous outer coat, which helps it float in water and travel for thousands of kilometres across seas and oceans. Water lily fruits are spongy, which makes them float in water and they are carried long distances by water currents.

Sycamore

Lotus seeds

Birds as pollinators

Birds and animals also help in dispersing seeds. Some plants, such as blackberry, cherry and apple, have juicy fruits that birds and animals like to eat. But only the juicy part of the fruit is eaten and the stones and pips pass through the animal's digestive system and are excreted. In this way they can reach far away from the parent plant. New plants can grow from these excreted seeds.

Some plants, such as the cocklebur, produce seeds covered with hooks or spines that get attached to the fur of animals or clothes worn by human beings. Eventually, the seeds fall off, or are brushed off in a location far away from that of the parent plant.

Balsam seeds

Seeds with spines

The seeds then germinate and give rise to a new plant.

Yet another method of seed dispersal is the sudden bursting of the dry seed pod with a jerk which scatters the seeds far and wide. The balsam and castor plants disperse their seeds in this way.

Brainteaser

How many rows of kernels does an ear of a corn cob have?

Answer: The number of rows on a corn cob is always even!

Revision Time

- Like all living organisms, plants also reproduce.
- Plants can reproduce in two ways: through asexual or sexual reproduction.
- Vegetative propagation is a type of asexual reproduction in which new plants can be grown from the roots, stems, leaves or buds without the need for seeds or spores.
- Flowering plants usually multiply by sexual reproduction. Flowers carry the reproductive parts of a plant.
- Unisexual flowers carry either only the male or only the female reproductive part.
- Flowers that carry both the male and female reproductive parts are known as bisexual flowers.
- Pollen grains produce male gametes.
- The pistil consists of the stigma, style and ovary. The ovary contains one or more ovules that contain the female gamete.
- The male reproductive part is called the stamen and comprises the filament and pollen containing anthers. The pollen grains produce the male gametes.
- The transfer of pollen grains from the anther of one flower to the stigma of the same or different flower of the same species is called pollination.
- In self-pollination, pollen from the anther of a flower is transferred to the stigma of the same flower.

* In cross-pollination, pollen from the anther of one flower is transferred to the stigma of another flower of the same species.
* Being light, pollen grains can be carried by the wind or water. Insects feeding on nectar also carry away pollen on their bodies.
* After pollination, the fusion of the male and female gametes leads to the formation of a zygote. This process is called fertilisation.
* After fertilisation, the zygote develops into an embryo, which ultimately grows into a fruit.
* The fruit of a flowering plant is actually the mature ovary—a structure of a plant that contains its seeds.
* Before they can grow into new plants, seeds need to be dispersed or scattered over a wide area, which is aided by wind, water, birds, insects and animals.
* Plants benefit by seed dispersal because it prevents overcrowding at one place, thus avoiding competition for sunlight, water and minerals between the parent plant and its own seedlings.

Quiz Time

1. Answer the questions.

a. What are the vegetative parts of a plant?

b. What is asexual reproduction in plants?

c. What are the advantages of growing plants by asexual reproduction?

d. How do common algae reproduce fast and spread over a large area of a pond in a short period of time?

e. What changes happen in a flower after pollination?

2. Fill in the blanks.

a. Flowers are known as the ____________________ parts of a plant.

b. The propogation of plants by growing them from a leaf, or 'buds' in stems, or shoots called 'eyes' in tubers, or roots is called ____________________ propagation.

c. In budding, the parent cell divides to form a new cell, which is called the ____________ cell.

d. Flowers that carry either only the male or only the female reproductive part are known as ____________ flowers.

e. Pollen grains produce male ____________, which take part in sexual reproduction.

3. Indicate whether the statements are true or false.

	Statement		
a.	Flowers are usually of two types—with either the male part only or the female part only.	True	False
b.	Plants that bear flowers usually multiply by sexual reproduction.	True	False
c.	The process of the fusion of male and female gametes to form a zygote is called pollination.	True	False
d.	When the pollen of a flower lands on the stigma of another flower on the same plant, it is called cross-pollination.	True	False
e.	The seed of most plants contains a gamete enclosed in a protective coat, which is capable of developing into another similar plant.	True	False

4. Project work

Look up reference books or the net for information on the different ways in which seeds of different plants are dispersed. Make a chart with pictures of seeds and brief notes about the method of their dispersal. From the chart, try to find out if there is a link between the structure of a seed and the mode of its dispersal.

Think it over

1. How are horticulturists able to grow flowers of different colours on a single rose plant?

2. How do peepal or banyan trees grow on the walls of old buildings?

13 Motion and Time

Whenever an object moves, it is said to be in motion. Everything in this universe is in constant motion. Even when an object is thought to be stationary on earth, it is still in motion because the earth itself is in continuous motion. The position of an object in motion constantly changes with respect to other objects in its surroundings. For example, when a person walks or a car moves, surrounding objects appear to move in the opposite direction.

Motion can be of three types. When an object moves in a straight line without any change in its direction, it is called **rectilinear motion**. When an object moves in circles, as people in a merry-go-round or a Ferris wheel, it is called **circular motion**.

If the motion of an object is repetitive, for example, the back-and-forth motion of a pendulum or a swing, it is called **periodic motion**.

pendulum: a weight hung from a fixed point with a thread so that it can swing freely

Explore

Observe various motions going on around you. For example, a car moving on a straight road, the blades of a running fan, a child on a swing, the hands of a person walking, the pedals of a bicycle in motion, the oars on a rowing boat, a person using a hand pump to lift water, and so on. In a table, make a list of the motions you observe and identify the type of motion in each case.

Speed

Motion can be fast or slow. A train normally moves faster than a bicycle. Of course, a train can also move slowly. On the road, a faster car can be easily distinguished from a slower one because the faster car overtakes all the slower vehicles. But if there is only a single car on the road then it is not easy to tell whether it is moving fast or slow unless there is some method of measuring speed. If the distance covered by a moving object in a given time interval can be measured, it is possible to identify its speed. The longer the distance covered in a given time, the faster would the motion of the object be. For example, a bus would cover a much longer distance in ten minutes compared to the distance covered by a person on a bicycle. Similarly, the bus would cover a distance of 1 km in much less time than the time taken by the cyclist. In both the cases it is clear that the bus moves faster, or has a higher speed, than the cyclist.

Commonly, the speed of an object is expressed in terms of the distance covered in unit time. For example, the speed of a car is usually expressed as kilometres per hour (km/h); that is, the distance it covers in one hour. A car moving at a speed of 60 km/h would cover a distance of 60 km in 1 hour. If the distances covered per unit time for two moving objects are known, then it is possible to tell which of them is moving faster.

But when we say that a car is moving at a speed of 60 km/h, it does not mean that the car moves at that speed all through. When the car starts from rest it moves slowly and then gathers speed. While driving, the driver may apply the brakes to slow down the car for turning or to avoid collision with another vehicle. In between, it may move faster than 60 km/h. So, generally speaking, speed means the average speed, which is the total distance covered divided by the total time taken.

$$\text{speed} = \frac{\text{total distance covered}}{\text{total time taken}}$$

speed: the rate at which an object moves

If an object always moves with a constant speed along a straight line, it is said to be in uniform motion. In such cases, the average speed of the object would be the same as its actual speed. But in reality, such a situation rarely exists. The speed of most objects we see around us that move along straight lines keeps changing. Such a motion is known as non-uniform motion.

Measuring time

In order to measure the speed of a moving object, it is essential to have a means to measure the distance covered as well as the time taken to cover the distance. There are several methods of measuring distance including the use of tapes or chains. Time can be measured by using a clock.

Before the invention of clocks, different ways of measuring time were used by ancient people. Most were based on the motions of the earth and the moon. For example, the time interval between one sunrise and the next, caused by the rotation of the earth, was called a **day**. The time interval between one new moon and the next one was counted as one **month**. The time taken by the earth to go around the sun in one complete circle was taken as a **year**.

Sundial

Clocks were invented later to measure intervals of time much shorter than a day. Many types of devices were built and used in different parts of the world for measuring time. They included sundials, **water clocks** and **sand clocks**, also known as the hourglass. But the most accurate clocks were those based on the regularity of the periodic motion of a simple pendulum. Later models of clocks used the periodic motion of a spring-driven oscillating balance wheel instead of the pendulum.

Hour glass

uniform motion: motion in which the speed remains constant
non-uniform motion: motion in which the speed keeps changing.
sundial: a time measuring device that indicates the time based on the shadow cast by a gnomon (triangular blade) on a calibrated dial
hourglass: a time measuring device with two connected glass bulbs containing sand that takes an hour to pass from the upper to the lower bulb

Simple pendulum

A simple pendulum is a device consisting of a small mass suspended by a non-elastic string from a fixed support. The suspended mass is called the **bob** of the pendulum and can be a small metal ball or any similar object that is free to move along with the string.

When the pendulum is at rest, the bob hangs vertically at position O. If the bob is moved slightly to one side, A, and released, it moves back to O and goes to the other side, B. Then it stops momentarily, comes back to O, and again goes to A, and the cycle is repeated. In other words, the bob starts moving to and fro, that is, it executes a periodic or **oscillatory motion**.

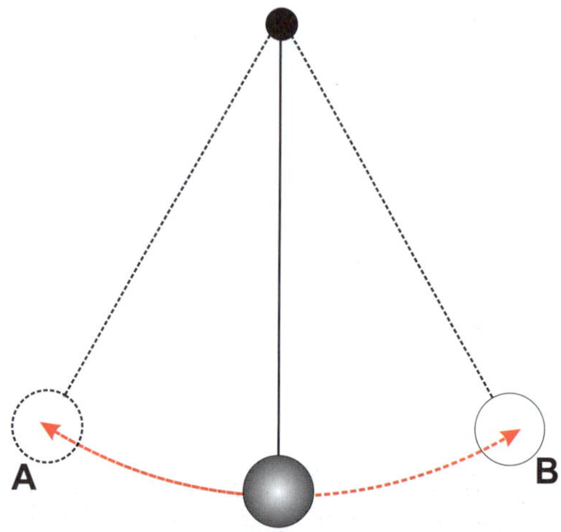

Simple pendulum

One oscillation, or the **time period** of the pendulum is the time that the bob takes to move from its mean position O to A, then to B and finally back to O. It can also be the time it takes the bob to move from A to B and back to A. During an oscillation, the maximum displacement from its mean position (the distance OA or OB), is called the amplitude of the pendulum.

The interesting thing about a simple pendulum is that its time period depends only on the length of the string with which the bob is suspended. The mass of the bob or the angle of the swing or amplitude has no effect on the time period. Even if the bob is made heavier or lighter, or the angle of swing or the amplitude is made larger or smaller, the time period of a simple pendulum will not change as long as the length of the string remains the same.

Explore

Aim: To demonstrate the working of a simple pendulum.

Material required: a heavy steel nut, string, stand, marker pen and a stop watch

Method: Take a heavy steel nut and tie it at one end of a long piece of string. Tie the free end of the string firmly to a stand. The length of the string should be about 20 cm. The bob should hang a little above the floor. Mark the mean position of the bob on

oscillation: a regular periodic motion about a mean position
amplitude: the maximum displacement of a bob in a simple pendulum

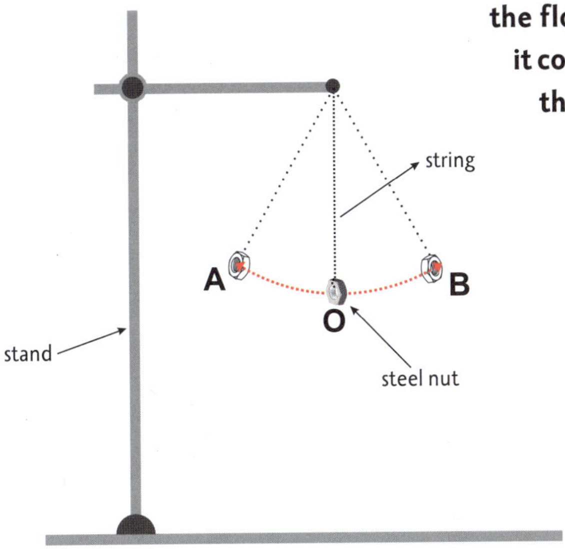

Simple pendulum

the floor with a piece of chalk or a marker pen when it comes to rest. Have a stopwatch ready to measure the time period of the pendulum.

The pendulum can now be set in motion by gently holding the bob, pulling it slightly to one side and then releasing it. Make sure that the string attached to the bob remains taut while the bob is moved. After being released, the bob will start swinging. The time period of the pendulum can be recorded by determining the average time it takes for the pendulum to complete a certain number of complete swings or oscillations.

You can record the time when the bob is at one of the extreme positions on the right or left. Every time it returns to the same position, it is counted as one oscillation. Measure the total time the pendulum takes to complete 60 oscillations. Repeat your observations a few times and find out the average time taken for one oscillation. It will give the time period of the pendulum.

You may repeat this activity with a heavier bob or with a string of a larger or shorter length. Record your observations. Does the time period change when a heavier bob is used? Does it change when a shorter or longer string is used?

Galileo's observations

It is said that while observing a chandelier hanging in a cathedral, the Italian physicist, Galileo Galilei, noticed that it was swinging with a constant time period even when moving at different angles. He counted his pulse beats to measure the time periods of the swinging chandelier and found that the time interval in which the chandelier completed one oscillation was almost the same, and did not change with the angle of the swing. In 1602, Galileo began conducting experiments with pendulums to verify his observation and found that the time period of a

Galileo

simple pendulum indeed depended only on the length of the string and not on the angle of swing. So a pendulum of constant length could be used as a reliable time-measuring device.

Motion of a chandelier

Galileo's observation led to the development of pendulum clocks, which later gave way to winding clocks and wrist watches in which an oscillating balance wheel is used in place of a pendulum. Modern clocks and watches use a vibrating quartz oscillator for measuring time and run on electric batteries. The quartz clock measures time much more accurately than the pendulum or winding clocks used in earlier days.

Units of time

The smallest unit of time in daily use is **second** (s). The other units of time commonly used are **minute** (min) and **hour** (h). Sixty seconds make a minute and 60 minutes make an hour. Twenty-four hours make a day. Thus, in a day, there are 86,400 seconds.

Explore

Start a stopwatch and immediately start saying aloud the words "one thousand and one" ten times, at usual speaking speed. As soon as you finish, stop the stopwatch and see how long it took for you say all the words ten times. Is it somewhere around 10 seconds? Do you find the time taken in saying aloud "one thousand and one" a convenient way to count seconds?

The commonly available clocks and watches used in our daily life are accurate for measuring time intervals of up to one second. For measuring shorter time intervals, special clocks are used. The time measuring devices used in sports to measure lap times can measure time intervals up to one-tenth or one-hundredth of a second. There are also quartz clocks available that can measure time intervals as small as one-millionth or even one-billionth of a second. One-millionth of a second is called a **microsecond** while one-billionth of a second is known as a **nanosecond**. Such high precision measurements of time are required in scientific research and also in satellite communication.

Winding clock

Pendulum clock

Quartz clock

Historical events can be dated in terms of hundreds or thousands of years, that is, in **centuries** or **millennia**. The ages of stars and planets lie in the range of a few billion years.

Different units of time are used depending on the scale of an event. For example, the duration of a TV commercial can be conveniently measured in seconds; a film song can be measured in minutes; a movie can be measured in hours; a season can be measured in months; and the age of a person can be measured in years. But if we try to measure the age of a person in seconds, or the duration of a season in hours, it would be absurd.

Measuring speed

The unit of speed has to be in terms of distance covered per unit time; that is, distance/time. The smallest unit of speed in common use is **metres per second**, or m/s. The larger units are m/min and km/h.

Factastic

To send a spacecraft beyond the earth's gravity, a rocket needs to have a speed of at least 11,000 m/s or 40,000 km/h.

The speed of a moving object can be determined by measuring either the distance it has covered in a specific interval of time or the time it has taken to cover a certain distance. For example, if a car travels 1/2 km in 1 minute, its speed would be 0.5 km/min, or 30 km/h. If a car takes 4 minutes to travel 1 km, its speed would be 1 km/4 min; that is, 0.25 km/min, or 15 km/h. So speed can be determined by measuring time if the distance travelled is known, or by measuring the distance if the time interval is known.

Circle Time

Mark two parallel lines with chalk powder or lime at a distance of 100 m from each other in your school ground. You will need a stopwatch to measure time.

Ask your friends to walk one by one from Line 1 to Line 2 as fast as they can. Note the time taken by each person to cover the distance. Calculate the walking speed for each person by dividing the distance (100 m) by the time taken (in seconds). Convert this into km/h and find out who walks fastest and who walks slowest and what their respective speeds are.

In every country, there are traffic rules that determine the highest speed at which vehicles can be driven on roads. In order to make it possible for drivers to know at what speed they are going, all vehicles are equipped with an instrument called a speedometer. It shows the speed of the vehicle in km/h on a dial on the dashboard.

Speedometer and odometer

If the speed of the vehicle is known, the distance travelled can be calculated by multiplying the speed by time. Of course, it will work only if the vehicle moves at the same speed throughout.

distance covered = speed x time

For example, if a car is moving at a speed of 50 km/h and travels at the same speed for 2 hours, the distance travelled will be 50 x 2 = 100 km.

In the same way, if the speed of a moving vehicle is known, it is possible to estimate the time it would take to cover a certain distance.

$$\textbf{time taken} = \frac{\textbf{distance}}{\textbf{speed}}$$

For example, if a car is moving at 60 km/h and it has to travel 120 km to reach its destination, it is easy to tell that it would take $\frac{120 \text{ km}}{60 \text{ km/hr}} = 2 \text{ hr}$, that is, 2 hours to reach its destination.

There is another dial on the dashboard that shows the distance covered by the vehicle. This instrument is called an odometer. The odometer reading displays the distance covered by a vehicle between any two points.

speedometer: an instrument fixed to a vehicle that measures and displays its speed
odometer: an instrument for recording the distance travelled by a vehicle

Time–distance graph

While travelling in a bus, if the odometer reading is taken when the vehicle starts at the point of boarding and then at intervals of every 30 minutes, a table, such as the one given below, can be prepared.

Time	Odometer reading	Distance from starting point
9.00 am	20,545 km	0 km
9.30 am	20,565 km	20 km
10.00 am	20,595 km	50 km
10.30 am	20,625 km	80 km
11.00 am	20,645 km	100 km

From the table, it is possible to find out at what distance the vehicle was from the starting point at intervals of every half hour. But it is not possible to find out from the table at what distance the vehicle was at 9.45 am or at 10.10 am. To be able to do that, a time–distance graph is necessary. A time-distance graph is a way of presenting a collection of data on time and distance in a visual form.

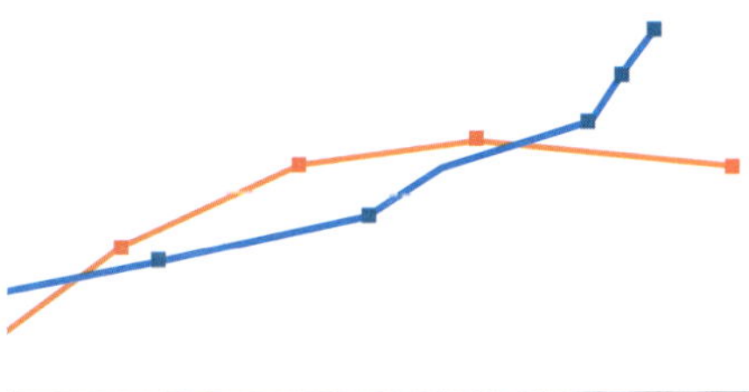

Line chart

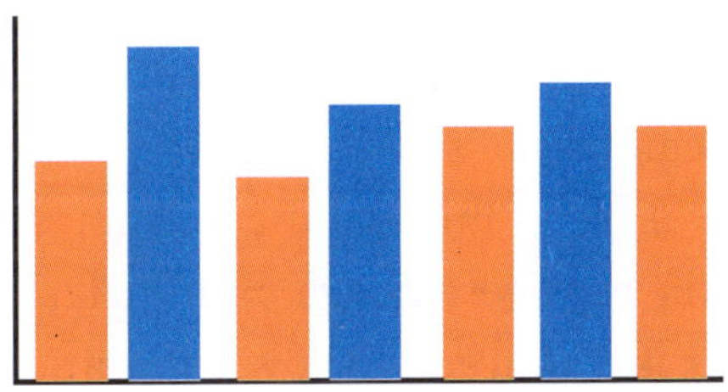

Bar chart

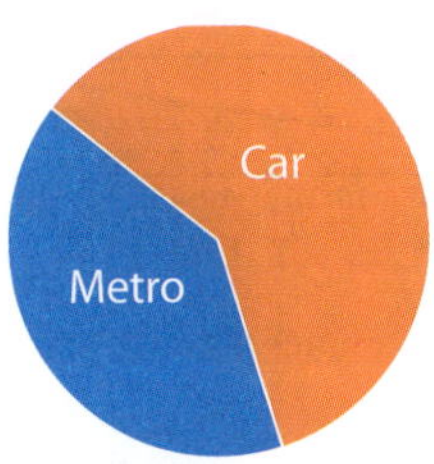

Pie chart

Types of graphs

time-distance graph: data on time and distance presented in a visual form

Graphs can be of various forms. Line graphs, bar graphs and pie charts are different forms of graphs in which data of various kinds can be presented in a visual form. A graph makes it easier to understand the relationships between the data that is otherwise not possible in the tabulated form.

A graph usually has two axes perpendicular to each other, usually shown as two straight lines intersecting at right angles. If two straight lines are drawn—one horizontally and one vertically—through the middle of a graph paper, they would intersect at the centre, dividing the graph paper into four parts. The horizontal line is termed the x axis and the vertical line the y axis of the graph. The point of intersection of the two axes is called the origin. The positive values of x are plotted on the right side and the negative values of x are plotted on the left side of the vertical line. Similarly, positive values of y are plotted above and negative values of y are plotted below the horizontal line. If only positive values are to be plotted, then only the top right part of the graph paper needs to be used.

Before drawing a graph, it is necessary to decide the scales for the two axes so that the entire data can be included. In general, a few points need to be kept in mind while choosing a suitable scale for drawing a graph. The scale chosen should be able to show the entire range between the highest and the lowest values of each quantity and also the intermediate values of each quantity. For example, if the x axis is required to show a time range from 9.00 am to 11.00 am and the length of the x axis is 5 cm, then a scale of 1 cm to show an interval of 30 min would be enough to show the complete range. Similarly, if the y axis is required to show a distance range of 100 km, then in a 5 cm-long y axis, a scale with 1 cm representing 20 km should be enough.

The chosen scale also should be such that the maximum part of the paper on which the graph is to be drawn is utilised.

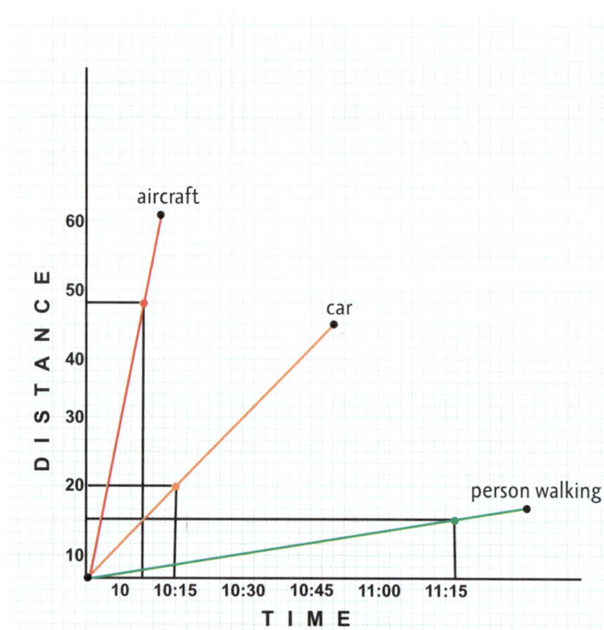

Time–distance graph

Once the appropriate scales of the x and y axes are chosen, the recorded values may be plotted on the graph paper. A line graph showing the relation between time and distance can then be obtained by joining the plotted points. The distance of a vehicle from the starting point at any time can now be determined from the graph by extending a vertical line from

origin: a fixed point from which coordinates in a graph are measured

the required time marked on the x axis up to the line graph and drawing a horizontal line to the y axis from the point on the graph where the vertical line intersects it.

If a vehicle moves with a constant speed, its time–distance graph would be a straight line, because it will be covering the same distances in the same amounts of time. But, if its speed keeps changing, the graph can be of any shape.

Explore

Draw a time–distance line graph using the data of time and distance covered by a bus, given on page 165. From the graph find out at what distances the bus was at 9.15 am, 9.40 am, 10.10 am and 10.45 am. Also find out the average speed of the bus from the graph.

Brainteaser

A sundial is a time piece that has the fewest number of moving parts. Can you name a time piece that has the most moving parts?

Answer: An hourglass!

Revision Time

- ✶ The speed of an object is the distance travelled by it in unit time.
- ✶ The basic unit of speed is metres per second, or m/s.
- ✶ If the distances covered per unit time for two moving objects are known, then it is possible to tell which of them is moving faster.
- ✶ If an object always moves with a constant speed, its motion is said to be uniform motion.
- ✶ If the speed of an object keeps changing, the object is said to have non-uniform motion.
- ✶ Before the invention of clocks, different ways of measuring time were used by ancient people based on the motions of the earth and the moon.
- ✶ Clocks based on the pendulum were invented later to measure intervals of time much shorter than a day.
- ✶ A time–distance graph is a way of presenting data about the motion of an object in a visual form.
- ✶ If an object moves with a constant speed, its time–distance graph would be a straight line.

Quiz Time

1. Answer the questions.

a. How will you define the speed of a moving object?

b. What is a simple pendulum and what is it used for?

c. How much time would a car travelling at 60 km/h take to travel a distance of 120 km and back?

d. How many nanoseconds make one second?

e. What is an odometer?

2. Fill in the blanks.

a. The position of an object in __________ constantly changes with respect to other objects in its surroundings.

b. Commonly, the speed of an object is expressed in terms of the __________ covered in unit time.

c. We can find out the speed of a moving vehicle by looking at the __________.

d. A simple pendulum displays periodic or __________ motion.

e. If the speed of the vehicle is known, the distance travelled can be calculated by __________ the speed by time.

3. Indicate whether the statements are true or false.

a.	The motion of a person on a Ferris wheel is called periodic motion.	True	False
b.	When we say that a car is moving at a speed of 60 km/h, it means that the car moves at that speed throughout.	True	False
c.	In order to be able to measure the speed of a moving object it is essential to have a means to measure time.	True	False
d.	The time period of a simple pendulum depends only on the length of the string with which the bob is suspended.	True	False
e.	Speed cannot be determined by measuring time if only the distance travelled is known.	True	False

4. **Describe the motion of the objects from the time–distance graphs given below.**

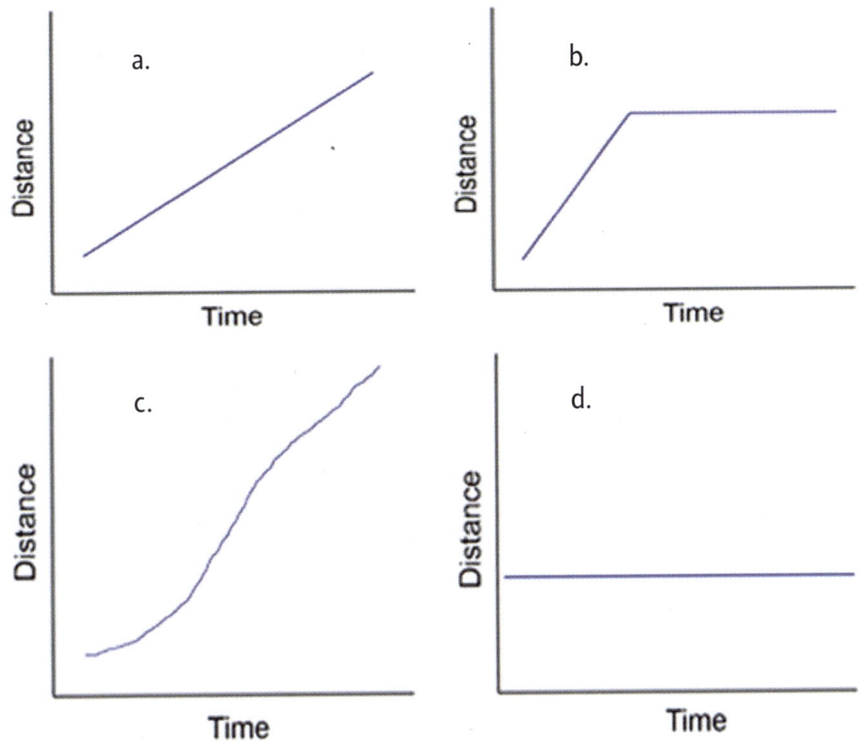

5. **Project work**

    a. Use an encyclopaedia or the internet to find the speeds at which different animals, such as the cheetah, deer, horse, camel, house lizard and snail, move. Make a table listing the speeds along with the names of the animals. Which is the fastest and which is the slowest animal in your list?

    b. Collect pictures of and information about the methods of measuring time used in ancient times. Use this data to make a chart on how the method of measuring time has evolved over the years.

Think it over

1. **How do scientists determine the speed of a spacecraft on its way to a distant planet?**
2. **How does the speedometer of a car measure speed?**

14 Heating and Magnetic Effects of Electricity

Electricity and electrical gadgets are part of our daily life. At home, electricity is supplied from power stations at a voltage of 220–240 volts, which is high and hence quite dangerous to handle. However, to study the effects of electric current, dry cells that deliver electricity at a low voltage of 1.5–9.0 volts, can be used since they are quite safe to handle.

Symbols of electrical components

A simple electric circuit can be created using a dry cell, a switch and a torch bulb with a few lengths of insulated wire. On paper an electric circuit can be depicted using symbols.

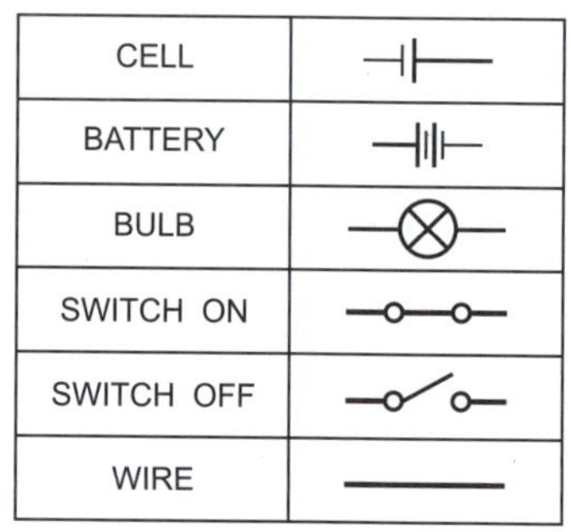

Electrical symbols

The symbols for electrical components are quite simple and easy to understand. For example, a cell is shown as two parallel lines, one short and one long. The long line represents the positive terminal and the short line represents the negative terminal. If two or more cells are to be connected together so that the negative terminal of one is connected to the positive terminal of the next one, a series of alternate long and short lines are used. Such a combination of two or more cells is called a battery.

electric circuit: a closed path around which an electric current can flow
electrical components: parts used to build an electrical circuit
battery: a power source made of several cells joined together

The symbol for a torch bulb is a loop within a circle. The loop represents the filament and the circle the glass envelope. A switch in the 'off' position is depicted as two short straight lines with a gap between them, while a switch in the 'on' position is shown as two short straight lines touching each other. A connecting wire is shown simply as a continuous line. It is more convenient to draw electrical circuit diagrams using these symbols than using actual pictures of the components.

Connecting cells

In many devices, such as torches, TV remote controls, transistor radios and toys, more than one dry cell is used to get a voltage higher than 1.5 volts. But the cells are not always arranged in a way that one cell touches the other. In a torch, of course, two cells are arranged one on the top of the other so that the positive terminal of the lower cell is in contact with the negative terminal of the top cell. The positive terminal of the top cell touches the middle terminal of the bulb, while the negative terminal of the bottom cell is connected through the switch to the other terminal of the bulb. Here the bulb gets a net voltage of 3.0 volts.

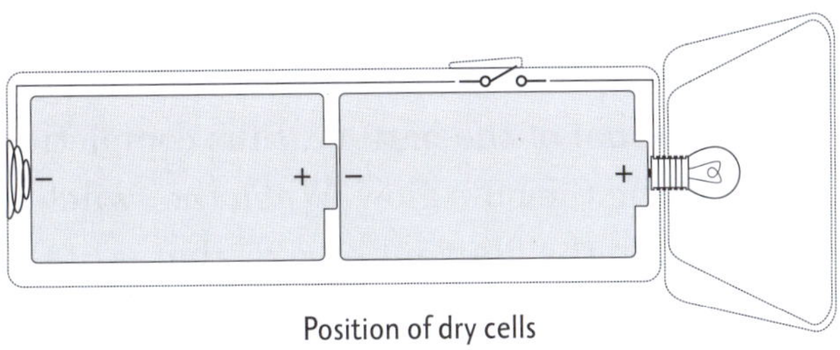

Position of dry cells

But when more than one cell is used, the cells are not always arranged one on top of the other. In a TV remote and transistor radio, for example, they are arranged side by side. However, in all these cases, the individual cells have to be so connected that the negative terminal of one is connected to the positive terminal of the next one because only then would the voltages of the individual cells add up to give the required voltage. This is achieved by using special cell holders in which direct connections between the negative and positive terminals of alternate cell compartments already exist. When the cells are inserted into the compartments, the connections are automatically made. In order to ensure that

cell holder: a device with built-in connections for holding several cells to make a battery

Cell holders of various kinds

the cells are placed in the holder correctly, the symbols + and – are usually marked on the respective ends in the battery compartment. By using cell holders, several dry cells can be joined together to give a voltage of up to 9.0 volts.

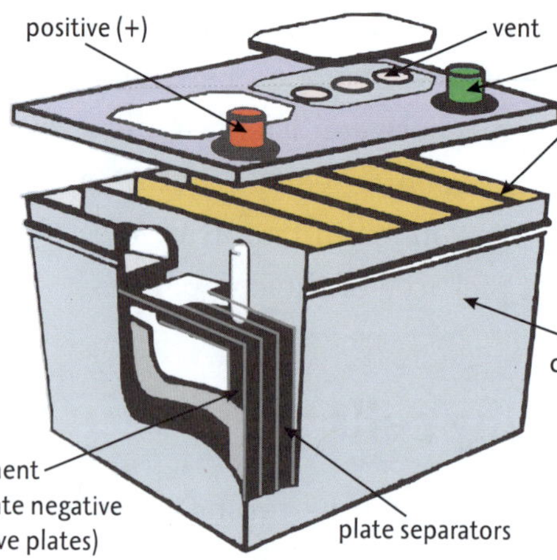

Car battery

The electrical circuit

An electrical circuit consists of a battery, a lamp and a switch connected by insulated wire. It is worth noting that the switch, which is used to control the current passing through the bulb, can be placed anywhere in the circuit. When the switch in on, the current can flow from the positive terminal of the battery through the filament of the bulb to the negative terminal of the battery, thus completing the circuit and making the bulb glow. When the switch is in the 'off' position or if the filament breaks, that is, if the bulb gets fused, the circuit is broken and the bulb stops glowing. Hence, for the current to flow in a circuit, the circuit has to be complete, without any break.

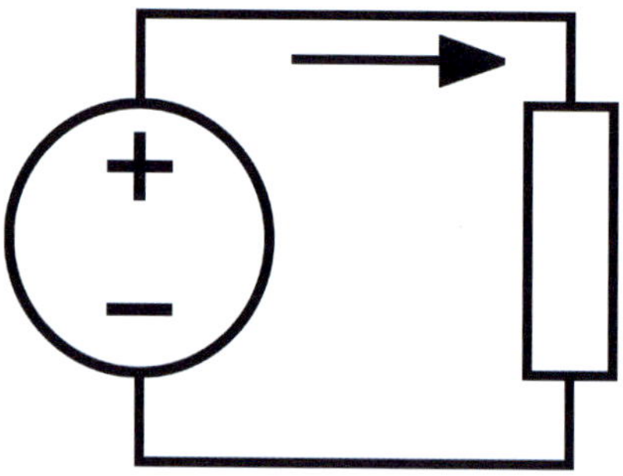

Electrical circuit

Heating effect of electric current

When electric current is passed through the thin tungsten filament of an electric bulb, the filament becomes white hot and emits light. All filament bulbs produce light in the same way. The heat can be felt if the glowing bulb is touched. For the same reason, it is dangerous to touch a lighted electric bulb connected to the mains. The bulb filament gets hot because of the heating effect of the electric current passing through it.

Filament in a bulb

heating effect: the production of heat in a wire on passing electric current through it

Factastic

The credit for the invention of the electric bulb is usually given to Thomas Alva Edison, although others before him had also worked on it. Edison conducted further experiments with thousands of different filaments to find just the right materials that would glow well and be long-lasting. In 1879, Edison discovered that a carbon filament in an oxygen-free bulb glowed and lasted for 40 hours. Edison eventually produced a bulb that did not burn out for over 1,500 hours.

In filament lamps, electricity is wasted as heat. But in a fluorescent lamp or a compact fluorescent lamp (CFL), light is not produced by a hot glowing filament and so very little electrical energy is wasted as heat. This is the reason why a CFL requires only a quarter of the amount of electricity that a normal filament lamp would consume to produce the same amount of light.

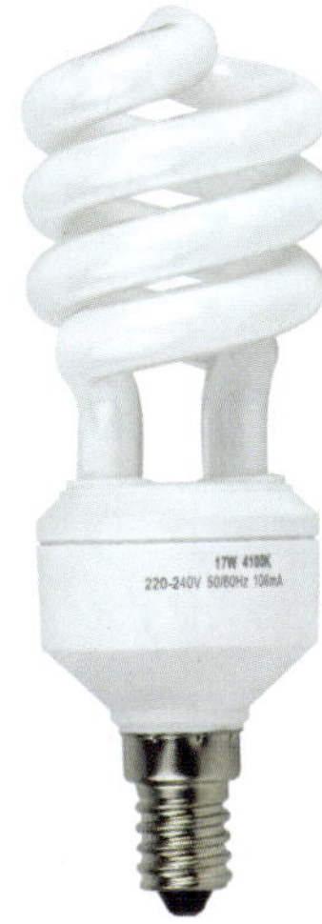

CFL

Heat is produced whenever an electric current is passed through a conductor, but the amount of heat produced depends on the material, its length and its thickness. For example, on passing an electric current through it, an iron wire would become hotter than a copper wire of the same size and thickness. Again, a thin copper wire will become hotter than a thicker wire of the same length.

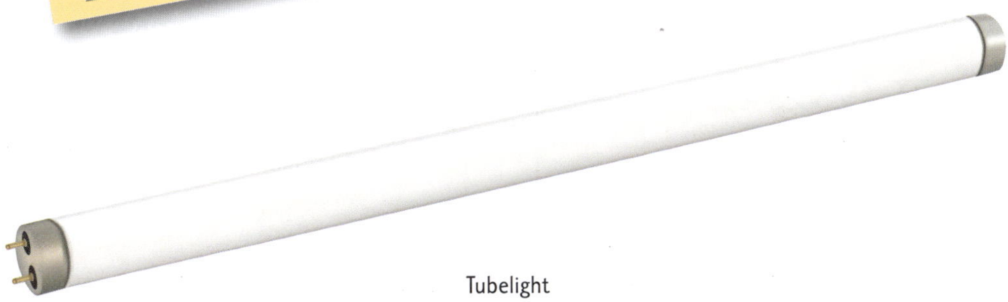

Tubelight

Copper wires used for house wiring and for making electrical circuits do not generally become hot. But, if too much current is passed through them, they too become hot. Hence, home electrical appliances, such as air conditioners, water heaters, washing machines and other appliances that need a lot of current to run, are connected to the mains by thicker wires while lights and fans, which require less current, are connected with thinner wires.

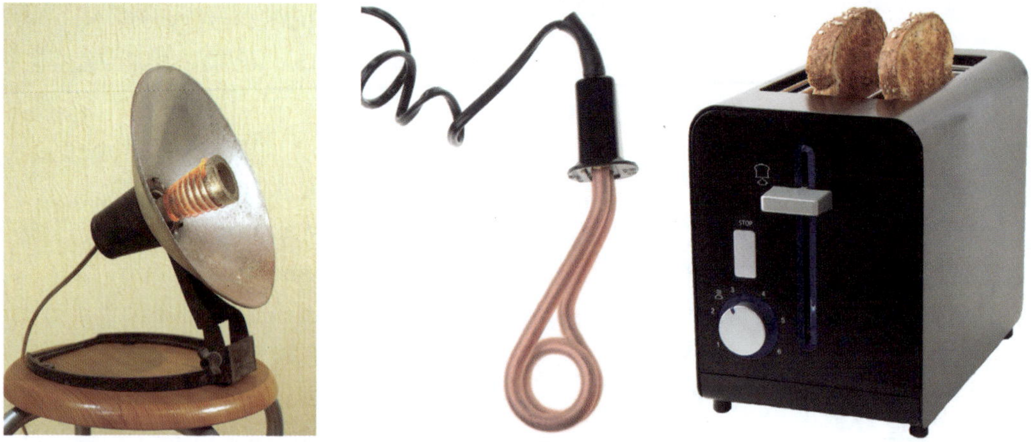

Electrical appliances in which the element is seen to glow

Electric heating appliances such as irons, toasters, stoves, room heaters, water heaters and hair dryers, have coils made of nichrome that get hot when an electric current is passed through them. Nichrome wire is made from a combination of nickel and chromium. The heating coil is also known as the element. The heating element can be seen glowing red hot when the power is switched on.

Explore

Aim: To study the effect of an electric current.

Material required: a wooden board, iron nails, switch, battery and a nichrome wire

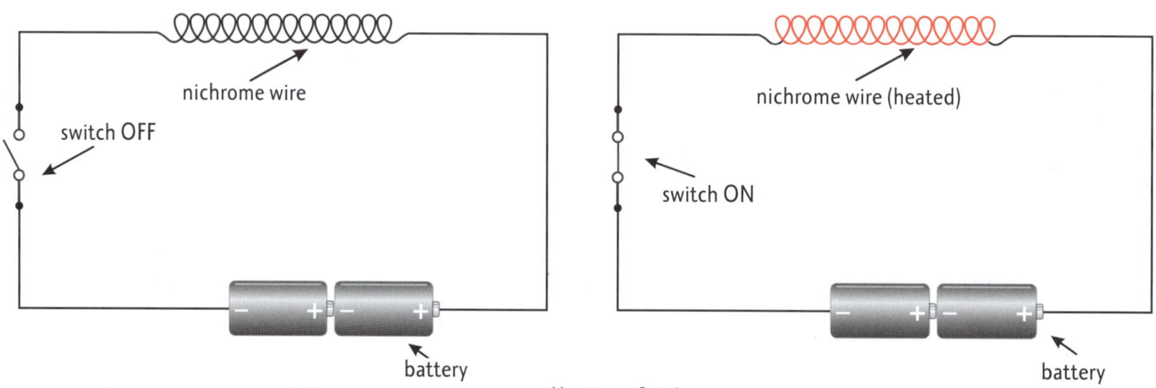

Heating of nichrome wire

nichrome: an alloy of nickel and chromium used for making heating elements
element: a part in a heater, or toaster which contains a wire coil that produces heat when electric current is passed through

Method: Take a wooden board about 10 cm^2 in size. Fix two nails on the wooden board about 1 inch away from one another. Make a circuit with a switch and a battery. Connect the switch to one of the nails and the free terminal of the battery to the

other nail. Get a 10-cm long piece of nichrome wire from an electrical repair shop and attach it to the electric circuit on the side opposite the battery, as shown in the diagram.

Touch the nichrome wire before allowing current to flow through the circuit. Turn the switch to the 'on' position and keep it on for a few seconds. While the current is on, touch the wire again. Touch the wire again a few minutes after switching off the current. Can you tell why the nichrome wire felt hot while the current was passing through it?

The amount of heat produced when an electric current passes through a wire depends on the length and thickness of the wire. Wires of different lengths and thicknesses are, therefore, used for different appliances. For example, an electric iron and a toaster need to produce much less heat than a water heater or a room heater. So the heating elements are designed accordingly.

Short circuits and overloads

If too much current is passed through a wire, it may produce a lot of heat such that the wire melts or causes a fire. The two possible reasons for a high current could be a short circuit or an overload. A short circuit may happen if the insulation on the wires gets damaged or comes off due to heat or wear and tear. This may cause two adjoining wires to come in direct contact and cause a short circuit or start a fire. On the other hand, overloading is caused by connecting too many appliances to a single socket. Sometimes fires are caused by short circuits and overloads.

Interestingly, the heating effect of an electric current that can cause fires can also be used for protecting electrical circuits from short circuits and overloading. For example, a short piece of wire, which melts easily when too much current flows through it, can be included in an electrical circuit. The moment too much current starts flowing through the circuit due to a short circuit or overloading, this piece of wire will melt, breaking the circuit and stopping the flow of current. As a result, there will be no risk of fire or damage to the electrical equipment. Special metals that melt easily on heating are used in making electric fuses. These wires melt (blow) and break the circuit in case of a short circuit or overloading.

electric fuse: a safety device consisting of a piece of wire that melts and breaks an electric circuit if the current exceeds a safe level

Electric fuses are part of the electric wiring in all buildings. Each fuse is designed to handle a certain amount of current flowing through the circuit safely. Due to some reason, if the current exceeds this safe limit, the fuse blows and breaks

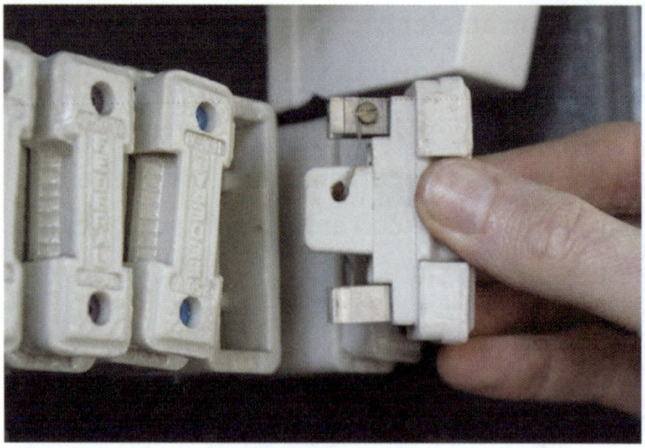

An electric fuse

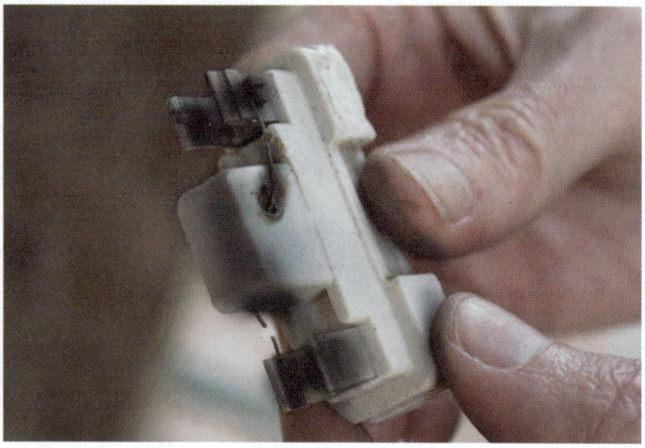

A melted electric fuse

the circuit. A fuse is thus a safety device that protects electrical circuits from damage and possible fires. After a fuse blows off it needs to be replaced with a fuse of the same rating. Replacing a blown fuse with a piece of wire or with a fuse of higher rating can be dangerous because doing that may allow much more current to pass through than is safe for the circuit. Different kinds of fuses are used for different purposes; some are used for protecting household wirings and other smaller capacity ones are used for protecting electrical appliances.

Nowadays, in most buildings, miniature circuit breakers (MCBs) are used in place of electric fuses. MCBs are switches that automatically turn off or trip if the current in a circuit exceeds the safe limit. They can be reset or turned on again after the problem of short circuit or overloading is sorted out. MCBs have the advantage that they can be manually reset without having to replace the wire as in the case of the traditional fuse.

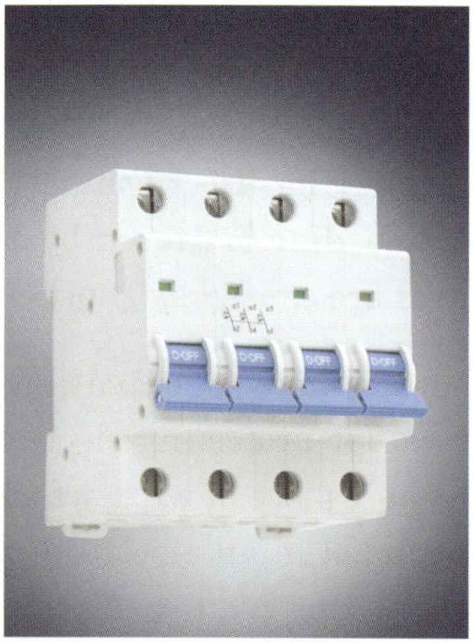

An MCB

Magnetic effect of an electric current

The needle of a magnetic compass points in the north–south direction because it is a tiny magnet. If a magnet is brought near a magnetic compass, the compass needle gets deflected from its original position because like poles of magnets repel and unlike poles attract each other. The same effect is observed if a wire carrying current is brought near a magnetic compass. The compass needle deflects in this case because when an electric current

miniature circuit breaker: a safety device that automatically switches off power if the current exceeds a safe limit
trip: disconnect automatically as a safety measure
reset: to restore to original position

is passed through a wire, especially a coil of wire, it behaves like a magnet. This relationship between electricity and magnetism was first observed by Danish physicist Hans Christian Oersted in 1820. He found that an electric current flowing through a wire deflects a compass needle and this effect lasts as long as the current flows through the wire. He showed that it is possible to produce magnetism even without a magnet. This is called the magnetic effect of an electric current.

Hans Christian Oersted

Explore

Make an electric circuit by connecting a torch bulb and a 1.5 volt dry cell through a switch with a long insulated wire. Get a small magnetic compass. Place the compass on the table. Now stretch a part of the wire of the circuit above the compass so that the wire lies north–south, parallel to the compass needle and above it. Observe what happens to the compass needle when the switch is turned on and the bulb glows. Does the position of the needle change? Turn the switch off and observe what happens to the needle. Does it come back to its original position? What does this activity show?

Electromagnets

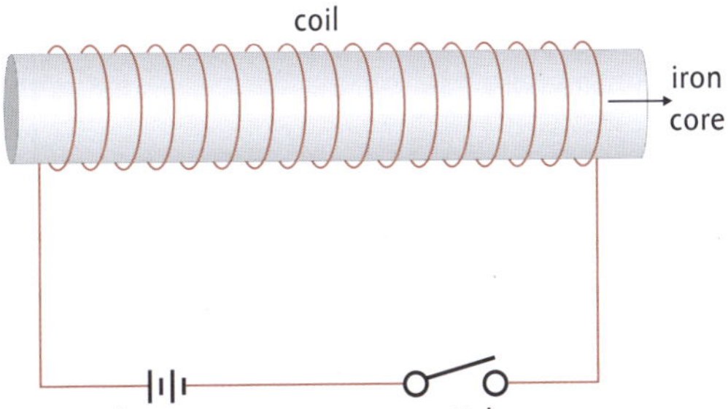

Electromagnet

magnetic effect: a coil of wire carrying current behaving like a magnet
electromagnet: a temporary magnet made by coiling wire around an iron core and passing current through the coil

When an electric current is passed through a coil of wire, the coil behaves like a magnet. This property is utilised for making electromagnets, which behave like magnets only when an electric

An electromagnet at work

current is passed through them. As soon as the current is stopped, an electromagnet loses its magnetism. Powerful electromagnets can be built if the coil is wound around an iron core. Electromagnets can be made very powerful by having a large number of coils and passing a larger current through them. Powerful electromagnets attached to cranes are used to lift heavy iron objects in scrap yards. Electromagnets are also used in MCBs and the common doorbell in homes.

Explore

Aim: To create an electromagnet.

Material required: copper wire (2 m), iron nail (7 m), a dry cell, switch and paper clips

Method: Take a 2 m long enamelled copper wire and a 7 cm long iron nail. Wrap a piece of paper on the iron nail and then wind the wire tightly on it in several layers, leaving a few centimetres free at the ends. Remove the enamel coating at the free ends of the copper wire by scraping or by rubbing them with a piece of sandpaper and connect the ends to a dry cell through a switch. Hold the head of the nail with the copper wire coiled around it near a few paper clips and turn the switch on. What happens? Are the paper clips attracted to the nail? Hold the nail upright and see if the paper clips still cling to the end of the nail. Observe what happens when the current is switched off. What does it show?

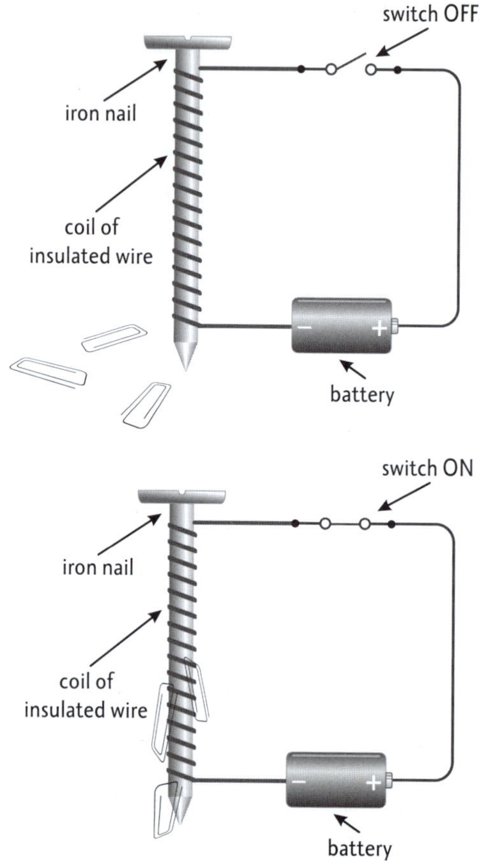

Making an electromagnet

The electric bell

The doorbell or common electric bell is a good example of an electromagnet. The electric bell consists of a coil of wire wound on a core of iron that behaves like an electromagnet when a current is passed through the coil. A gong is fixed at one side of the electromagnet. A spring-loaded hammer with a strip of iron is fixed in front of the electromagnet touching a contact screw in such a way that only when the iron strip is in contact with the screw will the current flow through the coil. The current stops when the contact breaks.

electric bell: a bell activated by the magnetic effect of an electric current

When current passes through the coil, the hammer with the iron strip is attracted to the electromagnet making it strike the gong. But as soon as the hammer is pulled towards the electromagnet, the contact of the iron strip with the screw breaks and the current flow through the coils of the electromagnet stops. As a result, it loses its magnetism and is not able to attract and hold the spring-loaded hammer, which returns to its original position. However, as soon as the hammer with the iron strip returns to its original position, it touches the contact screw and current flows again through the electromagnet, which again attracts the hammer and makes it hit the gong. Thus, the hammer strikes the gong every time the circuit is completed. This process is repeated in quick succession as long as the push button switch of the electric bell is kept pressed, which keeps the bell ringing. A buzzer also uses an electromagnet in a similar way, but it does not have a gong to give a ringing sound. It only makes a buzzing sound.

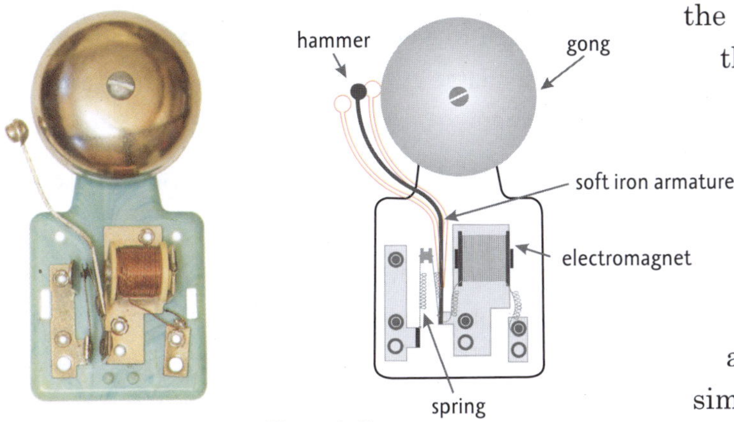

Electric bell

Brainteaser

Which component in audio speakers is commonly used as an electromagnet?

Answer: A voice coil is an electromagnet which is used in speakers to amplify sound.

buzzer: an electrical device that makes a buzzing noise

Revision Time

- ✶ Electrical components can be represented by symbols in diagrams of electric circuits.
- ✶ For current to flow in a circuit, the circuit has to be complete and should not have breaks.
- ✶ When an electric current flows through a wire, heat is produced due to the heating effect of an electric current.
- ✶ The heating effect of an electric current is used in many appliances such as electric irons, toasters, electric stoves, room heaters, water heaters and hair dryers.
- ✶ The heating effect of an electric current is also used in electric fuses, which are made of special metals that melt and break the circuit when large currents pass through them and thus prevent fires and damage to electrical equipment.
- ✶ Miniature circuit breakers are better than electric fuses because they can be reset and do not need to be replaced.
- ✶ When an electric current is passed through a coil of wire, the coil behaves like a magnet. This is called the magnetic effect of an electric current.
- ✶ An electromagnet behaves like a magnet only when an electric current is passed through it. As soon as the current is stopped, an electromagnet loses its magnetism.
- ✶ Electromagnets are used for lifting heavy iron objects in scrap yards. They are also used in MCBs and the common doorbell.

Quiz Time

1. Answer the questions.

a. What is the symbol of a battery used in depicting an electric circuit diagram?

b. What are the two main effects of an electric current?

c. What is a miniature circuit breaker and what is it used for?

d. Why does the needle of a magnetic compass get deflected from its north-south position when a wire carrying current is brought near it?

e. What kind of magnet is used in an electric bell?

2. Fill in the blanks.

a. In a torch using two cells, the ____________________ terminal of the lower cell is in contact with the negative terminal of the top cell.

b. A simple electrical circuit consists of a torch bulb, a switch and a ________________ connected by insulated wire.

c. The longer line in the symbol of a cell represents its ________________ terminal.

d. A ________________ may happen if the insulation on the wires get damaged or comes off due to heat or wear and tear.

e. An ____________ behaves like a magnet only when electric current is passing through it.

3. Indicate whether the statements are true or false.

a. To make a battery of 3.0 volts from two 1.5 volt cells, the positive terminal of one cell should be connected to the negative terminal of the other. True False

b. In an electrical circuit, the switch has to be placed only at a specific point in the circuit. True False

c. Electric heating appliances such as irons, toasters, stoves and water heaters have coils made of tungsten wire. True False

d. A fuse is a safety device that protects electrical circuits from damage and possible fires. True False

e. Electromagnets behave like magnets even when electric current is not passing through them. True False

5. Project work

a. You have learnt that an electric doorbell works with an electromagnet that makes a hammer strike a gong repeatedly. But how does a chime doorbell that produces a 'ding-dong' sound work? Does it also use an electromagnet? Get a chime doorbell and open the cover to see what is inside. In the presence of your teacher or an adult, connect the open chime doorbell to the mains and press the switch. Observe carefully what moves to produce the 'ding-dong' sound. Does this type of bell also employ an electromagnet?

b. Talk to your school electrician to learn how an MCB works. If possible, let him show you how an MCB looks from inside.

Think it over

1. How will you connect three dry cells, each of 1.5 volts, to get batteries of 1.5 volts, 3.0 volts and 4.5 volts? You have to use all the three cells.

2. Why are several MCBs used in the electrical wiring of a single apartment?

15 Properties of Light

Light is an essential part of our life. We cannot see without light. Normally, light is not visible unless it falls on an object. For example, when we look at the moon in the night sky, we cannot see the light from the sun travelling to the moon; we only see the moon illuminated by sunlight. Sometimes, if light travels through smoke, dust or mist, its path becomes visible as illuminated beams. Looking at the light beams, like those from a lighthouse or a powerful torch or a car headlight or in between leaves of trees, it becomes evident that light travels in a straight line. It is because light travels in a straight line that shadows are formed when light encounters an obstacle such as an opaque object.

Beam of light from the headlights of a car

Beam of light filtering through tree leaves

Explore

Take a 30 cm long straight piece of a garden hose that has a diameter of 4 cm. Look at a source of light such as an electric bulb or CFL through the tube. Can you see it clearly? Now bend the tube a bit and try to look at the same light source through the bent tube. Is it possible to see it? Can you explain why you cannot see the light source through the bent tube?

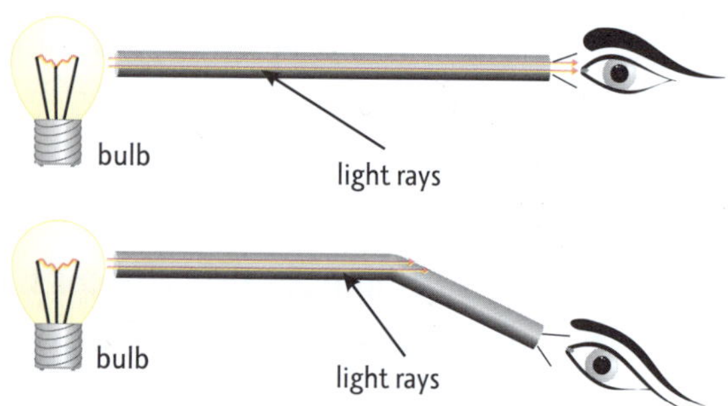

Light travels in a straight line

Reflection of light

Although light travels in a straight line, its direction can be changed by reflection. Light is reflected when it strikes a smooth and shiny surface such as that of a mirror, a clean stainless steel plate or spoon, even a sheet of clear glass or the still surface of water. The amount of light that is reflected depends on the type of surface. Shiny surfaces reflect more light, while dull surfaces, such as a matt surface, reflect very little light. The direction in which light is reflected depends on the direction from which the light beam hits the surface and also on the type of surface. For example, a plane surface reflects light differently from a curved surface. But whatever the shape of the reflecting surface, the reflected beam of light bounces off, or reflects back at the same angle that it hit the surface.

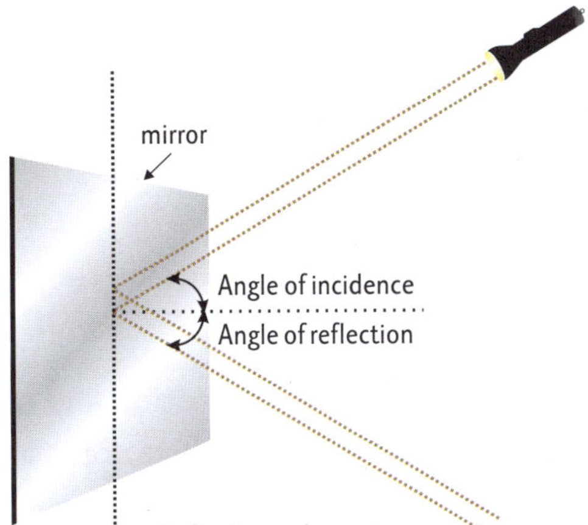

Reflection—plane mirror

Explore

Hang a plane mirror on a wall. Turn off the lights in the room. Take a torch and switch it on. Now shine the beam of the torch on the mirror from an angle so that its reflection falls on the opposite wall. Slowly change the angle at which the light beam strikes the mirror. What happens to the position of the reflection? Ask a friend to stand at the position where the reflected light beam falls on the wall and look into the mirror. What does she/he see? Does she/he see the reflected image of the torch?

Reflection from a plane mirror produces an image of an object that appears to be of the same size as the original object. The image appears to be placed behind the mirror at the same distance as the object is in front of the mirror. Also, the image appears upright, that is, the top and bottom of the image look the same as in the original object. Such an image is called an erect image.

reflection: the bouncing back of light from a shiny surface
plane mirror: a mirror with a flat surface
erect image: an image that is upright

Explore

Spread a sheet of white paper on a drawing board. Through the middle of the paper draw a line about 30 cm long. Mark the numbers 0 to 20 at intervals of 1 cm along this line, starting

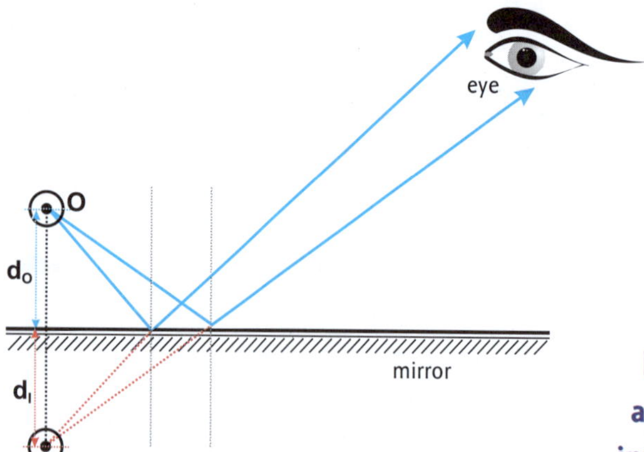

Distance between object and image

from one end of the line. Through the 0 mark, draw a short line perpendicular to the long line. Fix a small plane mirror vertically on the short line. In the mirror, the reflection of the line with the numbers marked can be seen extending behind the mirror.

Now, place a small object, such an eraser, on any of the numbers marked on the line. Looking into the mirror, where does the image of the eraser appear to be? Is it at the same distance as the eraser is in front of the mirror? Move the eraser nearer to a new position and observe. Does the position of the image also change? Is there any change in the distance it appears behind the mirror? Does the distance of the image behind the mirror always remain the same as the distance of the eraser in front of the mirror?

Factastic

During the Roman siege of Syracuse, a coastal city-state in Greece, from 214 to 212 BC, the Greek scientist Archimedes used bronze mirrors to focus sunlight on Roman ships and set them on fire!

The image formed by a plane mirror is not real because it cannot be focussed or projected on a screen placed in front or behind the mirror. So it is called a virtual image.

Right or left?

The image formed by a plane mirror is erect. The image is also of the same size as the object and also appears to be at the same distance behind the mirror as the object is in front of the mirror. But there is a big difference between the object and its image—the right side of the object appears as the left side in the image. This can be easily verified by standing in front of a plane mirror. If the right hand is raised, the image in the mirror appears to raise the left hand. Similarly, the pocket in most men's shirts , which is on the left side, appears to be on the right side in the image. So, in the image formed in a plane mirror, the 'right' appears to be 'left' and the 'left' appears to be 'right'. However, only the sides are interchanged; the 'top' and 'bottom' remain the same and the image does not appear upside down or **inverted**.

virtual image: an image formed by a mirror or a lens

Mirror writing is a form of writing backward, from right to left using letters that are also reversed left to right. However, when seen reflected in a plane mirror, the letters and words appear like normal writing. The famous Italian artist and inventor, Leonardo da Vinci, is famous for having written most of his personal notes as mirror images that could be read only by using a plane mirror. You would have noticed that the word AMBULANCE usually appears as a mirror image in front of these emergency vehicles. The reason for this is that drivers in cars in front of ambulances can read the word 'ambulance' the right way around as reflected in their rear-view mirror and can give way to them immediately.

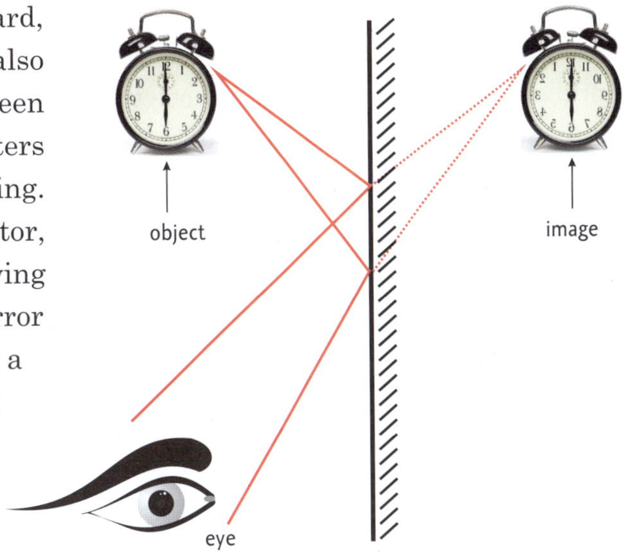

Reversal of object in an image

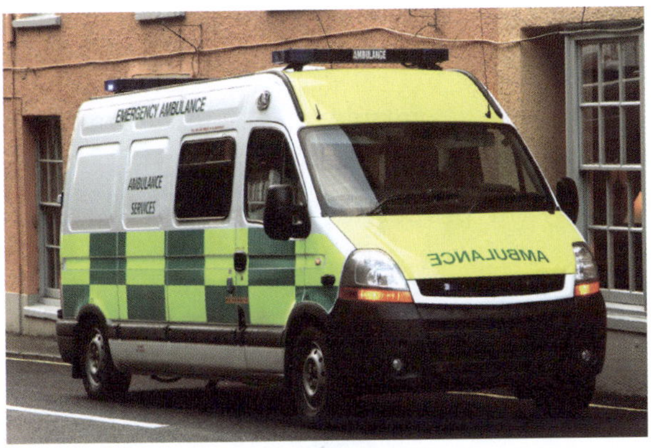

The word AMBULANCE written this way would appear normal in a mirror

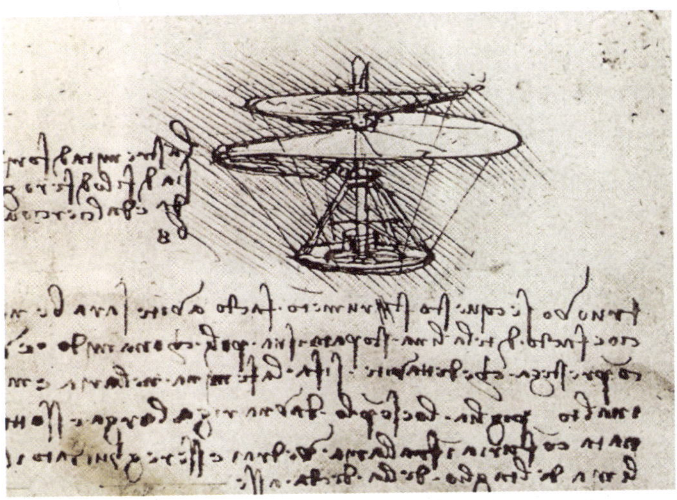
Mirror image writing

Leonardo da Vinci

Spherical mirrors

Another variety of mirrors are those that do not have a flat surface but are curved either inward or outward. For example, the side mirror of a scooter or a car is curved outward. This is an example of a **convex mirror**. Dentists use small mirrors that are curved inwards. They are called **concave mirrors**. Curved mirrors are called spherical mirrors.

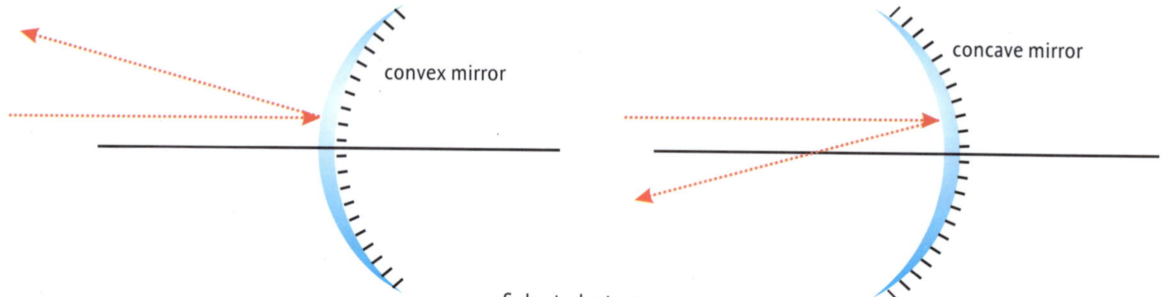

Spherical mirrors

Spherical mirrors can be seen in various shapes in articles of everyday use. A large stainless steel spoon or ladle has a convex outer surface and a concave inner surface. Although not of perfect shapes, these articles can be used to study the properties of spherical mirrors.

Concave mirrors

Spoons behaving like convex and concave mirrors

If the concave inner surface of a large stainless steel spoon is held close to the face, an enlarged upright image of the face (or part of it) can be seen. But if the spoon is moved a little distance away, a smaller, inverted image of the face is seen. A mirror that produces these kind of images is called a concave mirror. If an object is placed close to a concave mirror, the image appears erect and **magnified**. If the object is kept at a distance, the image appears inverted and **reduced**.

Unlike a plane mirror, which produces only a virtual image that cannot be projected on a screen, a concave mirror can produce a real image that can be projected on a screen. This can be easily tested by

spherical mirror: a mirror with a surface curved like the surface of a sphere
concave mirror: a spherical mirror that curves inward

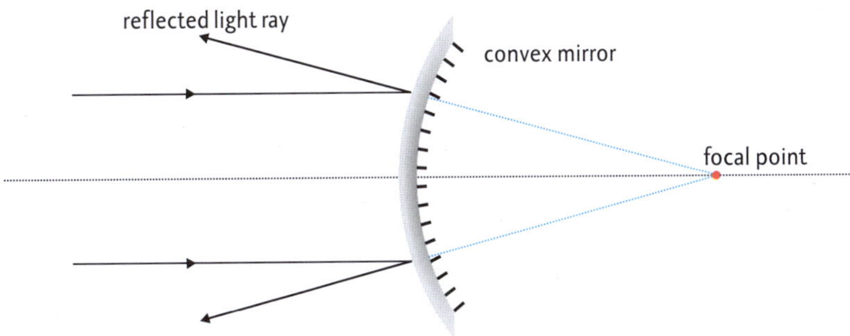

using a glass concave mirror from the science lab. If the mirror is held facing the sun, a sharp and bright image of the sun can be projected on a white sheet of paper as a bright spot. If the concave mirror is large, the spot will be hot enough to set the paper on fire in a few minutes.

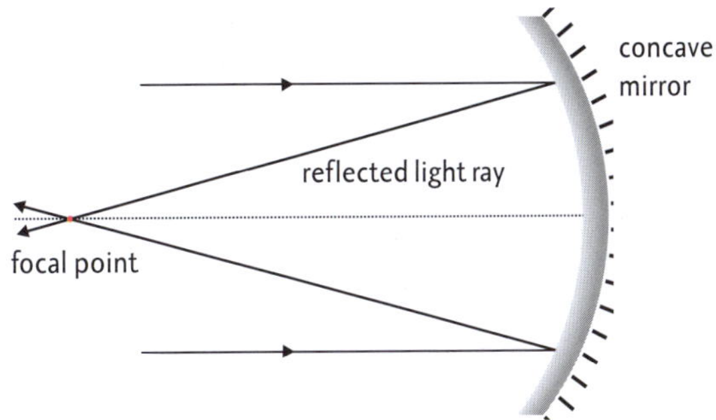

Explore

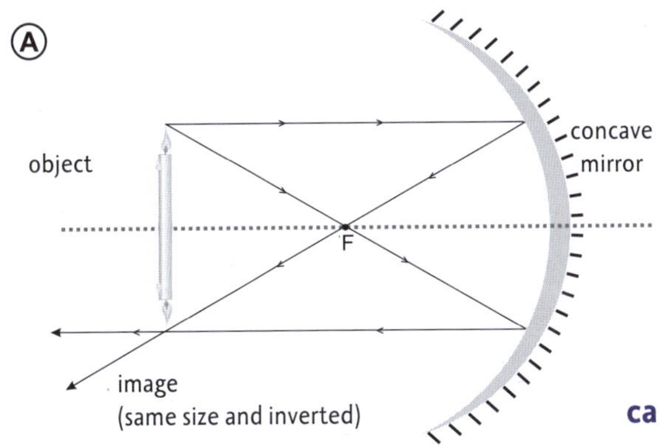

Mount a concave mirror vertically on a stand. On another stand, fix a board covered with a white paper to act as a screen. Fix a lighted candle on a stand. The heights of the three should be such that the centre of the mirror, the candle flame and the centre of the white screen lie on the same line. The candle should be in the middle of the white screen and the mirror.

Now place the candle closer to the mirror and keep the screen at different distances on the other side. Try to focus on an image of the candle flame on the screen. Move the screen away and look directly at the image of the candle flame in the mirror. Is it bigger or smaller? Is it erect or inverted? Is the image real or virtual?

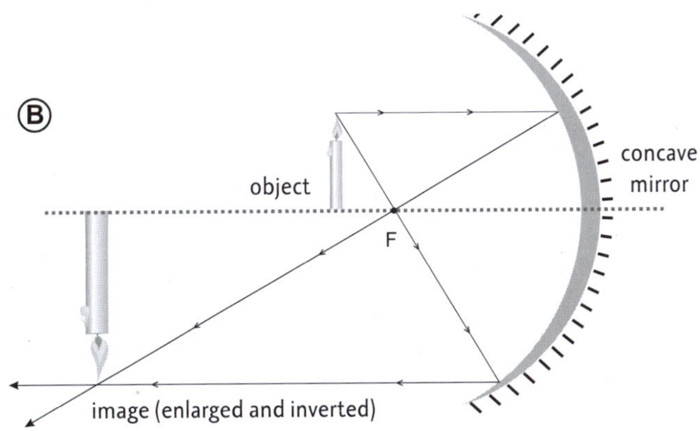

©

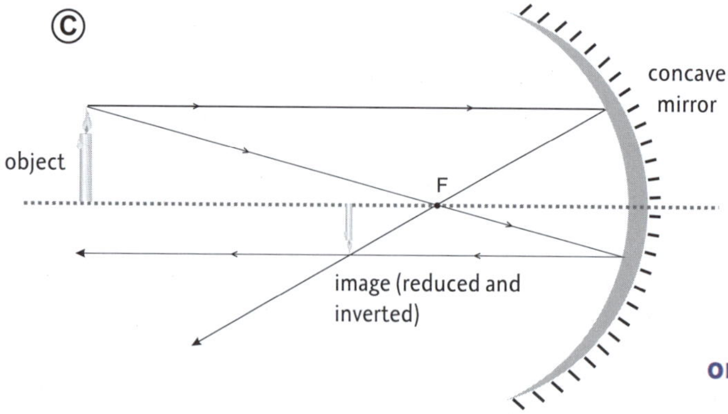

Move the screen back to its original position and move the candle slowly away from the mirror. Do you see an image of the flame on the screen? Is it bigger or smaller? Is it erect or inverted? Does the size of the image change if the candle is moved closer to or farther away from the mirror?

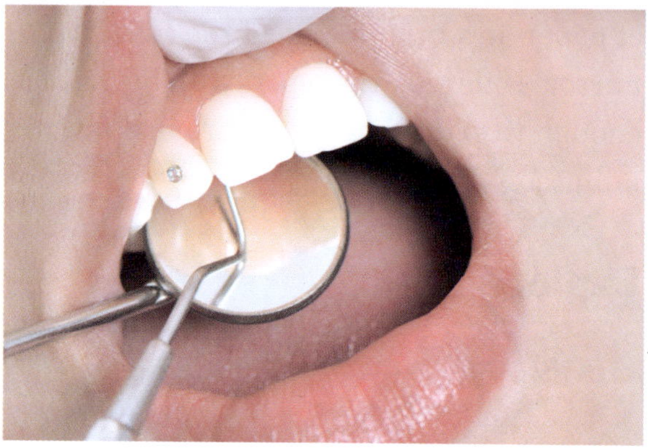

Concave mirrors used by dentists

A concave mirror produces a real and inverted image of a distant object, which is smaller in size than the object. This property of concave mirrors is used in making reflecting telescopes.

Concave mirrors are used for many purposes. Since concave mirrors can show magnified images, doctors use it for examining eyes, ears, nose and throat. Concave mirrors are also used by dentists to see a magnified image of the teeth to look for caries or cracks.

Concave mirrors of different shapes are used as reflectors in torches as well as in headlights of cars and motorbikes.

Concave mirrors—torch and car headlights

real image: an image formed by a mirror or a lens that can be projected on a screen
inverted image: an image that is upside down
reflecting telescope: a telescope that uses a concave mirror instead of a lens to gather light from the stars

Convex mirrors

Convex side view mirror

Unlike a concave mirror, which can produce a real image if an object is placed at the right distance, a convex mirror always produces a virtual image. The image is always erect and smaller in size than the original object. However, convex mirrors also have their uses. The side mirrors in cars and scooters are convex mirrors that can form images of objects spread over a large area. Such mirrors make it possible for drivers to see the traffic behind them.

Images formed by lenses

Factastic

The earliest lenses used by the Greeks and Romans were glass bowls filled with water, which were used as magnifying lenses of sorts and also as 'burning glasses' to light fires. They were made around 2000 BC, after glass-making was discovered.

A lens is a piece of glass or other transparent material with curved surfaces. Lenses with the surfaces curved outward, which feel thicker in the middle and thinner at the edges, are called convex lenses. Such lenses can be used as magnifying glasses to see small objects or writings clearly. Lenses with the surfaces curved inward, which feel thinner in the middle and thicker at the edges, are called concave lenses. Objects appear smaller when looked at through such lenses.

Unlike a mirror, which reflects the light falling on it, a lens is transparent and bends light as it passes through. A convex lens bends inward, or converges, the light falling on it and is called a **converging lens**. A concave lens bends outward, or diverges, the light and is called a **diverging lens**. Lenses are widely used to make spectacles, telescopes, binoculars, microscopes, cameras and also in CD and DVD players.

convex mirror: a spherical mirror that curves outward
concave lens: a lens that is thinner in the middle and thicker at the edges which makes light to diverge or spread out
convex lens: a lens that is thicker in the middle and thinner at the edges which makes light to converge or come to a focus

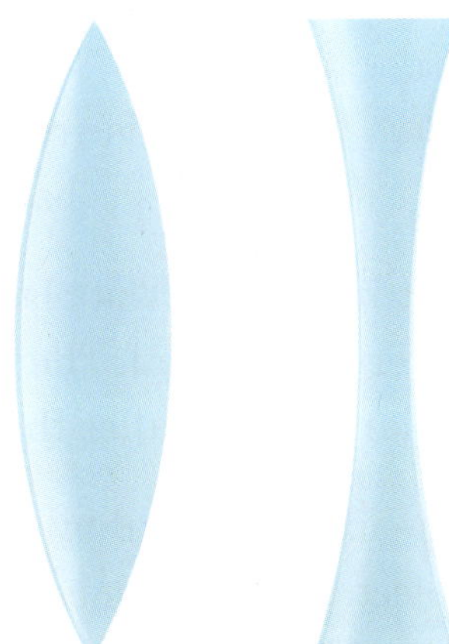

Convex and concave lenses

A magnifying glass is a common object available in many households. It can be used to study many properties of a convex lens. A magnifying glass can be used to focus the rays of the sun on a piece of paper. The sun's image appears as a bright spot. The image is formed by the lens converging the sun's rays into a bright spot, which can become hot enough to burn the paper.

A magnifying glass—convex lens

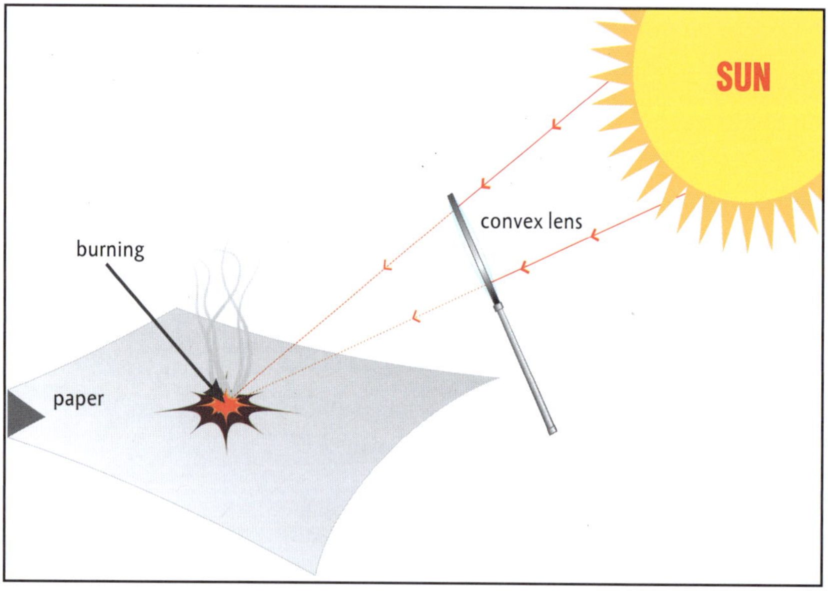

A magnifying glass—convex lens

A spectacle lens with a minus power through which objects appear smaller is a concave lens. If a concave lens is used in the same manner to focus the sun's rays, no image is formed because a concave lens diverges the sun's rays. The image formed by a convex lens can be virtual as well as real, depending on the distance between the lens and the object. If the object is held very close, the image is erect and magnified, but it is a virtual image and cannot be projected on a screen. This is basically how a magnifying glass works.

But if the object is placed some distance away from a convex lens, the image formed is inverted and real. The size of the image will depend on the distance from the lens—it can be larger or smaller than the object.

The image formed by a concave lens is always virtual, erect and smaller in size than the object. Hence, a concave lens cannot be used to focus an image on a screen. Concave lenses are widely used in spectacles, in door spy holes and in some types of telescopes.

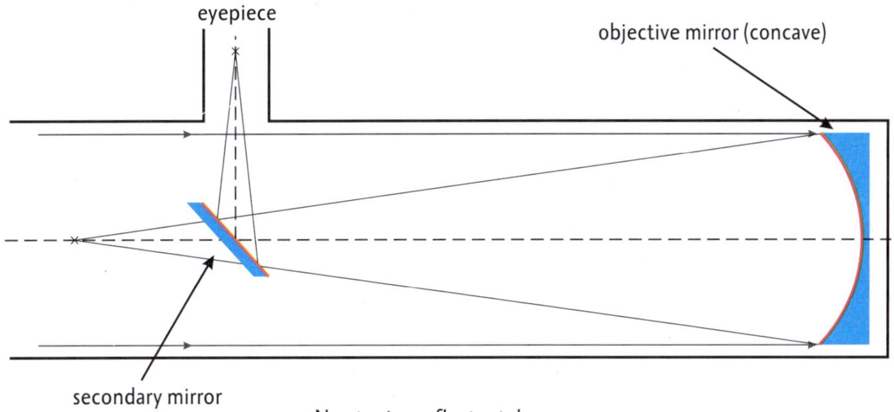

Newtonian reflector telescope

Explore

Mount a convex lens vertically on a stand. On another stand fix a board covered with a white paper to act as a screen. Fix a lighted candle on a stand. The heights of the three should be such that the candle flame, the centre of the lens and the centre of the white screen lie on the same line. Place the lens in the middle with the candle and the screen on its two opposite ends.

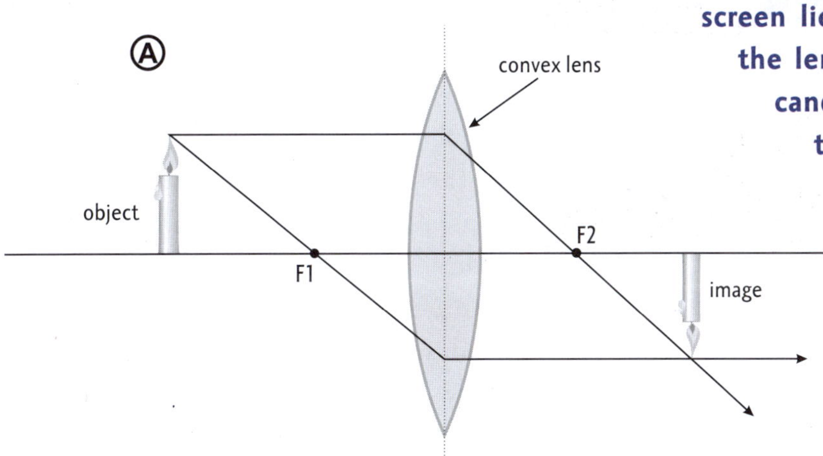

Keep the candle close to the lens and keep the screen at different distances. Try to focus an image of the candle flame on the screen.

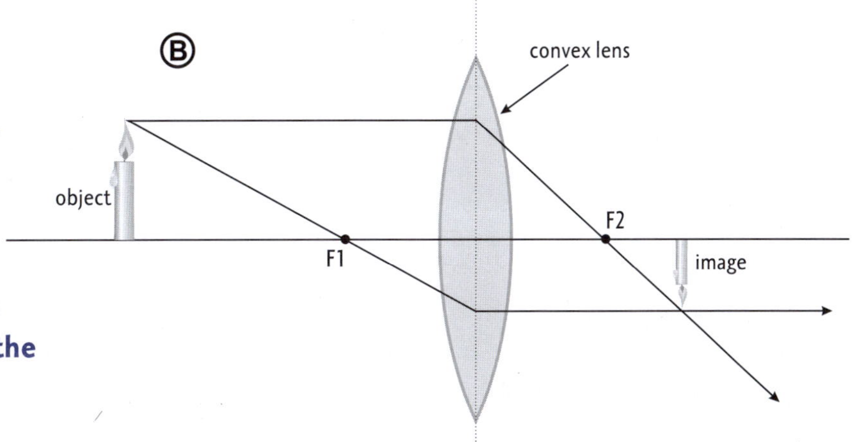

Move the screen away and look directly at the image of the candle flame through the lens. Is it bigger or smaller? Is it erect or inverted? Is the image real or virtual?

Move the screen back ot its original position and slowly move the candle away from the lens. Do you see an image of the flame on the screen? Is it bigger or smaller? Is it erect or inverted? Does the size of the image change if the lens is moved closer to or farther away from the candle?

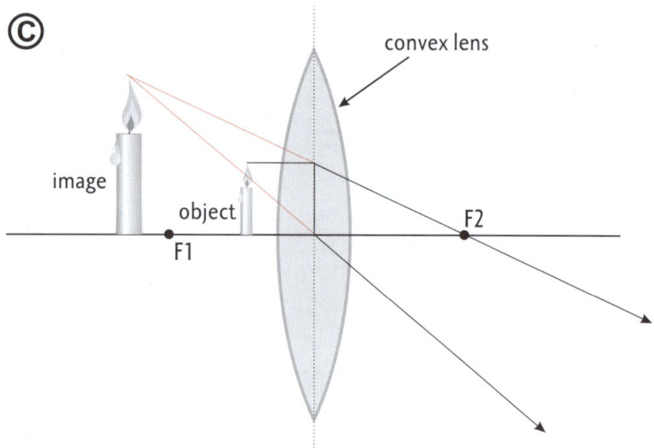

Colours of sunlight

A beam of light passing through a glass prism

It was the English physicist Isaac Newton who first showed that white sunlight is made up of seven colours. He performed a series of experiments in 1665 and 1666 and observed the formation of coloured bands when a narrow beam of sunlight was passed through a glass prism. The reason for the formation of colours is that a transparent medium (such as a glass prism) bends different colours of light at different angles. The amount of deviation for violet is maximum while for red is minimum. Sunlight is a combination of light of seven colours—violet, indigo, blue, green, yellow, orange and red (VIBGYOR).

This property of sunlight is responsible for the appearance of a rainbow when the sun comes out after it has rained. We always see the rainbow in the front

A rainbow

prism: a block of glass with three rectangular and two triangular faces that can break up white light into its components
rainbow: an arch of colours visible in the sky, caused by the refraction and dispersion of the sun's light by water droplets in the atmosphere

when the sun is low and behind us. The rainbow is created when sunlight is split into the seven colours by tiny raindrops in the air, which act as tiny prisms.

Explore

Select a room with sunlight coming in through one side. Close the windows on the sunny side leaving a small opening through which sunlight can stream in. Make the opening as small as possible by using black paper if necessary so that only a beam of sunlight enters the room. Place a glass prism such that the light beam passes through it and let the light coming out from the other side of the prism fall on a white sheet of paper. Do you see the seven colours of the rainbow? This is how Newton discovered that white light is a mixture of seven colours.

Rainbow colours on a CD

The colours of a rainbow can also be seen when a CD is placed in sunlight or in bright white light. Here the colours are produced by the fine groves on the CD, breaking up light into its seven component colours.

If white light can be broken up into seven colours, then it should also be possible to combine the seven colours into white colour. A simple device makes this possible. The device commonly known as Newton's disc is basically a disc about 10 cm in diameter and divided into seven pie-shaped segments each of which is painted in one of the seven colours of the rainbow in the same order as seen in a rainbow; that is, violet followed by indigo, followed by blue, and so on, up to red. When the disc is rotated fast in bright light, the colour of the disc appears whitish, as the individual colours appear to merge together.

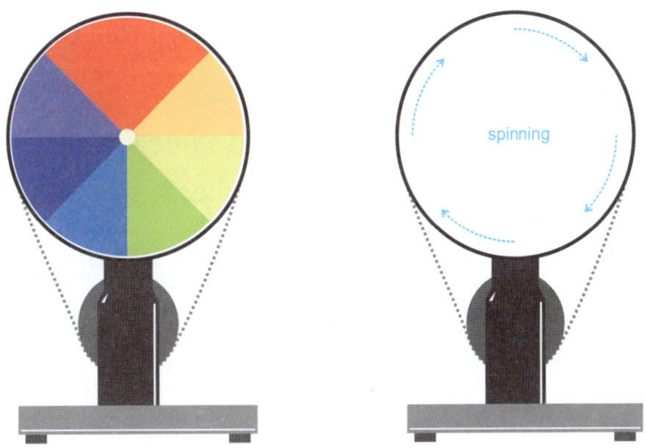

Newton's disc

Activity

Aim: To make a simple magnifying glass.

Material required: a card paper or a used broad sticky tape roll, scissors, cling film and tape

Newton's disc: a disc with segments painted in the seven rainbow colours

Procedure:

1. **Cut a strip of the card paper about 17 cm long. Bend it to**

form a circle and tape the ends together. You will get a ring shaped structure. If you have a used tape roll, you could use it instead of the card paper.

2. **Take a cling film and cover the ring tightly with it. Use tape to secure the cling film in place. The cling film should be stretched tightly over the ring.**
3. **While observing an object, place this ring shaped structure over it and gently put a few drops on water on top of the cling film surface. Look at the object through the water to see a magnified image.**

Revision Time

- ✶ Light travels in a straight line, but its direction can be changed by reflection.
- ✶ A plane surface reflects light differently from a curved surface.
- ✶ An image that cannot be projected on a screen is called a virtual image.
- ✶ An image that can be projected on a screen is called a real image.
- ✶ The image formed in a plane mirror is erect and virtual and is of the same size and appears at the same distance behind the mirror as the object is in front of it.
- ✶ In an image formed by a plane mirror, the right side of the object appears as the left side in the image.
- ✶ Mirrors that have curved surfaces are referred to as spherical mirrors. There are two types of spherical mirrors—concave (curved inwards) and convex (curved outwards).
- ✶ When an object is placed close to a concave mirror, the image is virtual and appears erect and magnified.
- ✶ When an object is placed some distance away from a concave mirror, the image is real and appears inverted and smaller in size than the object.
- ✶ The image formed by a convex mirror is always virtual, erect and smaller in size than the object.
- ✶ When an object is placed close to a convex lens, the image formed is virtual, erect and magnified. That is why a convex lens is used as a magnifying glass. But a convex lens forms a real, inverted and small image of distant objects.
- ✶ The image formed by a concave lens is always virtual, erect and smaller in size than the object.
- ✶ White light is composed of seven colours and can be split into the constituent colours by a glass prism.

Quiz Time

1. Answer the questions.

a. Why is a shadow formed when an opaque object is placed in the path of light?

b. Why cannot a plane mirror be used to produce a real image?

c. What does a convex lens do to a ray of light passing through it?

d. What kind of mirror is used by a dentist to have a closer look at a decayed tooth?

e. What happens when sunlight is passed through a glass prism?

2. Fill in the blanks.

a. A plane surface reflects light differently from a ______________ surface.

b. In the image formed in a convex mirror the 'right' appears as ______________.

c. If an object is placed close to a concave mirror, the image appears erect and ______________.

d. Objects always appear smaller when looked at through a ______________ lens.

e. We always see a rainbow in front of us when the sun is low and ______________ us.

3. Match the columns.

a. plane mirror	i. TV picture tube
b. concave mirror	ii. car side mirror
c. convex mirror	iii. car headlight
d. convex lens	iv. periscope
e. concave lens	v. camera
	vi. spectacles

4. Indicate whether the statements are true or false.

a. In an image formed in a plane mirror, the 'right' always appears as 'left'.	True	False
b. A concave mirror can be used to form an erect and magnified image.	True	False
c. A convex mirror produces a real image of an object placed very close to it.	True	False
d. A convex lens bends outward, or diverges, the light falling on it and is called a diverging lens.	True	False
e. The seven colours of sunlight can be combined to produce white colour.	True	False

5. Project work

a. Find information about half-silvered mirrors that reflect part of the light falling on them and allow a part of it to pass through. How do half-silvered window panes help keep interiors of buildings cool in summer? Also think of some novel ways of using half-silvered mirrors in science projects.

b. Set up a candle, a convex lens and a screen as described earlier. Begin by placing the candle very close to the lens on one side and the screen on the other side of the lens. Observe if an image is formed on the screen. If not, move the screen forward and backward till an image is formed, or look at the flame through the lens to see if there is a virtual image. Note down the distance of the candle from the lens and the character of the image.

Move the candle slowly away from the lens and also move the screen till an image of the candle flame is formed. Again note down the distance between the candle and the lens and the character of the image. Repeat the observation by moving the candle many times. Record the observations in the table given below.

Distance of candle from lens	Size of image (smaller/larger than object)	Character of the image	
		Real/Virtual	Erect/Inverted
5 cm			
10 cm			
20 cm			
30 cm			
40 cm			
50 cm			

From the table, try to find a relation between the distance of the candle from the lens and the type of image formed. Does the size of the image increase or decrease continuously as the distance increases, or does it increase up to a point and then decrease?

Think it over

1. **If you stand between two plane mirrors placed parallel to each other on either side, how many images of yourself would you see?**
2. **How does a concave mirror, used as a reflector in a torch, produce a beam of light in the forward direction?**

16 Water: A Precious Resource

The earth as seen from space

When observed from space, the earth looks blue because most of its surface is covered with water. In fact, oceans cover more than two-thirds of the surface of earth; yet water is a scarce resource. This is because ninety-seven per cent of all water available on earth is present in the oceans and is salty and hence is not fit for human or animal consumption or for agriculture. About seventy per cent of the freshwater that is available on earth, is present in the form of frozen ice in the polar regions. A large part of the remaining freshwater is stored in underground aquifers and has to be pumped out for use. Out of the remaining fraction that is available in the rivers, ponds and lakes, a whopping eighty per cent is used for growing food and raising animals. This leaves only about 0.06 per cent of the earth's total water for direct human use. The sad thing is that even this limited amount of freshwater is not

aquifer: an underground layer of rocks and soil saturated with water from where groundwater can be extracted

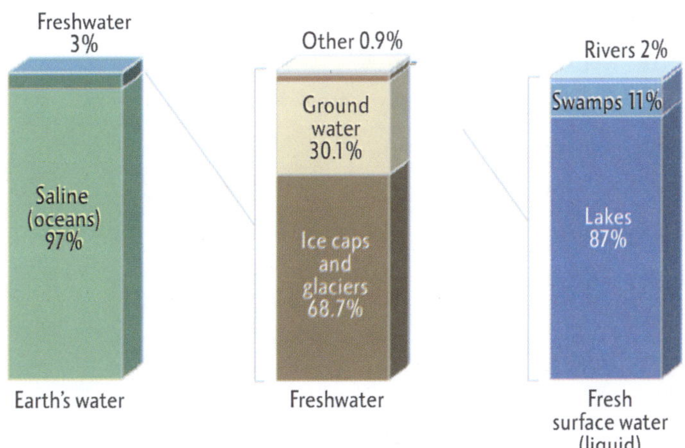

Distribution of the earth's water

clean; it is being polluted by reckless human activity, making the availability of freshwater for human use scarcer.

Life on earth is not possible without water. So there is an urgent need to protect and conserve this scarce resource. In order to make people aware of the importance of water and the need to conserve this precious natural resource, the United Nations General Assembly has designated 22 March of every year as **World Water Day**. The main purpose of this is to draw the attention of the world community, especially children, to the importance of conserving water and keeping it clean. In many cities all over India, water supply is severely restricted and the situation becomes more difficult in summer. According to the United Nations, every person should get at least fifty litres of water each day for washing, cooking and maintenance of proper hygiene. In everyday terms, this is about two and a half buckets of water per person per day. But in reality, not everyone on this planet gets this amount of water and the situation is becoming worse every day.

Water cycle

Water is a renewable resource; that is, it can be used again and again. But, the total amount of water on the earth does not change. Water only passes through different forms in nature and returns to the same form. The cycle starts with the evaporation of water from the oceans and land when heated by the sun, followed by the formation of clouds and rain and snow. Part of this precipitation seeps into the ground while the rest flows into the seas through rivers. In this cycle, water is present in all the three forms—solid, liquid and gas. Solid water can be seen in the polar regions as ice caps and on mountain peaks and glaciers as ice and snow. Liquid water is present in rivers, lakes, seas, oceans and even

The water cycle

evaporation: change of a liquid into vapour

in underground aquifers as groundwater. Water vapour is the gaseous form of water that is present in the air almost everywhere except in the extremely dry deserts. The continuous cycling of water among its three forms through the water cycle keeps the total amount of water on earth constant and maintains the supply of water on land.

Factastic

There is no such thing as 'new' water on earth. The volume of water on the planet has not changed in over three billion years. It has just been converted from water to vapour to ice to water to water vapour and back again. That means that the water that is in our oceans, lakes, our food and even our body today is the same water that the dinosaurs drank!

Circle Time

Take a 2 litre bottle filled with water, a clear, empty bottle and smaller glass containers. The water may be coloured with a dye to make it easily visible.

Out of the bottle measure out 1,940 ml of water with a measuring cylinder and pour it into the clear, empty bottle, labelling it as 'Salt water'. This represents how much of our planet's water is found in the oceans, which is about ninety-seven per cent of the total water on earth.

Pour the remaining 60 ml from the bottle, or 3% of the total, into another container. This represents the total amount of freshwater on earth. Label this container as 'Freshwater'.

Out of the container marked 'Freshwater', measure 40 ml into another container, labelling it as 'Water frozen in ice caps'. Next, from the remaining 20 ml, measure 19 ml into another container, labelling it as 'Water in air, soil and underground'.

The amount of water left in the container marked 'Freshwater', which should be about 1 ml, represents all of the freshwater available for human use out of the two litres that represents the total water available on earth.

Does this activity give an idea of the tiny fraction of the total water present on earth that is available for human consumption? Do you now understand why it is important not to waste and pollute water?

Depleting groundwater

groundwater: water held underground in the soil or in pores and crevices in rock

In big towns and cities, water is mostly made available through taps. The water from nearby rivers or lakes is treated and then supplied to homes through pipes. However, sometimes, the river or lake water is not enough to meet the total demand. At such times, water is drawn from deep tube wells to meet the demand for additional water. In villages, water is mostly obtained from open wells, tube wells and handpumps. This water comes from **groundwater**, which is an underground source of water.

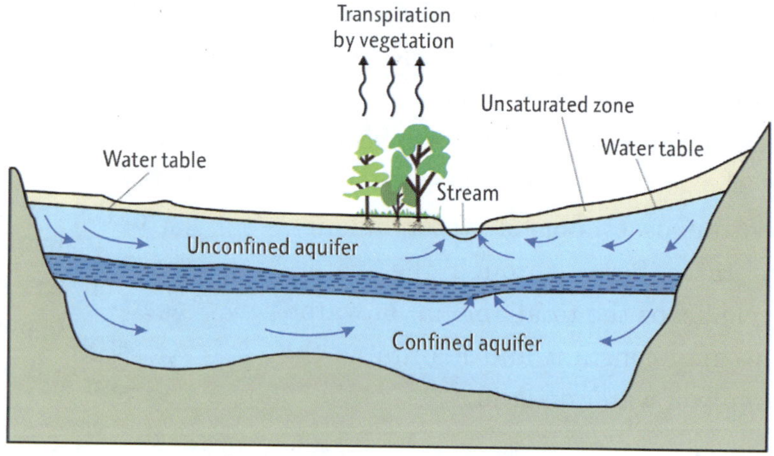

Occurance of groundwater in aquifers

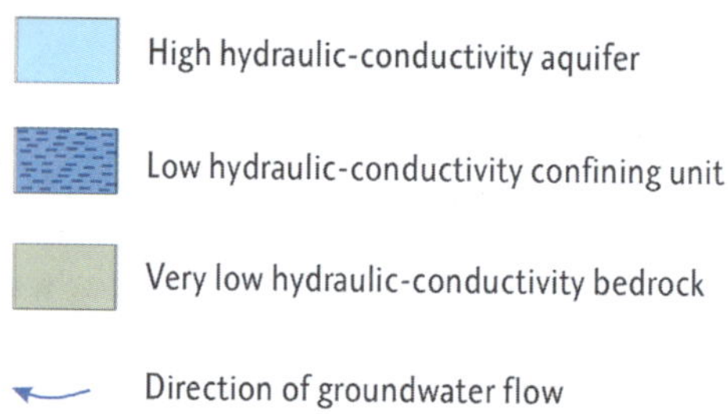

Groundwater is found below the ground in the cracks and spaces in soil, sand and rocks. The spaces where groundwater is stored and through which it moves slowly are called **aquifers**. Aquifers are made up of layers of soil, sand and rocks, which are quite porous.

If a hole is dug in the ground, water is normally found at a certain depth, depending on the place. At the depth where water is found, all the space between the particles of soil and gaps between rocks are filled with, or are **saturated** with, water. The level below which the ground is saturated with water, or below which water is found, is called the **water table**. So, if a well or a tube well is to be dug, it would be necessary to dig up to the depth of the water table to obtain water.

The depth of the water table varies widely geographically. In some places, the water table may be at a depth of less than a metre but there may be places where water may be found a few hundred metres below the surface of the earth. Even at the same place, the water table does not remain at a constant level. If too much groundwater is drawn out, the water table falls, making it necessary to dig deeper for water.

saturated: thoroughly soaked with water
water table: the level below which water can be found on drilling

Interestingly, all groundwater is actually stored rainwater. When rain falls to the ground, most of the rainwater flows along the surface to streams or lakes and some evaporates and returns to the atmosphere. But some of the rainwater seeps into the ground and is stored as groundwater. The process of seeping of water into the ground is called infiltration. Groundwater that is taken out by pumping is normally made up or recharged by the process of infiltration. As long as the volume of recharge water remains the same or is more than the volume pumped out, groundwater can be used almost indefinitely. But the problem is that more groundwater is being pumped out than is being replenished.

Nearly eighty per cent of the rural and fifty per cent of the urban population in India today depends on groundwater for drinking purposes. A large quantity of groundwater is also used for irrigation, especially in north India. This has led to a sharp drop in the water table in many parts of the country, which is a matter of concern.

Among the main factors responsible for the fall in the water table in India are increase in population, increasing industrial and agricultural activities and the occasional failure of the monsoon rains. The widespread cutting of forests, especially in the catchment areas, has also reduced the area over which effective seepage of rainwater and recharge can take place.

Increasing population

Whenever population increases, there is need for construction of more houses, shops, offices, roads and pavements on lands that were once open fields or forest areas. This, in turn, reduces the total area available for rainwater to seep through because buildings and paved roads block the seepage of water.

Even during construction work, huge amounts of water are required and groundwater is mostly used for this purpose. Thus, increase in population not only leads to increased consumption of groundwater, but also reduces recharge by preventing rainwater from seeping through paved structures. This leads to the depletion of groundwater and a drop in the water table. In fact, in recent years, the water table in some parts of many cities has gone down to alarmingly low levels.

Growth in the number of industries

Groundwater is used extensively for industrial purposes. Most manufacturing industries use water for washing, cleaning, cooling and in various stages of the production processes. Some manufacturers of soft drinks use huge amounts of groundwater for their products. As the number of industries increases, so does the consumption of groundwater.

infiltration: the slow passage of a liquid through a filtering medium such as soil
recharge: the replenishment of an aquifer by the absorption of water

Crop irrigation

Agriculture needs irrigation since crops cannot grow without irrigation. If water for irrigation is not available, crops die. Most farmers in India depend on rains for irrigating their crops, although canal irrigation is available in some places. But if the rains fail or canal water is not enough, farmers use groundwater for irrigation. With increasing demand for producing more crops through multiple cropping—the practice of growing two or more crops during a single growing season—the use of groundwater for irrigation is increasing day by day, leading to alarming drops in the water table levels in some areas.

Uneven distribution of water

The water available in different parts of the world differs widely. There are countries that have big rivers or lakes and receive plenty of rainfall. On the other hand, desert areas have hardly any source of water and receive little or no rainfall. In India, the north-eastern regions receive plenty of rain almost throughout the year, while in Rajasthan the availability of water is very limited. The uneven distribution of rainfall during the monsoons in different parts of India sometimes creates a peculiar situation. One part of the country may receive too much rain and may suffer devastating floods while in another part, the rains may fail and the region could suffer a severe drought. In such situations, the suffering of the people can be reduced to a large extent by the proper management of the water resources.

It is not only human beings and animals that suffer when there is scarcity of water, plants are also affected. During a drought, most plants die, leaving the soil exposed to erosion. Loss of plants also reduces the fodder available for animals. Prolonged scarcity of water may cause large green areas to turn barren and unfit for living.

Water management

While it may not be possible to prevent droughts, water resources can be managed to a large extent by making adequate provision of storing water in ponds or as groundwater when rainfall is normal. Floods can also be controlled to some extent by preventing deforestation in the catchment areas because forests prevent soil erosion and thus prevent the flow of silt into rivers that cause them to overflow their banks after heavy rains.

silt: fine sand, clay or other material carried by running water and deposited as a sediment in rivers or lakes

Wastage of water is a major cause of water scarcity. In

भारत मौसम विज्ञान विभाग
INDIA METEOROLOGICAL DEPARTMENT

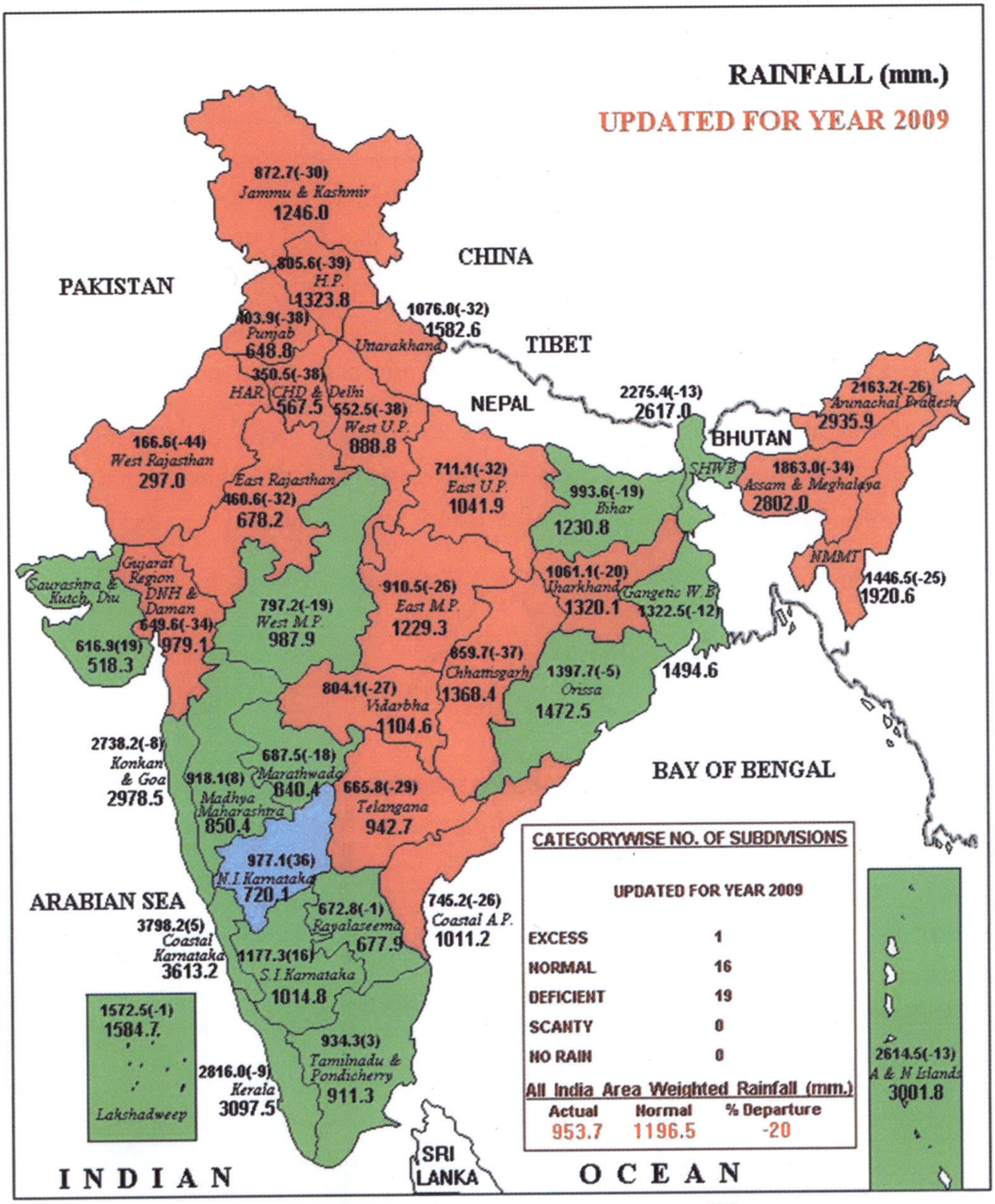

LEGEND: EXCESS (+20% OR MORE) NORMAL (+19% TO -19%) DEFICIENT (-20% TO -59%) SCANTY (-60% TO -99%) NO RAIN (-100%) NO DATA

NOTES:

(a) Rainfall figures are based on operational data.

(b) Small figures indicate actual rainfall (mm.), while bold figures indicate Normal rainfall (mm.) Percentage Departures of Rainfall are shown in Brackets.

Annual rainfall map of India

Wastage of water from pipes

cities where piped water is supplied by municipal authorities, it is quite common to see leaking water pipes with water flowing out of them, sometimes flooding roads nearby. If the leaks are not repaired promptly, water is wasted.

In homes, leaking taps and overflowing overhead tanks are a major source of water wastage. Keeping taps open when not required, such as when brushing teeth or shaving, also wastes water. While taking a bath, a lot of water can be saved by using a bucket rather than using the shower.

Rainwater harvesting is an effective method of increasing the availability of water. Normally, a large part of the rainwater received during the monsoons just flows away into the rivers and into the seas. This water is not used in any way and is wasted. In rainwater harvesting, the rainwater is collected either in tanks, ponds or traditional ***bawris***, or is used to recharge groundwater. In many cities today, rainwater harvesting structures have been made mandatory in all new buildings to save as much rainwater as possible. In some cities, the use of harvested rainwater to recharge groundwater has led to a substantial rise in the water table level.

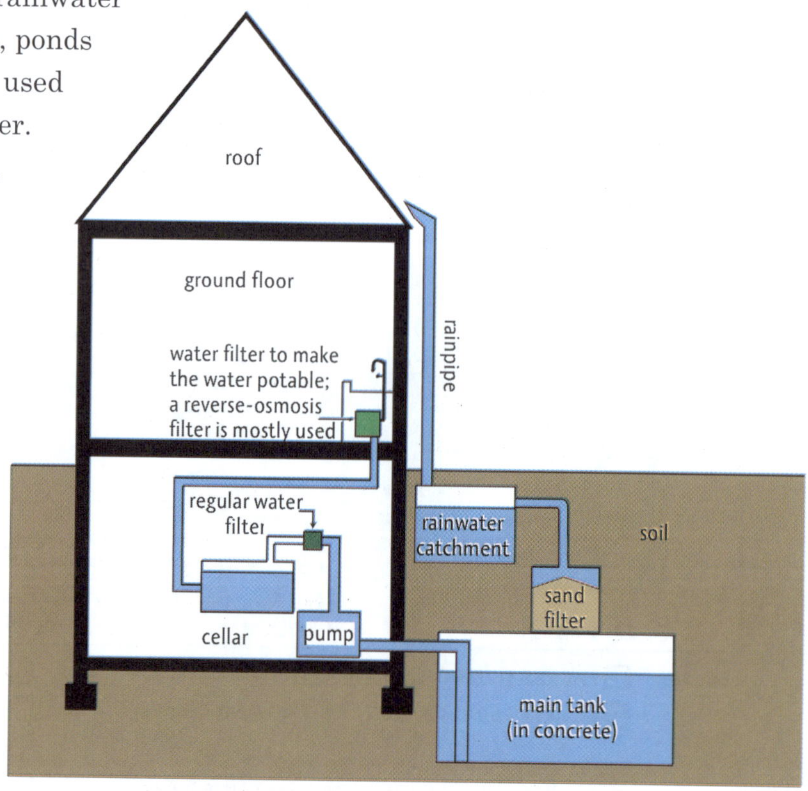

Rainwater harvesting system with potable water production

rainwater harvesting: a technique of collecting and storing rainwater for recharging groundwater

A success story

Ruparel is among the few rivers in India that has seen life after death. The area surrounding this river in Rajasthan receives very little rain. In the 1970s, the water level in the river began falling due to extensive deforestation and agricultural activities along its banks. By the 1980s, with almost no water in the river, the area was facing a drought-like situation. Then, the women living in the area were encouraged by some non-governmental organisations to take the initiative in building *johads* (round ponds) and dams to hold back rainwater. Gradually, as proper methods of conserving and harvesting rainwater were followed, water began coming back into the river. The revival of the river has transformed the ecology of the place and the lives of the people living along its banks. It has proved that if people put in an effort, the damage caused to nature can be undone.

A lot of water used for irrigation is wasted due to evaporation. When a field is irrigated, only a small part of the water used is actually taken up by the plants; the rest simply evaporates. Such wastage can be reduced considerably by using the technique of drip irrigation. In this technique, water is applied to a small area of the soil around the roots of the plants with the help of a network of plastic tubes. Since the water drips slowly on to the soil surface or directly on the roots, loss by evaporation is reduced considerably. If properly designed, installed and managed, drip irrigation can save a lot water by reducing water lost by evaporation and wasteful drainage when compared to other types of irrigation.

Water conservation at home

Each of us can contribute towards conserving water by using it judiciously and trying to cut back on its waste in our homes. In the long run, this will also help reduce the amount of water that must be treated by wastewater treatment plants. Repairing leaky taps at home and in school can also go a long way in saving water because a single dripping tap can waste as much as 10 litres of water or more each day.

drip irrigation: an irrigation method in which water is allowed to drip slowly on the roots of plants

Brainteaser

What am I?

I run but do not walk. I have a mouth but cannot talk and I have a bed but cannot sleep.

Answer: A river.

Revision Time

- ✶ Although seventy-five per cent of earth's surface is covered with water, only about 0.06 per cent of the earth's total water is available for direct human use.
- ✶ In order to make people aware of the need to conserve this precious natural resource, World Water Day is observed every year on 22 March.
- ✶ The continuous cycling of water through the water cycle keeps the total amount of water on earth constant and maintains the supply of water on land.
- ✶ There is water scarcity in many parts of the world. The water available in different parts of the world differs widely due to geographical and climatic reasons.
- ✶ Increase in population, rapid industrialisation, growing needs of irrigation and mismanagement and wastage are the major causes of water scarcity.
- ✶ Prolonged scarcity of water may cause large green areas to turn barren and unfit for living.
- ✶ Rainwater harvesting is an effective method of increasing the availability of water.
- ✶ Drip irrigation can considerably reduce the need for irrigation water by reducing wastage through evaporation.
- ✶ Repairing leaky taps at home and in school can also go a long way in saving water.
- ✶ Each of us can contribute to conserving water by using it judiciously and cutting down on its wastage.

Quiz Time

1. Answer the questions.

a. Why is World Water Day observed every year?

b. What helps maintain a constant supply of water on earth?

c. Where does groundwater come from?

d. What are the factors that lead to the lowering of the water table?

e. How can drip irrigation help in conserving water?

2. Fill in the blanks.

a. According to the United Nations, every person should get at least ____________ litres of water every day for washing, cooking and maintenance of proper hygiene.

b. ____________________ are the spaces where groundwater is stored underground and through which it moves slowly.

c. The process of water seepage into the ground is called ____________________.

d. The level below which water is found is called the ____________________.

e. In ____________________, water is applied to a small area of the soil around the roots of the plants through a network of plastic tubes.

3. Indicate whether the statements are true or false.

a.	Only about 0.06 per cent of the earth's total water is available for direct human use.	True	False
b.	As the population increases, the total amount of water on earth keeps getting less.	True	False
c.	All groundwater is actually stored rainwater.	True	False
d.	The total amount of water stored underground is much less than that present in the rivers and lakes of the world.	True	False
e.	In drip irrigation, water is applied to the plants from an overhead network of tubes.	True	False

5. Project work

a. Visit a building that has provision for rainwater harvesting. Study how rainwater is collected on the roof and sent to underground pits to recharge groundwater. How are dry leaves and other dirt removed from the water before it is sent to the recharging pit? Find out how the collected rainwater gets cleaned as it seeps through the layers of soil before it reaches the underground aquifers.

b. Look up reference books or the internet to find out about the traditional Indian systems of water harvesting. Prepare a chart with pictures and descriptions of the methods used in different regions of India.

Think it over

1. **Groundwater is sometimes found to be contaminated with pesticides or other toxic chemicals. How does groundwater get contaminated?**
2. **If all the rainwater is harvested for recharging groundwater, will it affect the flow of the rivers?**

17 The Importance of Forests

A forest is a collection of several hundred trees of various kind along with many species of wild animals. In fact, forests are home to over two-thirds of the known terrestrial species of plants, animals and insects, and are among the most notable storehouses of biological diversity on the land.

The forests of India have been present in nature since ancient times. Several ancient texts mention forests indicating their existence from ages ago. The people in earlier days revered forests which are worshipped even till date as sacred groves in parts of India.

India owes its rich biodiversity to its forests, which consist of evergreen tropical rain forests in the Andaman and Nicobar Islands, the Western Ghats and the north-eastern states. Dry alpine forests are found high in the Himalayas in the north. Due to the presence of these and other types of forests in various parts, India is considered one of the seventeen **megadiverse countries** in the world—a group of countries that harbour the majority of the earth's living beings. Apart from being the home to unique wildlife, flora and fauna, the forests of India are also a source of

A forest area

sacred grove: a grove of trees of great religious importance to a particular culture
biodiversity: the diversity of plant and animal life in a particular habitat

Forest biodiversity

sustainable livelihood to over 200 million people in the country.

Green lungs

Plants take in carbon dioxide and release oxygen

Just as our lungs exchange carbon dioxide with oxygen in blood, green plants in the forests absorb carbon dioxide and release oxygen into the atmosphere, purifying the air in the process. The forests are thus known as the world's lungs. We breathe in oxygen produced by green plants during photosynthesis. Plants take in carbon dioxide from the atmosphere. The source of this carbon dioxide includes carbon dioxide exhaled by animals (including humans), carbon dioxide produced by industries and by the burning of fossil fuels.

Autumn leaves

Factastic
Without forests we would have much less oxygen. One hectare of forest provides more than 15 tonnes of oxygen per year!

Forests usually have tall trees that prevent sunlight from reaching the forest floor, which results in the forest habitat often being shady, dark, moist and cool. Tropical rainforests have a humid and warm climate along with rainfall. Deciduous forests are found in warmer places. These have trees with big leaves that become dry and fall to the ground in autumn.

Any tree in a forest can often be recognised by the shape of its **crown**—the upper, extensively branched part that is often a characteristic of any particular species. In a tropical forest, the branches of the tallest trees, which look like a roof over the other plants, make up the topmost layer that is known as the canopy. The crowns of the smaller trees make up what is known as the understorey. Shrubs and herbs make up the lower layers of vegetation. Thus, there are several layers constituted by trees and plants in a forest. Various animals live in different layers to avoid competition for

Crowns of different trees

canopy: the uppermost branches of the trees in a forest, forming a more or less continuous layer of foliage
understorey: a layer of vegetation beneath the main canopy of a forest

food. For example, birds live in the upper layers of the trees. Many birds, such as the owl and the hornbill, make nests in holes dug in tree trunks. Large animals, such as deer, gaur, jaguars and tigers, generally live on the forest floor, but others, such as monkeys, gibbons, sloths and some snakes, live in tree branches. Insects are found almost everywhere and microbes are plentiful on the forest floor.

Different layers in a forest

Insects on the forest floor

The forest floor is the lowest level in the forest. Due to the lack of sunlight and humidity, only a few plants grow here that include mosses, a few herbs and fungi. The forest floor is mostly covered with a litter of rapidly decomposing vegetation and organisms that break down organic matter and provide nutrients to the soil. Many large mammals, such as pigs and boars, search for roots and tubers. Insects, such as termites, ants, cockroaches, beetles, centipedes, millipedes and scorpions along with earthworms and fungi, use the organic litter as a source of food.

The layered structure is, however, not the same in all forests. There are variations in the types of trees, plants and animals from forest to forest due to the difference in the climatic conditions.

In a forest everything is connected and nothing is wasted. The many different plants and animals that live in the forests interact with each other in many ways. Each layer supports another, providing specific animals and insects with food and shelter. Birds and insects spread seeds and pollens of certain plants for them to grow. Animals also disperse the seeds of certain plants through their droppings and help in forest regeneration.

The dry leaves shed by the trees, fallen branches as well as dead animals decompose and enrich the soil. Micro-organisms and fungi help in this process are known as decomposers. The decomposed leaves and dead organisms make up a layer of a dark-coloured substance called **humus** on the forest floor. The presence of humus ensures that the nutrients of the dead plants and animals are released into the soil. Trees absorb the nutrients in the soil and water through their roots. When seeds fall from the trees, the forest floor provides the right conditions for them to germinate and develop into seedlings and saplings and then trees. Together all these components make the forest a **dynamic living entity** that is full of life and vitality.

Forests also play a major role in preventing soil erosion. While the roots of trees and other forest plants hold the soil tightly, the uppermost layers of the forest canopy intercept the flow of raindrops and make them fall slowly often making them flow down through the branches and the stems of the trees. From the leaves the water drips down on the forest floor with little force and is immediately absorbed by the spongy layer of humus, thus protecting the soil from being carried

Forest rain and groundwater recharge

regeneration: renewed growth of something, a forest, for example
decomposers: organisms that break down dead organisms into their elements
soil erosion: the process of soil being eroded by wind or water

away even during the heaviest rainfall. This also helps more water to seep through the soil to recharge the groundwater and maintain its level.

Factastic
Forests maintain the global water cycle by returning the rainwater that they use to the atmosphere by way of transpiration. In the process of transpiration, a single tree may pump more than 360 l of water vapour into the air on a hot day.

Role of forests in our life

Forests have a variety of uses for humans. The wood obtained from trees is used for constructing buildings, for making furniture, as firewood, and in the paper and pulp industry. Other products of daily use that are obtained from the forests include medicines, honey, spices, resins, nuts, gums, oils and many others.

Timber

Plywood

Forests provide food, shelter, water and medicines as well as livelihood for many tribal communities. People living in or near forests also use

Rubber/Latex

Honey

Paper

forest land for grazing their cattle. Many tribal people have traditional knowledge about useful medicinal plants found in the forest. Unlike people living in cities, people living in forests practice a lifestyle that is in total harmony with nature.

Some trees are considered sacred by certain communities

The forest is a good example of existence of food chains. Just like humans, animals and insects also need food to live. Some eat other animals and insects and others just eat plants. Plants are the only living organisms that produce their own food and are hence called producers. Animals are called consumers as they depend directly on plants or other animals that eat plants for food. Herbivores live only on plants; carnivores live on herbivores; while omnivores can live on both plants and other animals. Plants are, thus, at the base of the food chain.

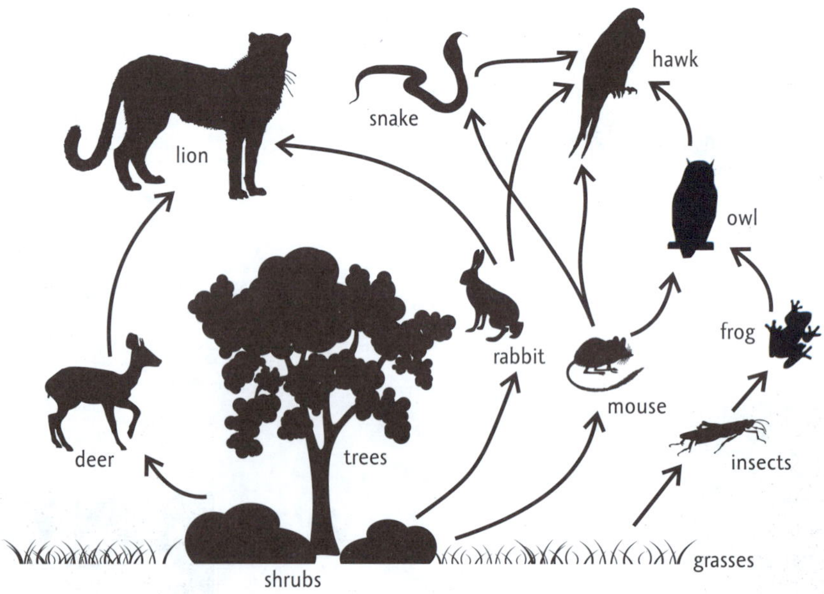

Forest food chain

food chain: a community of organisms where each member is eaten in turn by another member
producers: organisms that produce their own food
consumers: organisms that depend on food produced by other organisms

One example of a simple food chain is: insects eat grass while insects themselves are eaten by frogs. Snakes eat frogs and snakes are eaten by eagles, thus forming a food chain beginning with grass and ending with the eagle.

grass → insect → frog → snake → eagle

Many food chains exist in the forest and they are all linked. If any single species disappears, it can directly or indirectly affect the survival of other creatures in the forest. Why do you think projects to save the tiger should be encouraged and supplemented?

A walk through a forest

People who live in cities rarely get an opportunity to watch plants and animals in their natural surroundings in a forest. The best way to understand forests and the way it works is to walk into one and watch the activities going on there. By walking around a forest or a wooded park one can get an opportunity to watch the plants and animals in their natural habitat. A visit to a forest also provides an opportunity to collect a wide range of samples—of soil, bark, leaves, flowers, insects and much more—that give an idea of the diversity of nature.

Forests are not only enchanting but also exhilarating. Hearing animal and bird calls and watching their activity in a forest can often be an unforgettable experience. Every nook and corner of the forest harbours life. Turning a piece of deadwood on the ground, peeling the bark of a tree, or lifting a rotting leaf can reveal a plethora of organisms at work. Termites, beetles and ants are forever busy collecting their food and in the process recycling nutrients for the soil.

Most animals living in forests do not come out during the day; they come out only after dusk to graze or hunt for food. Their **footprints** and droppings on the forest floor provide clues about their presence. For example, in the forests of the Sunderbans in West Bengal, tigers are often identified by their pug marks left on the river banks and forest floors. Droppings also provide a clue to the presence of animals such as deer, rabbit, fox, tiger and many others.

Pug marks

Circle Time

droppings: the excrement of certain animals
pug marks: footprints of tigers

Discuss with your teacher and plan a trip to a nearby forest or national park. Carry binoculars, magnifying glass, a small spade and a notebook to record your observations as well as drinking

water. Also carry guide books on trees, birds and animals, if possible. You could apply a mosquito repellent on your exposed body parts to safeguard yourself.

A notepad

A paper bag

Observe the trees and try to identify them from the guide book or by asking your teacher. Do some of them have hanging roots? Record the characteristics of the trees, such as the height, shape of leaves, crown and flowers and fruits, if present. You may sketch the rough outline of the shape of the crowns of some of the trees and collect fallen leaves. Use binoculars to look closely at the top branches of the trees to see if you can spot any birds or animals. Try to identify them and record your observations. Photograph any animal you see if you have a camera or record your observation. Collect seeds or nuts if you find them and note down the tree or creeper from which they have fallen. Never collect bird eggs or disturb any bird nest if you find one.

A pair of binoculars

Using your observations along with those of the other students of your class, prepare a chart showing the main types of trees and animals that you have seen during your trip to the forest.

A magnifying glass

A spade

Disappearing forests

Forests are useful to humans because they provide oxygen and are a source of a host of useful everyday material. They are home to many endangered species of animals that are vital components of the earth's biosphere and key links in the food chain. However, the increasing population and the consequent need for large-scale industrialisation, construction of buildings for human habitation and increasing demand for food has led to the indiscriminate felling of trees in forests around the world. Forests are being cut not only for timber but also to clear the land for construction of factories, houses and roads. India had a large forest cover earlier, but the actual forest cover today is only about twenty-one per cent of the total land area. However, according to the State Forest Report 2009, in the last ten years, the forest cover has increased by 3.31 million hectares, showing an average increase of 0.46% of forest cover every year.

As forests are being cut down, the habitats of many large animals are becoming smaller. This is causing wild animals such as tigers, leopards and elephants to come into populated localities in search of food, which can sometimes result in violent encounters that lead to loss of property and human lives. Endangered wild animals also get killed in such encounters. This can be prevented by not destroying forests and conserving the habitats of these animals.

Extensive deforestation has also led to distinct changes in the rainfall pattern in many areas. It is now known that one of the major causes of global warming is deforestation, because with the destruction of forests one of the most effective natural sinks of carbon dioxide is lost. The burning of forest plants to clear land also releases large amounts of carbon dioxide in the air, which contributes to global warming.

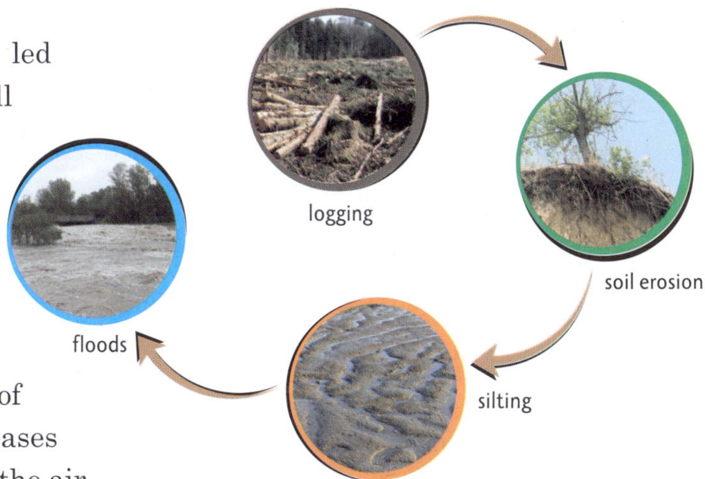

Effects of deforestation

Deforestation also affects the water cycle. Trees draw groundwater through their roots and release it into the atmosphere through transpiration. However, when forests are destroyed, there are no trees left to draw the groundwater and release it in the air leading to a much drier climate and less rainfall.

It is important to understand that forests take several decades and even centuries to grow, and once several trees are cut, the forest has little chance of being regenerated. A forest lost in this way is lost forever. The best alternative is to protect the forests from destruction and to lay more stress on **afforestation**. There is now an urgent need to preserve the forests at all costs so that the future of our planet can be secured.

deforestation: the act of clearing an area of forests and trees
afforestation: conversion of land into forest

Revision Time

- Forests are home to over two-thirds of the known terrestrial species of plants, animals and insects, and are among the most notable storehouses of biological diversity on land.
- Forests form an effective sink that remove carbon dioxide from the air and thus help in fighting global warming.
- Any tree in a forest can often be recognised by the shape of its crown—the upper, extensively branched part that is often a characteristic of a particular species.
- In a forest, the canopy forms the topmost layer followed by smaller trees that make up the understorey, and shrubs and herbs make up the lower layers of vegetation.
- Several animals live in different layers to avoid competition for food.
- The many different plants and animals that live in the forest interact with each other in many ways and nothing is wasted. Each layer supports another, providing specific animals and insects with food and shelter.
- When seeds fall from the trees, the forest floor provides the right conditions for them to germinate and develop into seedlings and saplings some of which grow into trees and become part of the forest.
- Forests play a major role in soil conservation.
- Forests provide food, shelter, water and medicines, as well as livelihood for many tribal communities.
- Forests sustain the water cycle. Trees draw groundwater through their roots and release it into the atmosphere through transpiration.
- Extensive deforestation is a known cause of global warming and has led to distinct changes in the rainfall pattern in many areas.
- The best alternative to prevent deforestation is to protect the forests from destruction and to lay more stress on afforestation.

Brainteaser

No matter what the size or thickness of a piece of paper, it can be folded into half not more than seven times. Try it!

Quiz Time

1. Answer the questions.

a. Why is India considered to be a megadiverse country?

b. In what way do forests act as green lungs?

c. Why do different animals live in different layers of the forest?

d. How do forests prevent soil erosion?

e. What is the role of decomposers in the forest?

2. Fill in the blanks.

a. The ancient people revered forests and even today they are ____________ in parts of India.

b. ____________ forests have trees with big leaves that become dry and fall to the ground in autumn.

c. The forest floor is a region where very little sunlight reaches and ____________ is very high.

d. Micro-organisms and fungi, also known as ____________, break down dead organic matter and enrich the soil.

e. Tigers are often identified by their ____________ left on the river banks and forest floors.

3. Indicate whether the statements are true or false.

a.	Forests are home to over three-fourths of the known terrestrial species of plants, animals and insects.	True	False
b.	Forests are called green lungs, because they absorb carbon dioxide and release oxygen into the atmosphere.	True	False
c.	The forest floor is a region where sunlight and humidity are very low.	True	False
d.	Tribal people have little traditional knowledge about medicinal plants found in the forest.	True	False
e.	Presence of some animals in a forest can be known from their droppings on the forest floor.	True	False

5. **Project work**

   a. Use reference books and the internet to find out about the different types of forests found in India and their locations. Also find out what typical animals or birds are found in those forests. On a political map of India show the forest areas, along with their descriptions and pictures of important animals and birds found in them. Do you find any animal common to all types of forests?

   b. In the rainy season, after it has rained for a few days, collect some wet deadwood from a wooded area in your neighbourhood or a nearby forest. Look at the piece of wet wood with a magnifying glass. Do you see any growth, worms or other organisms on it? Observe what happens to the piece of wood after several weeks.

Think it over

1. **Forest plantations are mainly aimed at producing timber and pulpwood for industry. Can they support the kind of biodiversity that natural forests do?**
2. **Why is it better for a forest to have a large variety of animal and plant species rather than a large number of plants and animals of a few varieties?**

18 Recycling Waste Water

Whenever clean water is used for any purpose—be it washing clothes or utensils, bathing, or in any industrial process, it turns into **waste water**. Urine is also a kind of waste water. Waste water is usually allowed to flow through the drain into sewers as sewage. We can afford to do this on earth because clean water is available from other sources. But astronauts who have to spend weeks on a space station are not so lucky. They have to make the most of whatever limited amount of water they carry or is available on the space station. And that includes recycling and reusing almost all the waste water produced, including urine.

Clean water: A scarce resource

Clean water is a basic human need. However, unfortunately it is a commodity that is becoming scarcer by the day. In many villages in India, people have to walk for several kilometres to fetch drinking water. The limited quantity of water that is available may not be clean. In many cities even the water supplied through municipal pipelines is not clean and safe for drinking. Presently, more than 880 million people around the world do not have access to safe drinking water, which makes them prone to water-borne diseases, some of which may be fatal. One way of making water available for human use is to clean and reuse waste water or sewage. Although clean water obtained by treating sewage may not be fit for drinking, this water can be used for other purposes such as gardening and flushing toilets and can also be released directly into the rivers without polluting them.

sewage: waste water and excrement carried in sewers
water-borne diseases: diseases caused by disease-causing micro-organisms that are directly transmitted when contaminated water is consumed

Sewage is a general term used for all types of liquid waste most of which is water. It is produced by homes, industries, hospitals, offices and other users wherever water is used. Sewage also includes rainwater that has been washed off the roads and rooftops during a storm or heavy rain and carries dirt and other harmful substances. Sewage usually has dissolved and suspended impurities in it, which are called contaminants. If the contaminants can be removed, sewage water can be used again for non-drinking purposes. Sewage that comes out of homes is quite different from the sewage that comes of industrial plants. Domestic sewage water contains human and animal waste including faeces and urine, kitchen waste, soap, detergents and disinfectants. Industrial sewage mostly contains a lot of toxic chemicals, acids, alkalis and metals. Sewage also contains substances such as phosphate and nitrogen and several types of microbes, which cause diseases like dysentery, typhoid, cholera and hepatitis.

Sewerage system

A manhole

To reuse sewage water that comes out of homes and public buildings, it is sent to **sewage treatment plants** through a network of big and small underground pipes, called sewers. The sewage has to be treated to make it safe for reuse or to be released into rivers and lakes. If raw sewage is directly released, it would cause serious water pollution problems. For regular cleaning and maintenance of the sewer lines, manholes are built at ground level at every 50–60 m, usually with iron or concrete covers.

In some small towns, that do not have sewerage systems, the sewage is often carried in open drains and directly released into a river, lake or swamp. Open drains carrying sewage always give off foul smell and are unhygienic. During the monsoons, the open drains often overflow, spilling the sewage onto roads and into houses, creating serious health problems. They often become the breeding grounds for flies, mosquitoes and other insects.

Sewage being released into a river

contaminant: a substance that makes water or something else impure
sewer: a pipe that carries away sewage and storm water
sewerage: a network of pipes for carrying away sewage

Treating sewage

In conventional sewage treatment, three stages are involved—primary, secondary and tertiary. The primary treatment consists of passing the sewage through bar screens to remove large objects such as plastic packets, rags, cans, sticks and similar objects. The sewage is then sent to a chamber where the speed of the incoming waste water is carefully controlled to allow sand, grit and stones to settle. After this stage, the sewage is temporarily held in a large settling tank where the heavy suspended matter settles to the bottom and oil, grease and lighter solids float to the surface. The settled and floating materials are removed and the remaining liquid called **clarified water** is sent for secondary treatment. For removing the settled solid matter or sludge, the settling tanks are usually equipped with mechanically driven scrapers. The sludge is transferred to a separate tank for further treatment with anaerobic bacteria when biogas is produced and manure is left behind. The biogas can be used as a cooking fuel or can be used to produce electricity.

Factastic

In India, the domestic sector is responsible for most of the waste water generation. According to a study by the Central Pollution Control Board, seventy per cent of the total municipal sewage and effluent from over 900 cities and towns is being released untreated into rivers, which are a major source of drinking water. This contributes to the high incidence of water-related diseases in the country.

During secondary treatment, the dissolved and suspended biological matter is removed from the sewage. In this process, air is pumped into the clarified water to help aerobic bacteria to grow and consume human waste, food waste, soaps and other unwanted matter still remaining in it. After several hours of aeration, the suspended microbes settle at the

sludge: the solid material that settles in tanks during sewage treatment
anaerobic bacteria: bacteria that do not live or grow in the presence of oxygen
biogas: gaseous fuel, especially methane, produced by the fermentation of organic waste
aerobic bacteria: bacteria that can grow and live in the presence of oxygen
aeration: passing air through water to add oxygen

Sewage treatment plant

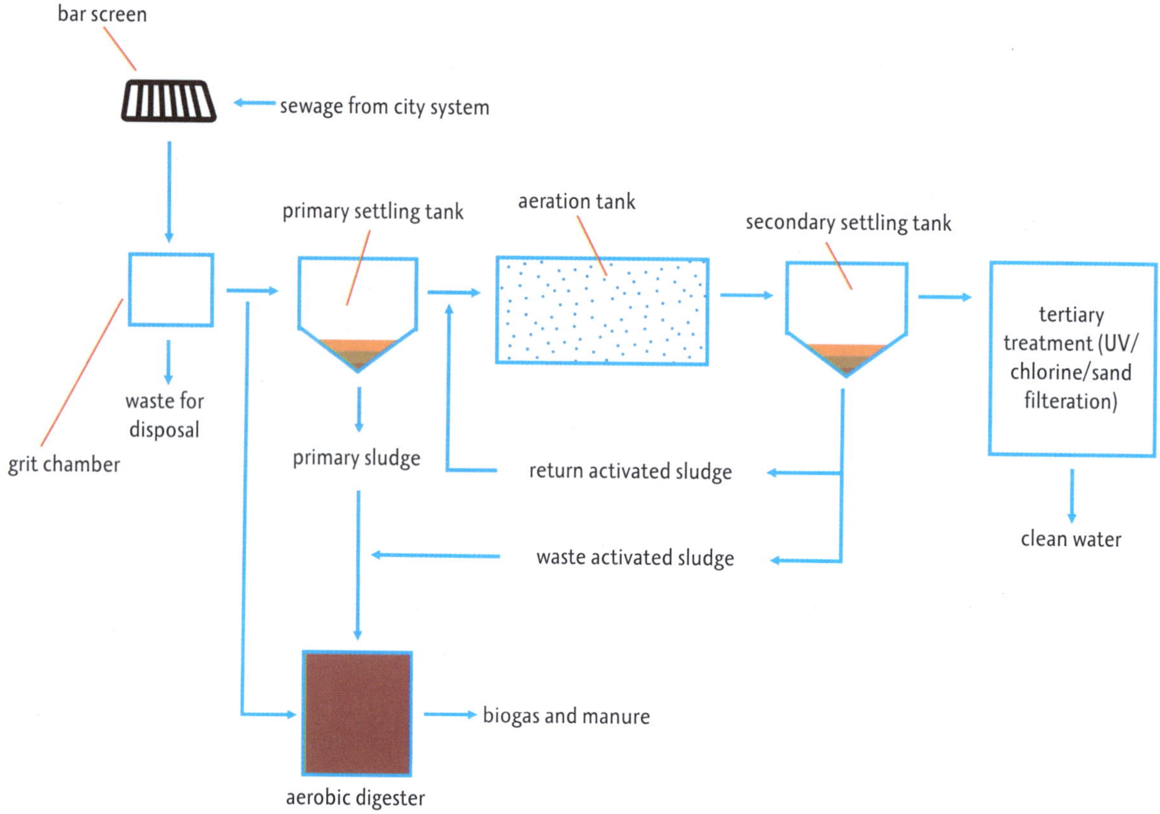

Sewage treatment plant

bottom of the tank as activated sludge. Activated sludge is different from primary sludge in that it contains many living organisms that can feed on the incoming waste water. The clear water, mostly free from harmful substances, is then removed from the top and can be discharged directly into a stream, river, bay, lagoon or wetland, or it can be used for the irrigation of a park or a garden.

Sometimes, after secondary treatment, the water is passed through a sand filter as tertiary treatment before it is released into water bodies. If it is sufficiently clean, the water can be used for groundwater recharge or agricultural purposes.

Circle Time

Carry out this simple experiment with your classmates to see how sewage treatment cleans dirty water.

activated sludge: biomass produced in waste water by the growth of aerobic bacteria in aeration tanks in the presence of dissolved oxygen

Fill three-fourth of a large glass jar with water. Add some dirty organic matter such as cow dung, straw pieces, vegetable peels,

a few pinches of detergent and a few drops of any colour, to make artificial sewage. Mix the contents of the jar well, cap it and keep it in a warm place for a two days.

After two days, stir the mixture well and pour about 20 ml from it into a test tube. Label this test tube as Sample 1. Note its smell and colour.

Get a small air pump, as used in an aquarium, and use it to bubble air through the remaining mixture in the jar for several hours. If an air pump is not available, a mechanical stirrer may be used to agitate the mixture, but this also has to be done for several hours to allow the material in the mixture to come in contact with air.

After sufficient aeration has been done, pour the mixture from this jar into a second test tube. Label it as Sample 2. Note its smell and colour.

Fold a filter paper into the shape of a cone and place it in a funnel mounted on a stand. Pour medium gravel, fine gravel and sand in the funnel in layers in that order.

Pour the remaining liquid from the jar through the filter into beakers. Take care that the liquid does not spill over the filter. You may need to repeat the filtration a few times till you get clear water.

Pour a sample of the filtered water from the beaker into a third test tube labelled Sample 3. Note its smell and colour.

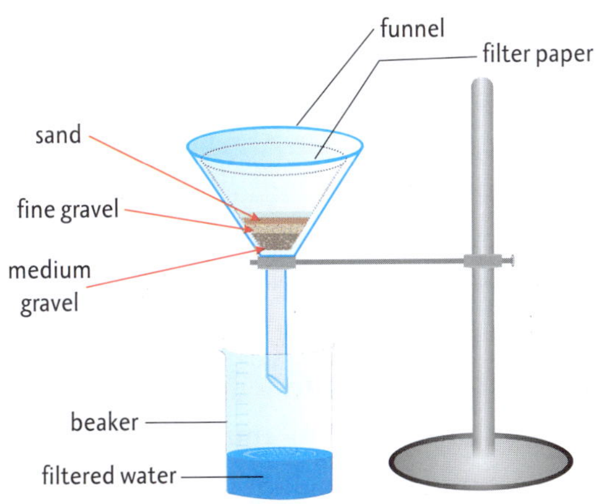

Water filtration

Pour another sample of the filtered water into a fourth test tube and add a chlorine tablet in it. Stir the tablet well until it dissolves in the water. Label the test tube as Sample 4. Note its smell and colour.

Observe carefully the changes in clarity, colour and smell that occurred in the samples at each of these stages and record them. Do not try to taste the water in any sample at any stage. From the steps carried out, do you get an idea of the processes involved in sewage treatment?

Types of wastes

The types of wastes that go into sewage water depend largely upon what is thrown into the drains, which also determines the load on waste water treatment plants. Indiscriminate dumping of waste material into drains also creates problems by choking drains or clogging

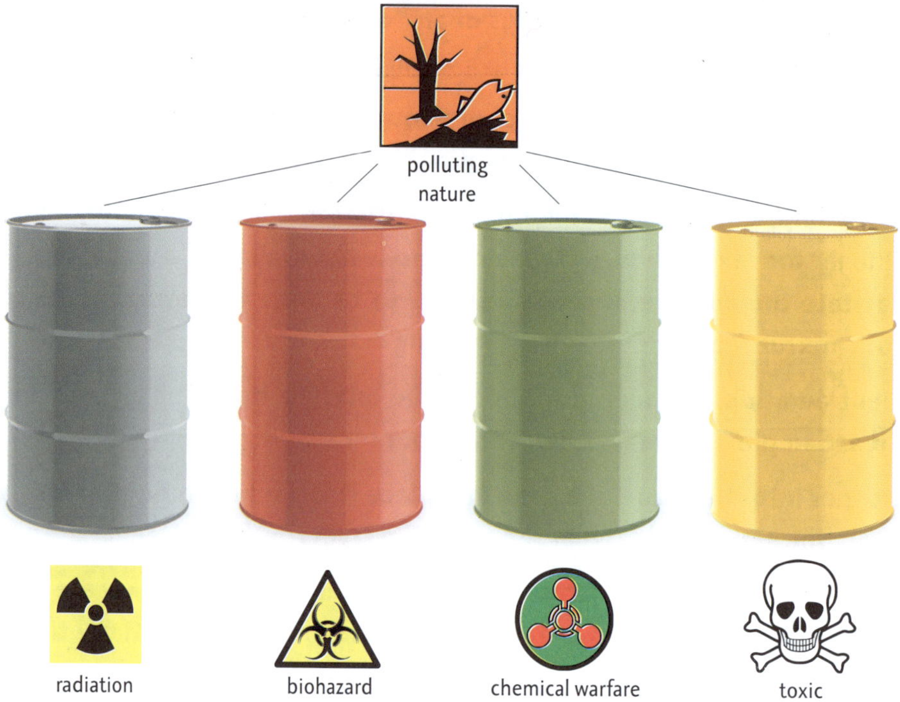

Harzardous waste

pores of filtrations beds in treatment plants. By preventing some types of wastes from going into the sewage, the sewer lines can be prevented from getting choked and the load on waste water treatment plants can be reduced.

It is better to throw substances such as cooking oil and fat into the garbage bin than into drains because they can sometimes cause fibrous material like hair to clump together and clog pipes. Substances such as solvents, insecticides, motor oil, chemicals like paints and medicines, when thrown into the drain, can kill microbes that help in purifying water. Solid wastes like used tea leaves, food remains and vegetable peels should also be thrown in the garbage bin rather than in the drain. These wastes can choke the drains and block the flow of oxygen, which can hamper the degradation process.

Materials that need to be recycled

Learn More

The eucalyptus plant is among the world's biggest and tallest as well as one of the quickest growing tree species around. The eucalyptus tree's ability to efficiently take up water from the soil can be made use of in extracting water from sewage or waste water. The tree can take up water from sewage and waste water and convert it to water vapour through transpiration. This water will eventually land on earth as rain.

Sanitation and disease

Polluted water is a major cause of disease and death in many developing countries including India, where a large percentage of the population does not have access to proper sanitation. Several diseases in the developing countries are caused by contaminated water. Water-borne diseases, such as diarrhoea, cholera and typhoid, cause the deaths of hundreds of thousands of children every year in these countries.

The practice of open defecation is also a major cause of water contamination. Even in cities where public latrines are available, people are seen defecating in the open. This practice is highly reprehensible since it leads to surface water as well as groundwater getting polluted. Since groundwater is a source of water for wells, tube wells as well as many rivers, it becomes the most common route for transmission of water-borne diseases. When particles of faeces from a person suffering from a water-borne disease are passed on by water, the disease can be transmitted to other people.A tiny amount of faeces is enough to spread the disease because it may carry thousands of millions of micro-organisms. Although most of these micro-organisms may be harmless, only a few of the dangerous ones can cause infection. Polio is a crippling disease that spreads by infected water.

Alternative sewage disposal methods

Sanitation can be improved even without a conventional sewage disposal system. The important thing is to make sure that human waste does not come in contact with water sources. This can be done by setting up septic tanks, **composting pits** or **chemical toilets**. A septic tank consists of a covered underground concrete tank, which is sealed from outside air. Waste water containing faeces enters the tank where the solids settle and the scum floats. In the absence of air, anaerobic bacteria slowly digest the faecal matter and turn it into odour-free sludge, which is

sanitation: conditions relating to public health like the provision of clean drinking water and adequate sewage disposal
septic tank: a large tank where solid matter or sewage is decomposed by bacteria

taken out periodically. The clear water from the tank is usually let into an open drain field where it soaks into the soil.

A composting pit or a toilet involves the collection of human waste in a pit and covering it repeatedly with soil for composting. Such pits do not need scavenging and are ideal for rural areas where open spaces are available for digging. Once filled up, a pit can be used for planting trees and another pit can be dug to collect human waste. The main objective of a composting toilet is to achieve controlled decomposition or waste disposal without polluting the environment.

A chemical toilet uses chemicals to treat the waste and remove the smell from the waste rather than simply storing it in a pit.

Sanitation in public places

Kumbh Mela

In India, social and religious gatherings are common on occasions like the Kumbh Mela, Makar Sankranti and solar eclipses when people gather at river banks, sea shores and ponds for bathing. Fairs are also organised at these places where thousands of eating places and hundreds of toilets are set up. In addition, there are places like railway stations, bus depots and hospitals that are also visited by thousands of people every day. A large amount of waste is generated in all these places, but unfortunately, a proper method of waste disposal is not always followed. Even public toilets are not properly used or maintained, creating unhygienic conditions and often posing risk of epidemics. Unless each individual makes a conscious effort not to litter and to throw waste material only in garbage bins, not to defecate or urinate in the open and maintain cleanliness in public places, keeping our water sources clean and in a healthy state may remain a distant dream.

Brainteaser

Nurdles make up ten per cent of the ocean's trash. What is a nurdle?

Answer: A nurdle is a smalll piece of plastic!

Revision Time

- ✶ Whenever clean water is used for any purpose, it turns into waste water.
- ✶ Waste water is usually allowed to flow through drains into sewers as sewage and is never used again.
- ✶ One way of making more water available for human use is to clean and reuse waste water or sewage.
- ✶ Sewage is a general term used for all types of liquid waste most of which is water.
- ✶ Sewage water can be cleaned in sewage treatment plants and used again for non-drinking purposes.
- ✶ Sewage is carried to a central treatment plant through a network of big and small underground pipes called sewers that form the sewerage.
- ✶ Sewage treatment plants produce sludge and biogas as by-products. The sludge can be used as manure and the biogas can be used for energy generation.
- ✶ Open drains carrying sewage always give off foul smell and are unhygienic.
- ✶ The practice of defecating in the open is a major cause of water contamination. Both surface water and groundwater get polluted by open defecation.
- ✶ Sanitation can be improved even without a conventional sewage disposal system by preventing human waste from coming into contact with water sources.
- ✶ Septic tanks, composting pits and chemical toilets are alternatives to sewage treatment plants than can dispose off human waste hygienically.

Quiz Time

1. Answer the questions.

a. What is sewage and why does it need to be treated before it is released into a river or a lake?

b. Why are open drains for carrying sewage considered unhygienic?

c. What are the main stages involved in sewage treatment?

d. What is sludge from settling tanks used for?

e. How does a septic tank work?

2. **Fill in the blanks.**

   a. Sewage usually has dissolved as well as suspended impurities in it, which are called __________________ .

   b. The sludge from settling tanks is transferred to a separate tank for further treatment with __________________ bacteria.

   c. During the secondary treatment of the sludge, the dissolved and suspended __________________ matter are removed from the sewage.

   d. The practice of open __________________ is a major cause of water contamination in India.

   e. Solid wastes, such as used tea leaves, food remains and vegetable peels, should be thrown in the __________________ .

3. **Indicate whether the statements are true or false.**

a.	Waste water is produced whenever water is used for domestic or industrial purposes.	True	False
b.	Sewage is a general term used for all types of solid waste.	True	False
c.	Sewage that comes from homes is quite different from the sewage that comes from industrial plants.	True	False
d.	The biogas produced from the sludge cannot be used as a cooking fuel.	True	False
e.	During secondary treatment, the heavy and suspended matter is removed from the sewage.	True	False

5. **Project work**

   a. With the help of your school try to arrange a visit to a sewage treatment plant in your city and observe the different stages through which sewage is made to pass. Also observe and note down the changes that take place in the character of the sewage at each stage. Prepare a brief report on your visit.

   b. Find the manholes in your neighbourhood and try to draw up a plan of the sewerage in your area. Find out if the storm water drains also connect to the sewerage.

Think it over

1. **When lakhs of people bathe in a river, a large pond or a lake at the same time, are they not taking a bath in waste water?**
2. **Why is river water in the mountains considered less contaminated than in the plains?**

Evaluation Sheet

Name: ____________________

Date: ____________________

Skills	Remarks
Work habits	
Observation skills	
Recollection of scientific terms, facts and definitions	
Understanding and co-relation of concepts and processes	
Application and integration of different concepts	
Diagrammatic skills	
Acquisition of required dkills	
Representation or explaning processes or observed phenomena	
Numerical ability	
Analysis of information	